STRENGTH TRAINING

FOR

BASKETBALL

Library of Congress Cataloging-in-Publication Data

Names: Gillett, Javair, editor. | Burgos, Bill, editor. | National Strength
  & Conditioning Association (U.S.)
Title: Strength training for basketball / NSCA, Javair Gillett, MS, CSCS,
  RSCC*E, Bill Burgos, MS, CSCS, RSCC*D Editors.
Description: Champaign, IL : Human Kinetics, [2020] | Includes
  bibliographical references and index.
Identifiers: LCCN 2019029446 (print) | LCCN 2019029447 (ebook) | ISBN
  9781492571490 (paperback) | ISBN 9781492594079 (epub) | ISBN 9781492571506
  (pdf)
Subjects: LCSH: Basketball--Training. | Weight lifting. | Physical
  education and training.
Classification: LCC GV885.35 .S77 2020 (print) | LCC GV885.35 (ebook) |
  DDC 796.323--dc23
LC record available at https://lccn.loc.gov/2019029446
LC ebook record available at https://lccn.loc.gov/2019029447

ISBN: 978-1-4925-7149-0 (print)

Senior Acquisitions Editor: Roger W. Earle; **Managing Editor:** Miranda K. Baur; **Copyeditor:** Bob Replinger; **Indexer:** Ferreira Indexing; **Permissions Manager:** Dalene Reeder; **Graphic Designer:** Whitney Milburn; **Cover Designer:** Keri Evans; **Cover Design Associate:** Susan Rothermel Allen; **Photograph (cover):** Jonathan Daniel/ Getty Images; **Photographs (interior):** © Human Kinetics, unless otherwise noted; **Photo Asset Manager:** Laura Fitch; **Photo Production Coordinator:** Amy M. Rose; **Photo Production Manager:** Jason Allen; **Senior Art Manager:** Kelly Hendren; **Illustrations:** © Human Kinetics ; unless otherwise noted; **Printer:** Sheridan Books

We thank Matthew Sandstead, NSCA-CPT,*D and Scott Caulfield, MA, CSCS,*D, RSCC*D at the National Strength and Conditioning Association in Colorado Springs, Colorado, for overseeing the photo shoot for this book.

Human Kinetics books are available at special discounts for bulk purchase. Special editions or book excerpts can also be created to specification. For details, contact the Special Sales Manager at Human Kinetics.

Printed in the United States of America   10 9 8 7 6 5 4 3 2 1

The paper in this book is certified under a sustainable forestry program.

Human Kinetics
1607 N. Market St.
Champaign, IL 61820
Website: www.HumanKinetics.com

In the United States, email info@hkusa.com or call 800-747-4457.
In Canada, email info@hkcanada.com.
In the United Kingdom/Europe, email hk@hkeurope.com.

For information about Human Kinetics' coverage in other areas of the world,
please visit our website: **www.HumanKinetics.com**

E7412

STRENGTH TRAINING
FOR
BASKETBALL

NSCA®
**NATIONAL STRENGTH AND
CONDITIONING ASSOCIATION**

Javair Gillett, MS, CSCS, RSCC*E
Bill Burgos, MS, CSCS, RSCC*D

EDITORS

HUMAN KINETICS

PART I: PRINCIPLES OF SPORT-SPECIFIC RESISTANCE TRAINING

PART II: EXERCISE TECHNIQUE

PART III: DESIGN GUIDELINES AND SAMPLE PROGRAMS

PATRICK EWING

As a former player and coach in the National Basketball Association (NBA) and currently a collegiate coach, I understand the significance of strength training. Strength training defines and characterizes an athlete's motivation to succeed as well as to protect him- or herself from injury. Furthermore, strength training creates a strong foundation to overcome the daily stressors experienced during practice and games.

Strength training prepares for activities such as squatting, pushing, and pulling movements. Basketball is a physical sport that includes plenty of contact. For that reason, a basketball athlete must be ready and strong to take on this sort of contact. A poorly trained athlete will incur nagging injuries and extended recovery periods from an injury. After all, to be a team player, a basketball athlete must do his or her part to ensure that the team is healthy and prosperous.

In conclusion, then, it is imperative to include an excellent strength and conditioning program that involves the latest science and a winning attitude. The inclusion of the latter defines discipline, character, and the purpose of what a sound strength program can do for a basketball athlete on and off the court.

INTRODUCTION

JAVAIR GILLETT AND BILL BURGOS

Feats of strength are frequently displayed on the basketball court. An athlete must have a strong mind and be strong physically in the face of his or her competitor. An athlete should show the same strength in the fourth quarter as he or she does in the first quarter. A good athlete often looks strong. A winning team finishes games looking strong. The term *strength* is often referred to in evaluation and can have several meanings to a basketball athlete, but what truly makes a basketball athlete strong? What type of strength and how much strength does a basketball athlete need?

What is strength?

- Newton's first law of motion states that an object will remain at rest until an external force changes its state.
- Newton's second law of motion states that the acceleration of an object depends on the object's mass and the external force acting on that object.
- Newton's third law of motion states that for every action there is an equal and opposite reaction.

Based on Newton's laws and in broad terms, strength is the ability to produce or exert force.

Departing from a textbook-based definition and looking at strength from a coach's empirical point of view, strength can also be described in an applied, practical way as the ability to

- withstand a load without failure,
- overcome an obstacle,
- generate force,
- resist attack,
- endure, and
- show resilience in the face of adversity.

The game of basketball is dynamic and presents various challenges in an ever-changing environment. Therefore, *applied* strength is complex. It is not solely determined in the weight room or defined by how much weight a person can lift. For the basketball athlete, strength is effective only when it can successfully be applied on the court. Resistance training is important for the basketball athlete because it causes changes in the central and peripheral nervous system and in skeletal muscle that result in enhanced muscular force output. With added strength acquired from a basketball-specific resistance training program, an athlete will become better conditioned to take on the highly stressful workload experienced during practice or a game.

The purpose of this book is to provide the coach or strength and conditioning professional with a resource that can guide the design of resistance training programs, based on science, that lead to improved application of strength on the basketball court. To reach her or his true athletic potential, a basketball athlete needs a well-planned resistance training program strategically designed to optimize strength. Adaptations made from effective resistance training protocols will result in increased work capacity, improved jumping ability, faster acceleration and deceleration, and quicker changes of direction.

This book also provides an overall analysis of the game and the mechanical demands it presents, and it offers an update of the most appropriate approaches to guide basketball-specific strength development. General and specific guidelines to sport-specific program structure and exercise selection are presented along with sample resistance training programs that can be used to help the athlete optimize strength and successfully transfer that strength to the basketball court.

PART I

PRINCIPLES OF SPORT-SPECIFIC RESISTANCE TRAINING

1

IMPORTANCE OF RESISTANCE TRAINING

BILL BURGOS

Basketball requires multiplanar movements to be executed in an ever-changing environment at various forces, angles, and speeds, and over various lengths of time. As a result, the adaptations made from resistance training help the athlete to meet the physiological and mechanical demands encountered in basketball and thus optimize athletic performance. Resistance training will improve physical attributes pertaining to body composition, strength, power, change of direction, and speed. Ultimately, the goal of resistance training is to maximize these physical attributes in such a way that it improves overall athletic performance and transfers to movements required on the basketball court.

REDUCE INJURY

The general purpose of resistance training is to enhance the development of strength and power by adding external forces to human movements. Regardless of the sport, the benefits of resistance training are multifaceted. For one, resistance training can help reduce the likelihood of injury. One injury that resistance training may help prevent is tendinopathy. A significant risk factor of tendinopathy in sport is an excessively high training load (18). Resistance training leads to adaptations that will help the athlete take on higher game workloads. The **overload principle** states that to increase muscle size, strength, or power, a muscle must be forced to take on a higher workload than it was accustomed to (17). The athlete will take on a specific workload above his or her current threshold and become accustomed to that workload over time. To make further improvements, the athlete must gradually take on a higher workload. Therefore, properly introducing a resistance training program and implementing a higher training load progressively throughout the training macrocycle can aid in tolerating the workload brought on by the sport more effectively and help reduce the risk of overuse injury.

Wolff's law states that bone adapts to the stress it is exposed to. The body's tissues are subject to high mechanical stress and strain during a basketball game. If a bone is not subject to appropriate loading to prepare it during landing phases, it will be more susceptible to injury. Mechanical loading influences both soft-tissue and bone strength. During growth, children are more susceptible to bone fractures. Children with higher bone strength are less likely to experience fractures. Resistance training will not stunt growth, but contrarily, and if prescribed properly, will improve peak bone mass and enhance strength to combat rapid bone growth stints in youth. Furthermore, resistance training early in adolescence will evolve to greater bone mass in adulthood. Resistance training has also been shown to improve bone mineral density. For example, Duplanty and colleagues (19) reported that including external resistance exercises at least once per week improved BMD in distance runners. Interestingly, Baptista and colleagues (3) reported that children with a below average bone mineral density demonstrated significantly lower vertical jump power. Therefore, resistance training can augment bone mineral density, which may decrease injury risk and be related to performance.

Duplanty and colleagues (19) examined the effects of a resistance training program (once per week) in distance runners and found that resistance-trained runners had higher bone mineral density than distance runners who did not resistance train. To maximize adaptation, bone loading needs to be intermittent, induce high strain, and be applied rapidly (5). Furthermore, bone cells can desensitize with repetitive loading (i.e., long-distance running) but are stimulated under dynamic (i.e., multidirectional movements) loading (5). Based on these conditions, the stress of basketball activity by itself should then be enough to strengthen bone. It is plausible, however, that a dynamic resistance training program may further enhance bone strength and remodeling.

IMPROVE JUMPING, ACCELERATION, AND CHANGE-OF-DIRECTION ABILITIES

Explosive basketball athletes require optimal muscle elasticity. Reactive strength is reliant on eccentric force development, elastic energy storage and release, and muscle reflexive properties. Concentric force production is also correlated with the reactive strength index (4). Training to increase reactive strength involves the stretch-shortening cycle and, therefore, serves as another mode of resistance training. Performance in agility tests may also be related to reactive strength attributes. In another analysis, female athletes who exhibited faster agility times had shorter ground contact braking times when compared with slower athletes (59). The ability to move quickly around the basketball court is highly related to the athlete's ability to interact with the ground properly. Stronger athletes exhibit higher ground reaction forces. In many instances a basketball athlete must stop very quickly and move in another direction. Other times, a center will jump vertically to rebound a ball that bounces around the rim. The delay will require the athlete to land and quickly jump up a second time. People with superior lower body strength have higher peak power output during jumping activities (10). As a result, the stronger athlete will be able to minimize ground contact time while still being able to reach near maximal jump height in the second jump.

Over the total distance covered in a game, a basketball athlete can experience various movement demands that place a tremendous amount of mechanical stress on the body. To grasp the importance of resistance training for the basketball athlete, a coach must understand that performance attributes like agility, power, and speed rely heavily on strength. The neuromuscular adaptations brought on by mechanical stress will be specific to the manipulation of several resistance training variables such as load, sets, repetitions, tempo, and rest period length.

Each quality of strength is unique and plays a role in injury prevention and reaching optimal physical performance. Change of direction involves multiple components of strength including eccentric (braking), isometric (planting), and concentric (propulsive) phases (59). Movements such as jumping and cutting rely on the ability to absorb the forces effectively in order to redirect

Courtesy of the Minnesota Timberwolves.

Resistance training improves a basketball athlete's ability to jump, accelerate, and change directions in the face of an opponent.

those forces and produce maximal concentric power. Therefore, the ability to decelerate and reaccelerate quickly is related to eccentric strength. Accentuated eccentric overload training appears to improve muscle architecture, strength, power, and velocity more than traditional resistance training does (12, 30). As a result, eccentric training should also play an integral role in a basketball athlete's resistance training program.

The stretch-shortening cycle plays an important role in countermovement activities. Stronger muscles are able to contract and store elastic energy better than weaker muscles. Elastic energy, which is stored in the muscle-tendon unit, is created in the eccentric phase. Naturally, this form of stored energy can be transferred into the concentric, acceleration phase. The greater an athlete's ability to transfer this energy, during what is called the amortization phase, the greater her or his ability will be to perform explosive countermovement activities. For example, Bridgeman and colleagues (7) showed that lower body eccentric strength is highly related to overall jump performance. Resistance training increases eccentric strength, and combining eccentric resistance training with traditional, concentrically focused training modes can have positive effects on jump performance (41). Furthermore, although type II fibers may be recruited regardless of load when sets are performed to failure, heavy loads require type II fiber recruitment. In addition, heavy loads appear to be more effective for eliciting neural adaptations that, in turn, facilitate strength improvements (31, 45, 36). Therefore, heavy or explosive resistance training may be an effective means by which to augment power production during the countermovement activities encountered in basketball.

Muscle architecture influences the athlete's ability to move explosively. When looking at dynamic movements such as the countermovement jump, jump height, peak force, and peak velocity are all related to greater vastus lateralis thickness and gastrocnemius pennation angle

(32). In general, resistance training improves muscle thickness, pennation angle, and fascicle length (12, 32). Regardless of training goals, an important goal is to bridge the gap between injury prevention and reaching optimal performance. Carefully designed resistance training programs performed in combination with ballistic, high-velocity basketball-specific movements may optimize muscle geometry and enhance performance in a dynamic, explosive sport such as basketball.

ENHANCE TORSO STIFFNESS

According to McGill (42), greater torso muscle strength (referred to as torso **stiffness**) enhances load-bearing capability and facilitates movement and a full transfer of force to the shoulder and hip joints, allowing greater force output and speed of the lower and upper limbs. After all, the ability to withstand higher external forces and resist changes in muscle length or joint position is important in movements like cutting, jumping, and battling opponents for a rebound.

Isometric exercise improves the ability to withstand the external forces applied during an activity (6). Therefore, isometric muscle actions maintain posture and facilitate the transfer of force through the torso to the limbs, and thus play an integral role in both injury prevention and performance. For example, a basketball athlete might not be required to accelerate a barbell with weight on the court during a game, but at times he or she must push or pull against an opponent to gain a better position. To put it another way, an athlete will still require enough strength to resist and overcome opposing forces while attempting to move forward or jump. Those opposing forces are difficult to replicate in controlled settings. Purposeful, basketball-specific resistance training programs and the exercises that are prescribed should attempt to mimic such an environment.

INCREASE FORCE PRODUCTION

In basketball-specific scenarios, load is only a part of the equation. For the basketball athlete, a higher force needs to be generated quickly, so coaches who implement largely dynamic, quick, powerful concentric and eccentric movements should also monitor progress through the rate of force development during a dynamic muscle action. Slowly developing force application, albeit against an extremely high load, does not occur often in a basketball game. As an example, using the isometric midthigh pull (IMTP) exercise executed for three seconds, an athlete might be able to generate an extremely high peak force in the later phase of the exercise, not just because peak force is achieved late in the exercise but also because it is static. As a result, this exercise might not ultimately transfer to a basketball-specific setting. Using research as a guide, this exercise can be more useful to the basketball athlete if peak force is attained more quickly. For instance, peak force and the rate of force production in the IMTP have been shown to be a predictor of linear sprint performance. Basketball athletes (men and women) who display higher average force and power over the first 5 meters (5.5 yd) of a 20-meter (22 yd) sprint also had a significantly higher rate of force production in the IMTP (40). Therefore, including the IMTP exercise into a resistance training program will not only allow progress to be monitored but also allow strength and conditioning professionals to train initial acceleration effectively if limited space in the weight room is a concern. Educating the athlete on the reasons why specific exercises are being programmed and how they can transfer into improved performance on the court will lead to better intent and follow-through.

IMPROVE POWER DEVELOPMENT

Purposeful selection of exercises will have a major influence on the success of a resistance training program. Accelerations make up a large portion of a basketball athlete's movement. Most exercises within a typical resistance training program have a concentric focus. Although primary exercises are typically emphasized, even assistance exercises in the later stages of an individual workout routine deserve attention. For example, the hip extension force production achieved in a barbell hip thrust exercise may effectively enhance horizontal force production, improve gluteus maximus hypertrophy, and increase linear sprint speed (13).

For the basketball athlete, resistance training aims to improve the rate of force development, improve concentric velocity, and therefore enhance power production. For example, Campbell and colleagues determined that athletes with a history of participating in a power training program achieved greater peak power, attained greater forces, and improved the velocity-time curve (10). Furthermore, Frost and colleagues (23) divided two groups into either a free-weight resistance or a pneumatic resistance group (resistance applied through air compression) for eight weeks. The pneumatic resistance group experienced significantly greater improvements in power (+33.4%) when compared with the free-weight resistance group (+22.5%). So although a pneumatic machine might not effectively improve some aspects of strength (i.e., maximal, eccentric) optimally, it may be used in phases of the resistance program that focus on strength applied in explosive, concentric movements. To maximize strength gains and transfer, the coach needs to know what modes of training work best and when to apply them over the course of a macrocycle.

In more traditional forms of resistance training, loads are prescribed as a percentage based on the athlete's 1RM and are often performed without attention to movement velocity. Throughout a macrocycle, resistance training programs should not focus solely on peak force output. But in cases where appropriate strength and power gains have been achieved, more attention can be placed on effort and velocities based on the load-power-velocity relationship. In velocity-based resistance training, the load is predicated on the movement velocity to be achieved during the exercise, which depends on the time of year, the training age of the athlete, and the training effect desired. Training with a low load and high velocity has been shown to improve countermovement jumping ability (10). Further, peak concentric velocity in a 1RM squat relates to linear sprinting ability (20). A true 1RM will be performed under 0.20 m/s (27). According to Fahs (20) when training to improve absolute strength, average concentric velocity should be between 0.15 and 0.30 m/s. On the other hand, when training to improve explosive strength, lighter loads should be used with an average concentric velocity between 1.0 and 1.5 m/s (40). Therefore, velocity-based training used in basketball can encourage individualized programming and reduce the effects of fatigue for upcoming training and competitive events.

INCREASE REACTIVE STRENGTH

The **reactive strength index** (RSI) measure is most commonly derived from dividing jump height by contact time in the drop jump (4). The purpose of reactive strength for the basketball athlete is to acquire the ability to transfer strength qualities into explosive actions so that he or she can move quickly and precisely while under a high amount of stress. The **amortization phase** is a point where energy derived from an eccentric muscle action is then quickly transferred to a concentric muscle action (17). According to Haff and colleagues (29), the amortization phase is the time between the eccentric and concentric phases, when zero velocity occurs. Essentially, the amortization phase reflects the athlete's ability to change direction moving from the eccentric phase to the concentric phase. The time spent in this amortization phase is highly related to the reactive strength index (4). For example, in a countermovement jump, increased time spent in the amortization phase will cause energy to dissipate and ground reaction forces to decrease, subsequently hindering reactive strength. Even when able to apply a high force rapidly into the ground, movements called on in a game often occur under delayed or mistimed sequences. Because of the reactive nature and cognitive processing required in the sport, basketball athletes need to work on their ability to stabilize and store elastic energy, while still processing information and delivering an explosive action after making a final decision. For instance, a cutter might need to pause while in the middle of a cut to throw a defender off course. Strength will allow this cutter to make the desired cut more explosively and create additional separation from the defender.

ENRICH WARM-UPS

Resistance training can also provide acute improvements in muscular performance. Sole and colleagues (58) concluded that warm-ups consisting of prolonged static stretching before competition can impair muscular performance, reducing force and power output. On the other hand, resistance training protocols implemented as warm-ups before competition have shown to improve linear sprint speed and agility. McBride and colleagues demonstrated that performing a squat for 1 set at 90% of the 1RM improved 40-meter sprint time (41). More important, implementing a back squat protocol with a load of 50%, 60%, and 90% of the 1RM for 3 repetitions before performing a 10-meter agility shuttle showed a trend toward improved times (34). Coaches are now aware that warm-ups consisting of static stretching alone hinder muscular performance. More proactive approaches to warm-ups consider the use of traditional strength exercises. **Postactivation potentiation** (PAP) is a physiological phenomenon that involves a maximal or near-maximal muscular contraction followed by an explosive, high-velocity exercise. For instance, resistance training can be used to elicit PAP by prescribing a near maximal load such as 4 repetitions at 90% of the 1RM immediately followed by a countermovement jump. Both contraction frequency and load have shown to elicit a PAP response. In fact, Hernández-Preciado and colleagues reported that using the French contrast method, for example, improved baseline countermovement jumping levels and including PAP training before an activity can improve power production (33). Thus, training professional basketball athletes before a game can give them the advantage against their opponents. Besides, resistance training should be viewed not only as a fatigue-inducing activity but also as a necessary performance-improving activity before a game, perhaps especially important for higher-level athletes who play more games and travel more frequently. Regardless of level, coaches should be aware of resistance training techniques and exercises that can be used in nonfatiguing ways to help improve mobility and assist in the warm-up process before a game or practice.

IMPROVE AEROBIC ENDURANCE AND ANAEROBIC CAPACITY

Conversely, other resistance training programs throughout a macrocycle should be designed to induce fatigue. For example, muscular endurance resistance training in combination with aerobic endurance exercise has been shown to improve aerobic capacity (21). This mode of training allows the body to adapt and fight against fatigue. For instance, performing a two-arm kettlebell (16 kg [35 lb]) swing for 12 minutes has shown to improve $\dot{V}O_2$ max (13). Although the improvement of $\dot{V}O_2$ max did not affect the overall gas exchange, it did improve specifically the onset of blood lactate accumulation (21). High-volume, low-load velocity-based training can offer an optimal environment for the athlete to take on a higher workload over longer periods and meet the metabolic demands specific to the sport. Merriam-Webster defines strength as the "power to resist attack." With that in mind, a basketball athlete has to resist "attack" many times over the course of a game. Common equipment implemented into these programs may be dumbbells, kettlebells, landmines, barbells, and so on, with movements executed at various velocities. These exercises can be initiated during the off-season in the general preparatory period. Mimicking in-game demands in the weight room during this time is extremely difficult. Ultimately, low-load resistance training can be used to improve a basketball athlete's overall conditioning level with higher transferability than other forms of conditioning.

IMPROVE BODY COMPOSITION

High-intensity resistance training will also increase lean body mass and help reduce body fat percentage. Body composition can influence muscular performance. Resistance training increases postexercise energy expenditure, influences metabolism, and increases a muscle's cross-sectional area, which shows its advantages as they relate to improved body composition. Recently, Mitchell and colleagues (44), Jenkins and colleagues (35, 36), and Schoenfeld and colleagues (57) have reported that higher and lower loads induce comparable hypertrophy in both men and women. Cholewa and colleagues (11) reported that women assigned to a heavy- or moderate-load resistance training group experienced similar increases in lean body mass and decreases in body fat percentage.

Metabolic stress brought on by resistance training can have a positive influence on development. Both high-load resistance training and fatigue-inducing low-load resistance training regimens have been shown to enhance mitochondrial protein synthesis posttraining (28). The metabolic and hormonal response that follows in postexercise recovery stages may also contribute to muscular development. Training causes an elevation in testosterone, growth hormone, and insulin-like growth factor (IGF-1) levels (37). Research has not been conclusive in showing that changes in circulating hormones influence the adaptive response to training, however (66).

Appropriate loading and exercise selection is essential to induce a proper metabolic training effect. For growth to occur, muscles must be stimulated in a manner that provokes them to hypertrophy. De Freitas and colleagues (16) examined several different resistance training modes with preferential intensity and volume to enhance metabolic stress and trigger an anabolic hormone response:

1. Resistance training only (moderate repetitions)—70% of the 1RM, 10 to 12 repetitions
2. Resistance training only (high repetitions to failure)—30% to 50% of the 1RM, 25 to 35 repetitions
3. Resistance training with blood flow restriction (100-200 mmHG)—20 to 30% of the 1RM, 30 repetitions or failure
4. High-intensity interval training (cycling)—100% of max power, 4 sets for 30 seconds

The age, training level, and goals of the athlete will influence the load and intensity prescribed and will be powerful determinants of what resistance training mode is most appropriate. For instance, an older, injured athlete might not be able to handle higher loads. With restored function in the midst of the rehabilitation process, resistance training with blood flow restriction or high-intensity interval training on a cycle ergometer might be an effective form of loading to provoke metabolic stress and thus may be the most appropriate form of resistance training. In contrast, the neuromuscular and mechanical adaptations acquired under heavier loads might be more beneficial for the younger, healthy athlete.

IMPROVE MOOD, ALERTNESS, AND RETENTION

For the basketball athlete, exercise is important not only in terms of muscular growth and maturation but also in terms of general health. Specifically, the rise in the level of hormones (and other substances) can improve energy and mood. Costigan and colleagues (15) found that in adolescents, various forms of exercise positively influenced cognitive function and overall feelings of psychological wellness. Their results, at the very least, suggest the need for inclusion of strategically designed exercise programs into the curriculum of the student.

Exercise increases endorphin levels, mitochondrial function, and hypothalamic pituitary-adrenal response that contribute to mental health, so both aerobic and resistance training protocols can have a positive influence on mood (decreased anxiety scores) (figure 1.1, 43). Nonfatiguing exercise protocols can improve mental performance before a practice or game, especially following a loss or in the presence of other stressors. In the days that follow a loss, sympathetic nervous system activity can then improve energy and overall mood. It is not clear what type of exercise specifically improves cognition, but if light to moderate exercise can improve alertness and memory, certain types of resistance training protocols before practice may be specifically designed to improve mood, alertness, and retention in subsequent, schematic film and practice sessions. Certain forms of exercise or an excessive volume or intensity of resistance training sessions might not be beneficial before competition. For instance, Neto and colleagues (46) recently found that low-load resistance training under restricted blood flow performed before a basketball game had a negative effect on mood.

OTHER BENEFITS OF RESISTANCE TRAINING

In an effort to speed recovery, a common practice after a game is to explore the use of parasympathetic activities. Active recoveries might also be useful because the athlete's mood might be altered following a loss or a poor individual performance or because of the physiological stress of a game or season. Activities that induce a parasympathetic nervous system response might help reduce stress and elicit a relaxation response. Studies have shown yoga or other mindfulness-based activities to be an effective method to reduce stress and improve memory by reducing sympathetic activity (24, 49). Although not a resistance training technique, parasympathetic methods like these, executed at the right times, might help to restore homeostasis and speed recovery after intense resistance training sessions. A careful balance between aggressive resistance training practices and proactive recovery modalities is needed if the athlete is to avoid injury and maximize performance over the entire course of a season.

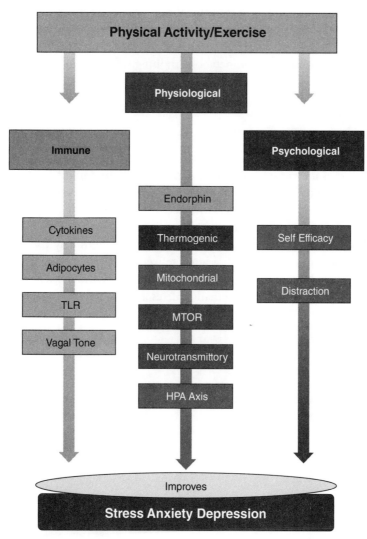

Figure 1.1 Exercise and mood. TLR = toll-like receptors, MTOR = mammalian target rapamycin, HPA Axis = interaction between the hypothalamus, pituitary gland, and adrenal glands.

Adapted by permission from K Mikkelsen et al., "Exercise and Mental Health," *Maturitas* 106 (2017): 48-56.

As explained in the introduction, resistance training for the basketball athlete involves complex application. Metabolic adaptations made through a concurrent training model are necessary. The learning and adaptations involved can last a lifetime. Resistance exercise may augment free fatty acid use and insulin sensitivity. As a result, resistance training may effectively improve cardiometabolic function and lower the risk for cardiovascular disease (26, 22). From a cardiovascular perspective, the athlete should know how modified resistance training protocols can influence metabolic demands and have a greater effect on cardiovascular function. For example, although a push-up might require minimal oxygen cost, Ratamess and colleagues (51) found that adding a lateral crawl to a push-up significantly increased mean oxygen consumption. Furthermore, these authors showed that burpees and battle rope exercises had a higher metabolic demand than traditional resistance training exercises under moderate loads. Instead of performing aerobic exercises that might result in low transfer on the court (e.g., biking, stair climber, and treadmill), resistance training exercises that may have a higher transfer can be modified for a higher metabolic training effect, promoting general health and perhaps weight loss.

CONCLUSION

Strength plays an integral role in injury prevention and maximizing on-court performance. Resistance training is a form of central and peripheral conditioning that uses external resistance to elicit a desired training effect and is essential for proper physiological and mechanical development. In terms of basketball performance, resistance training and its various modes have been shown to improve body composition, strength, power, speed, muscular endurance, agility, and change-of-direction ability. Enhanced muscle strength may also reduce the risk of injury. The adaptations to a strategically designed resistance training program can also positively affect overall health and improve energy and mental wellness. Ultimately, resistance training is an essential tool for the success of basketball athletes and their ability to endure a season and a healthy and productive lifestyle after competition.

2

ANALYSIS OF THE SPORT AND SPORT POSITIONS

STEVE SMITH, ROBBY SIKKA, AND TYLER A. BOSCH

Basketball, similar to other team field or court sports, can be defined as acyclic, reactive, and random. When successive repetitions are rarely identical the process of analyzing movement becomes extremely challenging. Movements are generally not preprogrammed, cyclic, or repeatable as is the case in sports such as cycling, rowing, or long-distance running, for example. Movements occur in response to a stimulus, context is required to understand why athletes are moving certain ways, and from there a coach can identify if other movement solutions would have been more effective, efficient, or successful. This chapter introduces the primary movements and physiological requirements of basketball, and it discusses athlete- and position-specific considerations. Finally, the chapter outlines some of the demands of the game based on developments in athlete-tracking technology.

GENERAL BIOMECHANICAL ANALYSIS

The following primary movement categories are outlined in this section, although numerous subcategories of these movements exist. The goal is to highlight these movements and focus on ways to think of them when analyzing basketball. Standing and walking, although making up a significant percentage of each game (30), will not be discussed in any detail.

Jumping

Jumping is defined as any movement or activity whereby an athlete initiates a jumping action and breaks contact with the playing surface (26). In basketball, athletes can jump in several different ways and typically choose the movement solution depending on the situation. An athlete going up for an uncontested rebound will most often jump and land on both feet. A contested rebound, however, often occurs with many different takeoff and landing strategies based on the needs and the environment. An athlete may need to jump off one leg while extending with one arm vertically and one arm horizontally. Athletes jump on both the offensive and defensive ends of the court while at different angles and heights. Consequently, athletes need to be able to create force to jump from a variety of positions as well as handle forces and stabilize their bodies in several different landing positions to minimize injury risk. The majority of jumps will be submaximal in nature, but as will be discussed later in this chapter, basketball athletes have unique body types and even low-intensity jumping places stress on the body.

Linear Movement

Linear movement in basketball is often composed of jogging, running, and sprinting forward or backward on the court. Biomotor abilities or qualities such as speed, acceleration, and deceleration are important to describe and categorize these movements. **Speed** is defined as the distance traveled per unit time. **Acceleration** is classically defined as the rate of change of velocity of an object or person with respect to time. By definition, the slowing down of an athlete, commonly referred to as **deceleration**, is actually a negative acceleration. For ease of terminology, the deceleration term is used as part of movements in which athletes are cutting or changing direction. An important component of all these actions in the game of basketball is that although they are primarily linear in nature, most of them occur in a curvilinear context. Rarely are these movements completed in a directly linear fashion, because athletes are working to create space and passing angles during offensive movements and working to disrupt spacing while on defense. Additionally, these movements may be occurring with the head and torso rotated to search for the ball or for athletes entering the space. These small but meaningful deviations away from pure linear movements are critical to the game of basketball.

In-game examples of high-intensity, forward acceleration are typically seen when an offensive player is driving to the basket with the ball, in transition offense and defense, on fast breaks, or when a defender closes out on a shooter. The *closeout* is probably the most direct, high-intensity linear acceleration. This brief movement creates an explosive acceleration and deceleration toward an opponent. But in other such instances athletes take a curvilinear path that creates or takes away options while adjusting their body position to avoid opponents. Additionally, these movements also include some rotational components, such as dissociation of the trunk and lower body. Rarely are those movements produced from a standing stance; instead, they occur in the midst of moving in some capacity. In these cases, athletes are constantly perceiving their opponents and adjusting their actions accordingly. Many of these high-intensity acceleration movements are coupled with varying deceleration techniques that allow the athlete to change paths quickly and keep defenders off balance. Common linear decelerations patterns seen in basketball are jump stops, breakdown stops, lunge stops, reverse lunge stops, and angled lateral stops. The *jump stop, breakdown stop, lunge stop,* and *lateral angle stop* are associated with forward, linear movement. The *reverse lunge stop* is associated with backward, linear movement

Vaughn Ridley/Getty Images

The closeout.

and can be done with either a *vertical heel technique* or a *T-stop technique*, both of which are commonly used by defensive backs in football.

Combined acceleration and deceleration movements are generally referred to as **change of direction**. Change-of-direction movements involve the reacceleration of the athlete's body mass into the same or a different movement direction or vector. The two combined directions or vectors of movement can both be linear or lateral or a combination of the two. All the primary deceleration patterns described earlier can be used to change from one movement vector to another depending on the need or reaction to what is happening around the athlete. Examples include a lateral slide to a linear acceleration or sprint as would be the case with running the floor as an offensive player after a turnover was created or a 45-degree speed cut being used to evade a defender. Athletes are required to have a variety of linear movement strategies, and through trial and error they can identify successful strategies for different situations within the game. No single answer or movement provides a solution to any situation; the answer will depend on a variety of contextual information in that moment.

The *lateral slide pattern* is the most widely used and viewed lateral movement in basketball and can also be thought of as lateral acceleration. Like other movements or activities, it can be categorized by the intensity of the movement. It is most widely used as a defensive tactic to guard an opponent with or without the ball. When high-intensity lateral acceleration is needed, the athlete often uses a crossover step initially so that he or she can cover more ground and stay in front of or get back in front of the athlete he or she is defending. The most common lateral deceleration tactic used is the *shuffle stop*.

Upper Body Movements

Upper body movements include movements or skills like reaching, passing, and dribbling. **Reaching** specifically involves the projection of one or both of the upper extremities in the horizontal or vertical plane to defend, rebound, shoot, and so on. Upper body movements are often centered on the action of the ball. As in most team-based ball sports, the ball is critical to

The defender performing a lateral slide pattern.

Tim Warner/Getty Images

both understanding and describing movement patterns. The ball becomes the contextual key to most movements. On offense, the athlete with the ball has to perform these movement skills while also dribbling, passing, carrying, shooting, or catching the ball. Given the relatively small dimensions of a basketball court compared with the playing area of other sports, the ball can go anywhere, at any time, to anyone. All these movements will be completed with knowledge and intent of where the ball might go. This is the link between perception and action; competitors perceive to act and act to perceive (9). The actions of athletes are based on the perception of their environment, and each action is constantly changing the perception (9, 10, 11).

Movement analyses in basketball and the subsequent training and development of these skills requires a high degree of contextual information. Athletes have to be able to sprint, jump, cut, and reach from a variety of positions; some are ideal, but most are not. An interwoven development plan that teaches sound mechanical strategies, combined with the chaotic nature of basketball, provides an ideal learning environment for athletes to explore the necessary movement skills to be successful in basketball. A whole field of work dedicated to this strategy is known as **ecological dynamics**, but it is outside the scope of this chapter. One of the founders of this area was Nikolai Bernstein, who famously explained movement and sport as a problem-solving activity that has many possible solutions and through variable repetition, the body and brain can coordinate to identify the best solution based on current perception (4). Thus, within the analyses of movement it is necessary to describe not only how athletes move but also why athletes move a certain way. What did the athlete perceive to create that movement, pass, or shot? In analyzing movement, coaches can learn to identify environments to encourage new strategies for the athlete to evaluate and improve or develop new movement skills to be executed successfully during games.

Evolution in Movement Analyses

Recent technological advances have allowed athletes to be monitored during both practices and games. These sensors have provided living lab scenarios to understand the movement demands within the sport of basketball. Triaxial accelerometers, gyroscopes, and magnetometer microsensors have been developed to track movements. Additionally, visual tracking from local positioning camera systems or radio frequency identification (RFID) can also be used to provide real-time data on athletes' accelerations and movement patterns. Strength and conditioning professionals, athletic trainers, and coaches can use this information to compare movement data with what they see from visual observation and film study. Moreover, coordinates from visual or RFID tracking can be mapped to visualize structure and tactical strategy within a team.

In addition to tactical analysis, quantifying the distance, velocity, and acceleration that occur during practice and game play has provided greater insight into the demands of the sport and the way that athletes are training and recovering. Many teams have started to use tactical periodization strategies in which they are interweaving the physical requirements of the athletes with the technical and tactical requirements. Wearable devices also have given insight into the jump patterns and volume for basketball athletes in training sessions and games at different levels. Over time these data can provide individualized insights into athletes' training and recovery strategies to keep them available and their performance optimal.

GENERAL PHYSIOLOGICAL ANALYSIS

The ideal characteristics of a basketball athlete, regardless of age, sex, or skill level, are twofold. They need the ability to exhibit high, repeated power outputs and to do so with a low fatigue index, or a low performance decrement, from the first explosive bout to the last.

Energy Production

It has been reported that the work-to-rest ratio of basketball is approximately 1:4 to 1:5 (6), where for every 1 second of high-intensity activity, 4 to 5 seconds of medium- and low-intensity activity accompany it. Generally, the high-intensity bouts last far less than 10 seconds (6). Thus, basketball athletes essentially fall into the category of repeated sprint athletes in which **sprints** can be defined as any explosive, high-intensity bout of short duration done repeatedly with incomplete rest between bouts. As a broad definition, sprints are considered to be bouts greater than 1 second in duration when using tracking data, and accelerations are often categorized by the acceleration speed but are considered to cover at least a distance of 1 meter (1.1 yd).

During active game play the average heart rate is frequently at or above 85% of maximal heart rate with high blood lactate concentration. The many stoppages (rest) that occur result in large fluctuations in heart rate during the entirety of the game. In the second half, free fatty acid concentration in the bloodstream increases, associated with increased lipolytic activity (1), which is indicative of aerobic metabolism. This increase in free fatty acid concentration is partially contributed by a decrease in exercise intensity as a result of accumulated fatigue. Because the body is unable to maintain higher intensities, it shifts toward more aerobic metabolism and fatty acid oxidation. Average VO_2max values for female and male basketball athletes have been reported in the range of 44 to 54 and 50 to 60 mL^{-1} · kg^{-1} · min^{-1}, respectively (34). Guards were noted to have a higher aerobic capacity than centers in the aforementioned study.

Physiologically speaking, then, the demands for energy production are placed primarily on the ATP-PCr and aerobic systems. The ATP-PCr system is relied on to provide energy for the quick explosive movements of the sport, and the aerobic system is most important for recovery between bouts. But during game play, with each successive high-intensity bout of activity, the aerobic system becomes more and more dominant in regard to total energy contribution (22). This shift to a higher proportion of the aerobic system is an inevitability of accumulated fatigue and decreasing intensity. Higher aerobic fitness, in theory, allows for a higher level of exercise intensity with less reliance on **anaerobic** (without oxygen) metabolism. Robustness and efficiency of the aerobic system allows the athlete to be able to sustain higher levels of power and explosiveness longer without fatiguing and, at a cellular level, to replenish the substrates needed by the ATP-PCr system. Thus, if coaches can improve an athlete's ability to meet energy demands using the ATP-PCr or glycolytic systems, he or she should be able to do more high-intensity work for a longer time. High-intensity interval training has been shown to improve not only the glycolytic capacity in skeletal muscle (2) but also aerobic capacity. Because of the use of all three energy systems by basketball athletes, training should focus on improving each as well as allowing the athlete to remain flexible and rely on all systems.

Anthropometrics

In today's sports environment, comments are often made about an athlete's body type or frame. In basketball, the term *long* is often used to describe athletes. Coaches and athletic trainers may try to identify an athlete's frame size to determine how much muscle mass he or she may be able to add or if he or she will continue to grow in height. But this approach was not always the case. In the early 1920s it was believed that the average height and average weight were ideal for all sports (7). As sports evolved and became more mainstream, however, unique body types that matched the demands of each sport emerged. In basketball, height and length (wingspan) are advantageous. In fact, on average, college and professional basketball athletes have an average wingspan 5 inches (13 cm) longer than their height (19c). (The average person has a wingspan that is the same length as her or his height). Figure 2.1 shows how rare it is for professional

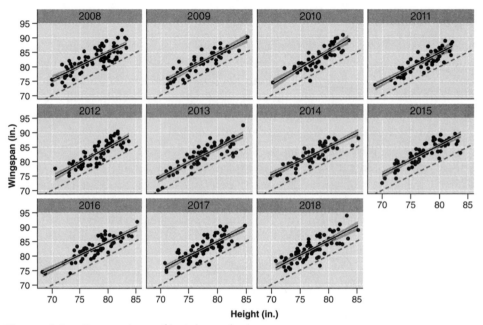

Figure 2.1. Comparison of height and wingspan.

athletes to have a wingspan equal to or less than height. In this plot, the solid line represents the linear relationship between height and wingspan, and the dashed line represents equal wingspan and height. In 10 years, only six athletes have ever had a wingspan less than their height. This unique anatomical feature allows a greater range both offensively (shooting over an opponent) and defensively (the area to guard). Additionally, with changes in the game and requirements of positions, specific injury risk may be associated with higher or lower wingspan. More examples are shown later in this section.

Within the same sport, even greater selection occurs between different positions. These differences emerge from positional requirements within the sport of basketball. Historically, basketball has five defined positions: point guard (PG), shooting guard (SG), small forward (SF), power forward (PF), and center (C). In both college and professional athletes, C and PF are on average taller and heavier than the other three positions (19c, 29). In fact, from data collected from a large sample of power-five universities from 2008 to 2016, a 2-inch (5 cm) decrease in height occurred, on average, with each change in position; C averaged 81.1 inches (206 cm), and PG averaged 73.2 inches (186 cm). The average heights for PF, SF, and SG are 79.5 (202 cm), 77.9 (198 cm), and 75.2 (191 cm) inches, respectively (29). NBA data taken from the scouting combine (19c) over the same time frame (2008-2016) mirror the collegiate data spread between positions but have slightly higher average heights across most positions: 82.2 inches (209 cm) for C, 80.0 inches (203 cm) for PF, 78.3 inches (199 cm) for SF, 75.8 inches (193 cm) for SG, and 73.0 inches (185 cm) for PG. Weights in both college and professional basketball athletes have much larger differences among positions. The average weight for a C in both college and professional basketball was 250 pounds (115 kg) from 2008 to 2016. The average weight for a PF at both levels was 233 pounds (106 kg). The biggest difference between college and professional athletes was at the SF and SG positions; collegiate SF and SG had an average weight of 202 pounds (92 kg) and 195 pounds (89 kg), respectively, versus 215 pounds (98 kg) and 203 pounds (93 kg) for professional SF and SG, respectively. Professional and college PG had similar average weights of 186 pounds (85 kg).

Table 2.1 highlights these comparisons.

Table 2.1 Anthropometrics* for College and Professional Combine Attendees

	College				
Position	PG	SG	SF	PF	C
Weight (lb)	187.7[b] (85 kg) ±20.7 (9 kg)	196.5[b] (89 kg) ±15.2 (7 kg)	202.6[b] (92 kg) ±13.2 (6 kg)	233.9[a] (106 kg) ±18.3 (8 kg)	253.0[a] (115 kg) ±36.9 (17 kg)
Height (in.)	73.2[a] (186 cm) ±1.5 (4 cm)	75.2[a] (191 cm) ±1.6[a] (4 cm)	77.9[b] (198 cm) ±1.5 (4 cm)	79.5[bc] (202 cm) ±1.1 (3 cm)	81.1[c] (206 cm) ±1.2 (3 cm)
Body mass index (kg/m^2)	24.3[a] ±1.8	24.4[a] ±1.8	23.3[a] ±1.5	25.9[ab] ±1.7[ab]	27.3[b] ±4.0
**Percent body fat (%)	14.4[a] ±3.8	12.4[a] ±3.2	12.0[a] ±3.1	14.8[a] ±4.2	15.5[a] ±4.9
	Professional combine				
Position	PG	SG	SF	PF	C
Weight (lb)	185.3[a] (84 kg) ±21.1 (10 kg)	203.0[b] (92 kg) ±12.1 (6 kg)	215.4[c] (98 kg) ±12.1 (6 kg)	233.3[d] (106 kg) ±15.5 (7 kg)	250.8[e] (114 kg) ±20.0 (9 kg)
Height (in.)	73.0[a] (185 cm) ±1.9 (5 cm)	75.8[b] (193 cm) ±1.1 (3 cm)	78.4[c] (199 cm) ±1.1 (3 cm)	79.9[d] (203 cm) ±1.3 (3 cm)	82.2[e] (209 cm) ±1.43 (4 cm)
Body mass index (kg/m^2)	24.5[a] ±2.8	24.9[ab] ±1.6	24.7[ab] ±1.6	25.7[bc] ±2.0	26.2[c] ±2.3
**Percent body fat (%)	6.2[a] ±1.8[a]	6.7[a] ±1.8	7.0[ab] ±2.2	8.4[b] ±2.7	8.6[b] ±3.2[b]

*Average ± standard deviation. The letter next to the average signifies that the value is significantly different from other positions. If positions do not share a letter, they are different at p <0.05 using a Tukey Honest significant difference test.

**Indicates that the method for measuring percent body fat is different between the groups. College was measured by DXA, and pro combine was measured by skinfold. These values should not be compared.

College data modified from Solfest and colleagues (29).

Professional combine data aggregated from NBA Advanced Stats (19c).

To pull together the data in table 2.1, the anthropometric data was scraped from the website and brought into Rstudio, and data were taken from Solfest and colleagues (29) and converted to imperial units for comparison. Means and standard deviations were calculated by position for the year ranges identified. The data were then analyzed according to the same methodology described previously (29). In brief, the effect of athlete position on the measured anthropometric variables was measured. If a significant effect of position was identified (p <0.05), posthoc comparisons were made among each of the positions using an honest significance difference test with an adjusted significance level of 0.01 using a Bonferroni adjustment (corrected p = α / number of tests; 0.01 = 0.05 / 5). Statistically speaking, both the heights and weights were significantly different (p <0.05) in the professional athlete, but in the college athletes, significant differences were observed only between PG, SG, and SF versus PF and C for both height and weight (29). These data suggest that the range of heights and weights between positions in college athletes is greater than what is observed in athletes from the pro scouting combine. There are two possible explanations for this difference. First, the increased similarity within a position could be driven by further self-selection of the most talented athletes (the sample was made up of those selected to the combine) having similar body types. Second, the increased diversity of body types within positions at the college level could be driven by differences in playing styles among individual teams or conferences. Either way, most basketball athletes represent a unique body type with similar mass distribution regardless of height. Note, however, that the sample included athletes invited to the NBA combine. Although these athletes are regarded as the top collegiate athletes, not all of them become successful NBA athletes.

Other important factors to consider when looking at body types in sport are related to **body composition** (the amount of muscle and fat relative to their total weight), the **distribution of mass** (where that mass is distributed, such as around the waist and abdomen versus on the hips), and **mass relative to height** (i.e., body mass index, fat-free mass index; see next section). Both composition and distribution patterns influence movement patterns and have the potential to influence the body's response to a given stimulus. In collegiate athletes, dual x-ray absorptiometry (DXA) derived body composition data suggest that, even though height and weight differ, significant differences are not found in relative body fat (%) among the different basketball positions (12.0% [SF] to 15.5% [C]; table 2.1) (29). This finding is in contrast to the professional combine data, which illustrated that C and PF positions have a significantly higher percent body fat than the SG and PG positions (p <0.05). Note that the methods for measuring percent body fat are different in these populations; the professional combine uses digital calipers. Skinfold assessment and DXA are alternative methods with different validities and reliabilities, and caution is warranted when interpreting any differences in body composition between the professional and college athletes presented in table 2.1.

Mass Indices

Differences in height are seen among athletes who play different basketball positions (3, 27, 29, 35). Height is an important factor in determining how much total mass a person will tend to carry. One way to compare mass between positions is to use indices that account for the height of the individuals. Three indices have been used to compare total mass, fat mass, and fat-free mass relative to a person's height. The **body mass index** (BMI) is commonly used to assess total mass relative to a person's height. Specific cut points have been identified and used for general health. A BMI >25 kg/m² is classified as overweight, and a BMI >30 kg/m² is classified as obese (19b). BMI, however, is a poor index in athletic populations, because it does not account for the type of mass. Because many athletes carry greater than normal fat-free mass, they can be misclassified as overweight or obese based on their BMI alone. To account for this, the fat mass index and the fat-free mass (or lean mass plus bone mass) index have been proposed as methods of comparing fat mass and fat-free mass relative to height. To calculate the fat mass index, an athlete's total fat in kilograms is divided by his or her height in meters squared (fat mass index = fat mass [kg]/height [m]²). The fat-free mass index, on the other hand, is calculated by dividing the athlete's fat-free mass in kilograms by his or her height in meters squared (fat-free mass index = fat-free mass [kg]/height [m]²) (31). To obtain absolute measurements of fat and fat-free mass, the coach should first measure the athlete's percent body fat. The coach can then calculate absolute fat mass by multiplying the percent body fat by the body mass (in kg). Finally, the athlete's absolute fat-free mass is calculated as the difference between fat mass (in kg) and body mass (in kg).

These indices can be used to identify whether an athlete has more (or less) mass relative to her or his height than other positions. Using the fat mass and fat-free mass indices, coaches can identify whether an athlete has more (or less) fat and fat-free mass, respectively. This information could be useful when attempting to modify an athlete's mass and pinpoint what areas to address. For example, if an athlete has a higher BMI relative to other athletes at his or her position, the coach might ask if this is a result of more fat mass or more lean mass. Using the fat-mass and fat-free mass index, the coach can determine which type of mass is contributing to the higher BMI. A higher lean mass (primarily muscle) may mean that no change to the athlete's body mass is necessary, but a higher fat mass may mean that an adjustment to weight or mass is needed.

These indices can be important in understanding the increased forces that may be placed on joints during basketball movements like jumping, cutting, and sprinting. Athletes with a high fat mass index are carrying nonfunctional mass that can cause increased internal stress (14). Table 2.1 shows the average BMI values for each position from the college and professional combine populations. These data suggest that, on average, PF and C are carrying more mass relative to height. The ideal BMI for an athlete depends on the team's playing style and their positional requirements. More mass can be beneficial in a traditional half-court offense or if playing teams that like to slow the pace and work the ball inside the post. But if the system emphasizes movement, spacing, and speed of play, lower indices can be beneficial to all athletes, because they are likely to be more efficient in their movements.

Mass Distribution Ratios

Indices can provide insight into how much mass (fat versus muscle) an athlete has relative to height, but they are in reference to total mass. One concept to understand regarding body types and composition is to compare mass distribution ratios. These ratios allow coaches and athletes to identify where fat and lean mass is distributed within the body and determine if a specific distribution pattern may be hindering movement or performance. To calculate these ratios, regional mass distribution must be determined first (e.g., leg mass, trunk mass, arms mass, and so on). Traditionally, this measurement has been possible only with DXA, but other modalities such as multifrequency bioelectrical impedance analyses and bioelectrical impedance spectroscopy provide regional mass measurements. Further, even the use of 3D body scanners or circumferences measurements can be used to estimate ratios of regional body volumes in athletes. One simple, common example of mass distribution is the **waist-to-hip ratio**. This ratio compares the circumference of waist (measured halfway between the lowest palpable rib and the superior border of the iliac crest) to the widest circumference of the hip and buttocks and provides insight into abdominal fat distribution. People with higher distribution of abdominal fat relative to hip fat storage (think apple shaped versus pear shaped) are at increased risk for metabolic disease and dysfunction (5, 8, 17), as well as increased risk of injury (20, 24). These ratios can provide another layer of context, because total mass may not change even while the distribution of that mass may be shifting.

From a performance standpoint, our lab has started to observe some interesting relationships between these mass distribution ratios with movement patterns in a variety of sports. Athletes with higher **upper to lower lean mass ratios** (a ratio of the total mass in the trunk and arms relative to the muscle mass in the legs) tend to have impaired force transfer during countermovement jumps with lower (relative) braking force, lower propulsive force, and lower propulsive rate of force development (unpublished data). Additionally, this top-heavy distribution is also associated with slow change-of-direction movements in both planned and reactive environments even after normalizing for total mass.

Physiological Evolution

A shift in the game has occurred at all levels as emphasis has been placed on spacing, increasing possessions, and taking quality shots. This change has included an increased emphasis on three-point shooting for all positions. In 2016, only 3 centers attempted over 100 three-point shots in the regular season. In the 2016-2017 and 2017-2018 seasons, 10 and 11 NBA centers (respectively) attempted over 100 three-point shots and 8 of them attempted over 200 three-point shots (13b). With these game-play changes have come body-type changes within positions. Figures 2.2a through c and 2.3a through c show the longitudinal averages for height, weight, and wingspan for traditional positions and for Bigs and Smalls. In both cases, height has remained fairly consistent between 2008 and 2018. But weight has been trending down for some positions, in particular PF, who on average weigh almost 20 pounds (44 kg) less. Similarly, the long positions (C, PF) are trending toward getting longer, but even PG have been trending up in wingspan. The increase in wingspan is more evident in figure 2.3c, which shows that Smalls (wings and guards) have increased their average wingspan by 2 inches (5 cm).

Basketball athletes represent a unique body type relative to the average person and to athletes in other sports. Basketball athletes tend to be long and lean, even at the larger positions. These attributes allow athletes to be explosive and cover a lot of space in a short time multiple times per game. Carrying excess mass can increase the stress on their joints with the numerous explosive actions that occur during a game. The evolution of the game has had an influence in some positions; some positions are getting lighter (e.g., PF), and others are becoming longer (e.g., guards and wings). Finally, note that most of the data presented are averages; the standard deviations presented in table 2.1 demonstrate a wide range of variability for each body type. Each athlete will be slightly different from others. Considering the athlete's body type in both performance and tactical contexts is preferable to identifying a standardized weight or index that an athlete needs to get to.

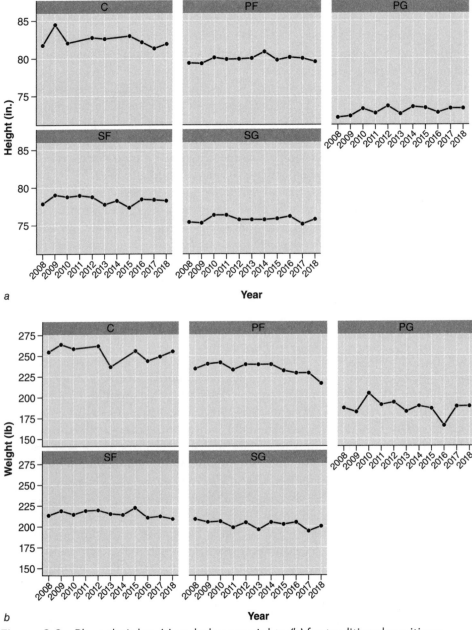

Figure 2.2   Player heights *(a)* and player weights *(b)* for traditional positions.

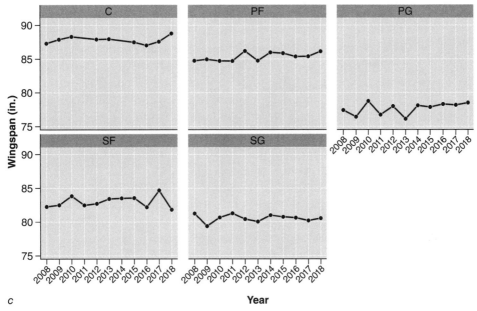

Figure 2.2 (continued) Player wingspan *(c)* for traditional positions.

POSITION-SPECIFIC ANALYSIS

The time length of basketball games depends on the level of play and ranges from 32 to 48 minutes between high school and professional games. The typical distance traveled per athlete during live games may range from 1.5 to 3 miles (2-5 km) (26, 30, 34). When considering the number of games that a collegiate or professional athlete may play in a given season, including

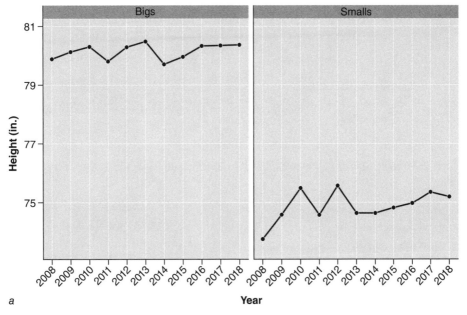

Figure 2.3 Player heights *(a)* for bigs and smalls.

(continued)

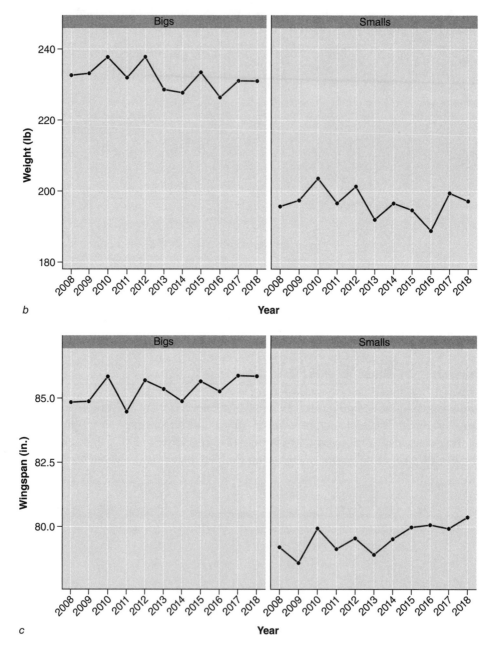

Figure 2.3 *(continued)* Player weights *(b)* and player wingspan *(c)* for bigs and smalls.

preseason and postseason games, some athletes may approach 250 to 300 total game miles (400-480 km) traveled over the course of a season. Practice sessions and lower-level tournaments in youth basketball can often result in even higher distances than this when athletes are playing multiple games in a day.

An analysis of collegiate basketball tracking data indicates that **high metabolic distance**, or distance covered within 20% of maximum speed, typically ranges from 5% to 15% of total distance. Guards typically are at the higher end of this range, and athletes typically average 10% of their total distance as high metabolic distance. Maximum speeds of athletes may range from 12 to 18 mph (19-29 km/h). The highest speeds are typically seen in transition situations, but athletes may sprint for shorter distances 50 to 80 times per game. Maximal acceleration and deceleration levels may reach 12 to 18 ft/s² (4-6 m/s²). Tracking and movement data suggest that athletes may spend 70% to 80% of their total time in "slow range," or 0 to 4 mph (0-6 km/h), 10% to 15% in moderate speed zones between 4 and 12 mph (6-19 km/h), and 5% to 10% in high speed zones greater than 12 mph (19 km/h). The total amount of time spent in maximal speed zones is 1% to 2%. Angular speeds and accelerations, however, may be more common. The number of accelerations and decelerations that a basketball athlete may have in a game can vary widely, but the number of high-speed accelerations is typically 10% of his or her in-game total (26, 30, 34).

During a game, guards may perform less standing and walking, as well as more sprinting and high-intensity lateral sliding when compared with forwards and centers (1, 30). Guards also reach higher maximal speeds and sustain higher speeds for longer periods. Analysis of collegiate athletes showed that they spent 34.1% of playing time running and jumping, 56.8% walking, and 9.0% standing (19). Athletes commonly sustain speeds greater than 12 mph (19 km/h) for only 10 to 15 feet (3-5 m) and at the most 20 to 30 feet (6-9 m). Such rapid changes in speed and direction lead to high accelerations and deceleration speeds in basketball. This pattern may be different in centers, who often sustain high speeds and accelerations for 10 to 20 feet (3-6 m) and have fewer total accelerations than guards. Such variations in activity demands likely account for the higher blood lactate concentrations and HR responses observed for guards compared with forwards and centers (30).

An analysis of temporal relationships within games indicates that high-speed activity declines during the fourth quarter. This change may be associated with lower blood lactate concentrations and HR responses toward the end of games. Furthermore, higher-level athletes perform a greater intermittent workload than lower-level athletes do (30). This circumstance may be changing, however, with the evolution of basketball and offensive strategies. Indeed, with the rising pace of play, greater emphasis on defensive switching, and increasing use of three pointers, fewer differences are seen between movement patterns of the different positions.

Jump mechanics and volume must also be considered in basketball athletes. Increasing evidence shows that the frequency and intensity (jump height) of jumping and landing can be reliably and validly quantified using commercially available inertial measurement units (IMUs) such as the G-VERT (Mayfonk Athletic, Fort Lauderdale, Florida, USA) (18, 28). In volleyball, jump count has been linked to injury (32). Similar studies have not yet been performed in basketball, but future studies may help illustrate the relationship between jump volume and jump intensity or load to injuries. Game-day jump volumes in the 100 to 200 range are commonly seen, with significant variation on practice days. Heavy days for some high-volume shooting on practice days may result in 1,000 repetitions. As the game evolves, forwards and centers are taking more three pointers and as a result are taking more practice shots, resulting in more jumping activity.

Understanding the unique factors for each athlete's jump mechanics is important. Single-leg jumping and landing tasks elicit less hip and knee flexion angles, stimulate larger knee joint forces and knee flexion moments, and therefore produce twice as much load as double-leg landings (16, 33). Thus, teaching an athlete to use both single- and double-leg jumping techniques, depending on the situation, can help reduce total jump load. Though not yet validated, these data may be able to be collected in-season through wearables worn on each limb. Poor landing mechanics, such as stiff-legged landings or dynamic lower-extremity valgus, may subject the athlete to injury risk and additional biomechanical load (12, 23). Screening tools such as Landing Error Scoring System (LESS) or Y balance may offer additional weighting to the measured values of jumping load and may guide strategies to prevent injuries. For example, in an athlete with a high preseason LESS score or Y balance, suggesting faulty movement patterns, each jump may register a greater load in comparison with an athlete with a lower score (15, 21). These metrics can then be considered and weighted to better individualize appropriate jump count and assess total mechanical load. Indeed, **mechanical load**, a metric frequently used in professional and elite basketball to assess practice intensity and volume, considers jump load. Analysis of jump mechanics can allow coaches to assess athletes for injury risk and provide significant insight into areas for performance improvement. Specific measures, including ground reactive forces, symmetry and landing mechanics, knee valgus, and hip and knee flexion angles can all be assessed in jumps. All of this must take into account an athlete's native anatomy and history of prior injuries. Timing of testing must also be considered because athletes may be assessed before or after games, during the season, during the off-season, or during breaks. Jump testing and biomechanical testing is optimally done in the preseason, as well as on a consistent basis in season after a period to adjust training. A late-season test may also then guide off-season programming.

Overuse injuries such as patellar, quadriceps, or Achilles tendinosis may be precipitated by sudden increases in jump load (32). Athlete-specific risk factors should be considered when developing a jump training or plyometric program and should account for range of motion or stiffness at the ankle, knee, and hip. Because basketball athletes are often subjected to higher jump volumes than other athletes, using the concept of acute-to-chronic load ratio may also be helpful, noting that higher injury risk may be associated with rapid changes in week-to-week load. In particular, this may also affect resistance training programs as well as the building of chronic load, which may be a consideration for strength and conditioning professionals and may help delineate specific time frames to increase load.

With the evolution of basketball and the corresponding changes in anthropometrics, injury patterns may begin to evolve as well. Indeed, ankle sprains are common in collegiate men's basketball (11.96 per 10,000 athlete-exposures [AEs]), women's NCAA (9.50/10,000 AEs) (25), and professional basketball (3.2/1000 AEs [13.2% of injuries and 8.8% of games missed]) (13). In-game strategies like switching on all screens and expectations for guards to defend centers and vice versa may place different strains and risks on athletes. Furthermore, expectations for faster accelerations and decelerations may affect the risk for hamstring and other soft-tissue injuries. Increasing emphasis on the three-point shot and jump shooting may increase the risk for tendinosis and overuse injuries. As the game continues to evolve, training and developing skills commensurate with a changing game will be necessary. Programs that incorporate balance, proprioception, strength, and agility training may all improve performance and reduce injury risk.

CONCLUSION

More data than ever are being collected on basketball athletes at all levels. These data may raise more questions than answers. Strength and conditioning professionals will be expected to understand such data and apply the results to improve the care of their athletes. Understanding how the game is evolving will be imperative for strength and conditioning professionals to provide the best possible care for their athletes.

TESTING PROTOCOLS AND ATHLETE ASSESSMENT

ANDREW BARR, ALEXANDER REESER, AND TANIA SPITERI

Performance tests are used for a variety of reasons depending on the situation. Among the most common reasons that performance tests are used (especially at the professional level) are the following:

- Identifying baseline strength levels and preferred movement strategies
- Ranking athletes during talent recruiting process
- Evaluating effectiveness of specific training programs
- Informing athlete development and injury risk reduction strategies
- Guiding return to play progression

The overarching goal of the performance testing in basketball is to provide athletes, coaches, medical and performance staff, and front office personnel with objective data. That said, the value of performance testing is not in the athlete's specific data, but rather in the correct interpretation of the data within the proper context. Moreover, because the knowledge of sport science and performance testing for basketball continues to grow, a detailed understanding of the foundational protocols described in this chapter is, and will continue to be, a necessary skill for strength and conditioning professionals.

GENERAL TESTING GUIDELINES

The value of a performance test lies in the analysis and conclusions drawn from the data collected during testing. To that end, the appropriateness of the conclusions drawn depends on the accuracy and reliability of the data obtained. To ensure accurate and reliable data, the following guidelines should be followed:

- Follow a manufacturer's setup and calibration guidelines for all equipment used during testing.
- Keep a log of the tests performed.
- Standardize the testing environment and protocols followed.
- Maintain consistency in the sequence of tests performed.

Although this list is not exhaustive, following these basic gui ines will help to safeguard the standardization of the testing process and to control the fact that could otherwise jeop- ardize the accuracy and reliability of the collected data.

TESTING PROTOCOLS

The testing protocols provided include instructions to promo   alidity and reliability and normative and descriptive data, when data are supported by rese   :h. Note that any data pro- vided are specific to the athletes who were evaluated and uniqu   the conditions of the test.

STRENGTH TESTS

Strength testing serves a variety of purposes in basketball.   rge-scale testing events, like the NBA combine, collect multiple athletes' performanc   aselines that can be used to compare athletes' strength capabilities. When performed   a regular basis, strength tests can be used to quantify performance changes from r   stance training programs and to monitor an athlete's fatigue status in-season.

ISOMETRIC MID-THIGH PULL

Purpose

The isometric mid-thigh pull (IMTP) is a valid and reliable total body, functional isometric strength test used to identify peak force, rate of force development, and impulse from a traditional power stance or ready stance (5). Despite limited research in basketball, IMTP peak force has been shown to be significantly correlated to change-of-direction performance in elite female basketball athletes (49). The rate of force development generated during the IMTP has also been shown to be significantly associated with initial acceleration kinetics during sprinting in Division I men's and women's basketball athletes (46). Given the positive relationship between IMTP performance and basketball performance, coaches and strength and conditioning professionals should consider the IMTP when designing basketball strength and power testing batteries.

Equipment

The fundamental equipment required for the IMTP includes a force plate and a stationary bar running parallel to the floor and the athlete. One setup example includes fixing a bar underneath the safety bars in a traditional squat rack, but many suitable options exist. When available, dual force plates may be used in preference to a single force plate to identify strength differences between limbs.

Setup

The bar should be placed in a fixed position equidistant from the hip and knee. Athletes should approach the bar with a shoulder-width, overhand grip, an upright trunk posture, neutral neck position, and slight hip and knee flexion. Previous studies suggest using a hip joint angle of 145 degrees and knee joint angle of 140 to 150 degrees (9, 14). As such, other athlete-specific measurements (i.e., the bar height from the floor) may be chosen to ensure reliability of results in different testing environments. Additionally, careful attention should be given to the sampling rate of the force plate and the effect it may impose on rate of force development and other time-derived outcome measures.

Testing Protocol

1. Calibrate the force plate based on unit-specific guidelines.
2. Ensure that the force plate is zeroed out following calibration.
3. Instruct the athlete to come onto the force plate and assume the ready "power" position using a self-selected grip technique.
4. Cue the athlete to initiate a maximum-effort pull as quickly as possible. Common cues include *drive the heels into the floor* and *pull the bar away from the floor*.
5. End testing when force plateaus or begins to decline.
6. Ensure that adequate rest periods of at least three minutes are provided for multiple trials.

Descriptive Data

Tables 3.1 and 3.2 provide descriptive data that can be used to evaluate the IMTP of high school and Division I college basketball athletes.

Table 3.1 Isometric Mid-Thigh Pull Test Values for Male High School Basketball Athletes

Variable	Value ± SD
Absolute peak force (N)	2,906 ± 428
Relative peak force (N/kg)	34.6 ± 2.9

SD = standard deviation.

Data from Scanlan et al. (2019).

Table 3.2 Isometric Mid-Thigh Pull Test Values for NCAA Division I College Men's and Women's Basketball Athletes

Variable	Value*	
	Men	Women
Peak force (N)	2,534.1 ± 368.0	1,248.0 ± 377.2
RFD** 0-50 ms (N/s)	5,643.1 ± 6,459.8	2,778.7 ± 1,708.0
RFD 0-100 ms (N/s)	6,161.4 ± 4,694.8	2,988.1 ± 1,831.1
RFD 0-150 ms (N/s)	5,811.0 ± 3,995.0	2,664.6 ± 1,439.0
RFD 0-200 ms (N/s)	6,015.8 ± 2,678.0	2,736.0 ± 1,176.5
RFD 0-250 ms (N/s)	5,603.0 ± 2,272.6	2,882.2 ± 1,105.2

*Mean ± SD. **RFD = rate of force development.

Data from Townsend et al. (2017).

HIP ADDUCTION AND ABDUCTION TESTS

Purpose

Maximal voluntary isometric contractions are a standard methodology used to identify muscle strength. Hip adduction (AD) and abduction (AB) muscles play an important role in optimizing hip and trunk movement control in the frontal and transverse planes. Strength asymmetries in hip AD and AB have been shown to correlate with increased risk of hip, groin, and knee injuries in multidirectional, quick-change-of-direction sports (10, 19, 44, 45). Given the high frequency of lateral and rotational actions in basketball, testing of the hip AD versus AB strength ratio (AD:AB) is important to consider for injury risk monitoring and performance development in basketball.

Setup

There are no specific set-up directions for hip AD:AB testing because certain instruments may require different calibration and setup procedures. That said, measurements should be taken at multiple limb positions (i.e., hip AD:AB at 0 degrees, 30 degrees, 45 degrees, and 90 degrees hip and knee flexion) to highlight potential strength deficiencies or asymmetries in variable positions. Similarly, the athlete's body position during testing (i.e., seated, prone, supine) is a confounding variable known to produce statistically meaningful differences in force output (33). Above all, retaining consistency in the testing procedure is important because no study has identified which positions or limb configurations are most relevant to basketball athletes.

Equipment

Equipment used for hip AD:AB testing is often determined based on availability. Isokinetic and isotonic dynamometers are the most commonly used instruments in laboratory-based settings. Previous studies on injury-free athletes have identified a hip AD:AB of 1.0 to be normal, whereas a ratio of less than 0.8 has generally been agreed on as a cutoff for increased risk of adductor-related groin injuries (43). Laboratory-based tools are not commonly used in applied settings, however, because of high cost and lack of convenience. Given these limitations, handheld dynamometers may serve as a more cost-effective and convenient option in a high-performance basketball environment. Moreover, instruments designed specifically for AD:AB testing are becoming increasingly popular in professional sports. Sphygmomanometers, although not commonly used, are another tool that provides valid and reliable data when assessing isometric hip strength (45).

Testing Protocol

Testing protocol for AD:AB testing is determined primarily from manufacturer guidelines. Regardless of the instrument or specific protocol used, accuracy and repeatability in testing are important to ensure reliable longitudinal between- and within-athlete comparisons.

Descriptive Data

No normative or descriptive data are available for hip AD:AB testing for high school, college, and professional basketball athletes. Coaches and strength and conditioning professionals can perform pre- and posttesting to monitor improvements in the hip AD:AB strength ratio.

NORDIC HAMSTRING ISOMETRIC TESTS

Purpose

The purpose of Nordic hamstring isometric testing is to identify single-leg hamstring strength capabilities. Assessing hamstring strength is important because the hamstring muscle group is the most frequently strained muscle group in basketball athletes (23) and strength deficits have been shown to increase risk of injury in sports that require high amounts of running, jumping, and rapid change of direction (43).

Equipment

As with hip AD:AB testing, equipment required for hamstring isometric testing is determined primarily based on availability. Handheld, isokinetic, and isotonic dynamometers are valid and reliable methods for the collection of isometric strength data (3, 43). In recent years, traditional instruments used for hamstring strength testing have been replaced by test-specific tools that provide easy access and storage of athlete data and analysis to track development and injury risk year round. Additionally, instruments designed specifically for Nordic hamstring testing are becoming increasingly popular in professional sports.

Setup

No specific setup directions for hamstring isometric testing are available because specific instruments require different calibration and setup procedures. Nevertheless, measurements should be taken at multiple limb positions (i.e., knee flexion at 90, 60, and 30 degrees) to highlight potential strength deficiencies or asymmetries in variable positions. Also, a neutral neck, trunk, and pelvic position must be maintained during testing. As with other tests, consistency in testing procedure is important because no study has identified which positions or limb configurations are most relevant to basketball athletes.

Testing Protocol

No standardized protocol has been established for hamstring isometric testing. That said, standardizing hip and knee flexion angles between testing sessions and athletes is important to ensure accurate comparison of data between athletes and across multiple testing sessions.

Descriptive Data

No normative or descriptive data are available for Nordic hamstring isometric testing for high school, college, and professional basketball athletes. Coaches and strength and conditioning professionals can perform pre- and posttesting to monitor improvements in isometric hamstring strength.

T, Y, AND I ISOMETRIC SHOULDER TESTS

Purpose

The purpose of testing end-range isometric shoulder strength is to identify one-arm shoulder girdle strength and at multiple end-range positions. Reduced overhead shoulder girdle strength is linked to scapular dyskinesia and increased risk of injury (3). Optimizing shoulder girdle strength at end-range overhead positions is advantageous for basketball athletes because of the high frequency of overhead reaching actions in basketball.

Equipment

A force plate is highly recommended when administering isometric shoulder extension testing in athletic populations. If a force plate is not readily available, a handheld dynamometer may be used, although debate exists on the reliability of handheld dynamometer-based testing in elite athletic populations (31).

Setup

The athlete lies prone on the floor using a pad or block to cushion the forehead. With palms on the floor, the athlete abducts one arm to 90 degrees relative to the torso. This position is referred to as the "T" position. When setting up for multiple trials, tape may be used to provide landmarks to ensure correct positioning. Establish tape landmarks for the "Y" (135-degree abduction) and "I" (180-degree abduction) positions. The working arm should be fully extended at the angle appropriate for all three testing positions. During the T and Y tests, the nonworking arm is placed behind the back. During the I test, the nonworking shoulder should be internally rotated and held close to the body with 0-degree abduction and the palm facing up (4).

Testing Protocol

1. Instruct the athlete to find the baseline "T" position (both arms at 90-degree abduction) to ensure optimal baseline positioning. Adjust the location of the force plate depending on limb length.

2. After establishing correct positioning, the athlete moves the right arm overhead to the "I" position (180-degree abduction) and rests the back of the wrist of the nonworking arm on the low back.

3. Cue the athlete to press as hard as possible into the force plate without gaining additional momentum from a countermovement. The athlete continues to push maximally into the plate for 3 seconds. Allow 20 seconds of rest between contractions.

4. If noticeable compensatory strategies are used during testing, immediately instruct the athlete to stop and repeat the test.

5. Collect three maximum values for each arm at each position to create an average score for both arms (nine trials per arm).

Descriptive Data

No study has yet to identify clinically significant end-range isometric shoulder strength between-limb differences or normative values in basketball athletes. Coaches and strength and conditioning professionals can perform pre- and posttesting to monitor improvements in isometric shoulder strength.

BALLISTIC PUSH-UP TEST

Purpose

The purpose of ballistic push-up (BPU) testing is to identify peak horizontal pushing force and potential between-limb asymmetries. Despite being a newer upper body strength test, BPU testing has been shown to be predictive of traditional 1RM bench press scores (48). The BPU imposes less stress on the body, making it a more appropriate test option for continued monitoring purposes. Upper body push strength is important for basketball athletes given the need for two- and one-arm push strength in chest and bounce passes.

Equipment

A force plate is required to collect kinetic data during BPU testing. When available, dual force plates may be preferred to identify between-arm force differences. When a force plate is not available, time photocell and contact mats may be used to calculate time-derived power variables.

Setup

The main testing position has the athlete lying in the prone position with the chest on the floor, the elbows flexed, and the hands underneath the shoulders, similar to the lowered position of a push-up. After the force plate has been zeroed out, athletes should lower themselves onto the floor in the ready position with force plates positioned underneath each hand. The test administrator may begin testing after the athlete establishes this position. If only one force plate is available, collect two trials so that limb asymmetries can still be identified.

Testing Protocol

1. Calibrate the force plate based on unit-specific guidelines.

2. Ensure that the force plate is zeroed out following calibration.

3. Instruct the athlete to come onto the force plate and assume the ready position (chest on the floor, shoulders and elbows flexed, hands slightly wider than shoulders).

4. Cue the athlete to push explosively off the floor with both arms and get as much airtime as possible.

5. Repeat the testing if the athlete prematurely shrugs the shoulders or tries to increase airtime during the push-up because this action could affect the accuracy of other time-derived power scores.

Descriptive Data

No study has identified clinically significant between-limb differences of mean values for the BPU test in basketball populations. Coaches and strength and conditioning professionals can perform pre- and posttests to evaluate improvements in peak horizontal pushing force.

BENCH PRESS TEST (MAXIMUM REPETITIONS)

Purpose

For most athletes, the bench press test uses a submaximal load to allow multiple repetitions to be performed. As a result, it does not measure muscular strength, but rather muscular endurance. Untrained individuals may not be able to perform many repetitions with the weight assigned for the test, so for them the test measures muscular strength.

Equipment

As with testing an athlete's 1RM, the bench press test for maximum repetitions uses a bench with upright safety racks, an Olympic bar and various Olympic weight plates, and a pair of collars (locks) to hold the plates in place during the test. In addition, a spotter is needed.

Setup

Explain and demonstrate proper exercise technique for the bench press (if needed, refer to the description on page 140 in chapter 7).

Testing Protocol

1. Direct the athlete to warm up with 10 push-ups, 60 seconds of rest, 5 repetitions with the warm-up weight, and then 90 seconds of rest. College men and NBA athletes use 135 pounds (61 kg), high school males use 95 pounds (43 kg), college women and WNBA athletes use 65 pounds (29 kg), and high school females use 45 pounds (20 kg) for the warm-up weight (29).

2. At the end of the second rest period, the test begins. College men and NBA athletes use 185 pounds (84 kg), high school males use 135 pounds (61 kg), college women and WNBA athletes use 95 pounds (43 kg), and high school females use 75 pounds (34 kg) for the testing weight (29).

3. For a repetition to count, the athlete must move the bar through a full range of motion (i.e., from full elbow extension, down to touch—but not bounce off—the chest and back up to full elbow extension). The test ends when the athlete cannot perform a full repetition.

Descriptive Data

Table 3.3 provides descriptive data for the bench press test for maximum repetitions for high school basketball athletes. Table 3.4 provides descriptive data for the bench press test for maximum repetitions for NCAA Division I college basketball athletes. Table 3.5 provides descriptive data from the NBA combine.

Table 3.3   Maximum Repetition Values for the Bench Press Test for High School Basketball Athletes

	Males	**Females**
Maximum	28	15
Average	12.2	9.8
Minimum	0	5

Data from National Basketball Conditioning Coaches Association (2007).

Table 3.4   Maximum Repetition Values for the Bench Press Test for NCAA Division I College Men's and Women's Basketball Athletes

	Males	**Females**
Average	10	16.38
SD	4.58	8.25
n	14	8

SD = standard deviation, n = sample size.

Data from National Basketball Conditioning Coaches Association (2007).

Table 3.5   Percentile Values of the Bench Press Test (Maximum Repetitions) From the NBA Men's Basketball Combine

Percentile rank	**Repetitions**	**Percentile rank**	**Repetitions**
100	27	30	8
90	18	20	6
80	15	10	3
70	14	Average	10.34
60	13	SD	5.55
50	11	n	1,081
40	9		

SD = standard deviation, n = sample size.

Data from National Basketball Association. https://stats.nba.com/draft/combine-strength-agility/ for the 2000-2020 seasons.

REACTIVE STRENGTH TESTS

An athlete's ability to move quickly from an eccentric muscle action to a concentric muscle action is an expression of reactive strength (16). The tests included in this section evaluate that ability, which is crucial to a basketball athlete.

DROP JUMP TEST

Purpose
The drop jump test is used to evaluate total body reactive strength capabilities (32) and simulates quick transitioning during land-jump actions performed in typical basketball play. The reactive strength index (RSI) is a typical calculation taken from the drop jump to measure stretch-shortening cycle capabilities. The calculation for the RSI is airtime (or jump height) divided by floor contact time (15). When measured over progressively intensified jumps, the RSI is an effective way to measure how well an athlete can quickly absorb and then redistribute forces.

Equipment
A time mat or photocell mat is required to collect airtime and floor contact time. The RSI and jump height, the two primary variables of interest, can be derived from this time series information alone. Drop jump testing may also be administered with a force plate and motion capture system to collect specific biomechanical variables of interest.

Setup
Specific setup directions depend on the type of instrumentation used during testing. When using a photocell or contact mat, ensure that correct pretest procedures are followed in collecting the key time variables, floor time and airtime, during testing. Moreover, ensure that the box used for testing is positioned close enough to the testing area that the athlete does not have to deviate from the desired movement strategy during jumping. Thirty centimeters (about 12 in.) is the most often used baseline box height for drop jump RSI testing in the literature, although this height can be increased or decreased based on expected performance capabilities and the experience, maturity, or size of the athlete (15).

Testing Protocol
1. Calibrate all instruments before testing.
2. Starting from a shoulder-width stance on the box, the athlete steps off with one leg.
3. The athlete lands with both feet hitting the floor simultaneously and immediately rebounds into a maximum-effort vertical jump. Redo tests with floor contact times above 0.25 seconds.
4. Allow at least 2 minutes of rest between attempts if multiple trials are desired.

Descriptive Data
The RSI is a valid and reliable determinant of total body reactive strength capabilities, but no normative or descriptive data are available for the RSI to be compared with (47).

REPEATED JUMP TEST

Purpose

The repeated jump test is used to identify lower body, ankle-dominant reactive strength capabilities. The ability to perform repeated jumps is an essential skill for a basketball athlete in performing basketball-specific actions such as rebounding and challenging a shot (20).

Equipment

A timing mat or photocell mat is required to collect airtime and floor contact time. Repeated jump testing may also be administered with a force plate and motion capture system to collect other biomechanical variables of interest.

Setup

Specific setup directions depend on the type of instrumentation used during testing. When using a photocell or contact mat, ensure that correct pretest procedures are followed in collecting the key time variables, floor time and airtime, during testing.

Testing Protocol

1. Calibrate all instruments before testing.
2. Starting from a shoulder-width stance on the floor, the athlete performs a maximum-effort countermovement jump.
3. The athlete lands with both feet hitting the floor simultaneously and immediately rebounds into another maximum-effort jump.
4. The athlete performs 10 consecutive jumps. Of the 10 jumps performed, identify the 5 jumps with lowest floor contact times. Use the data from these 5 jumps to create an average RSI value for the trial.
5. Allow at least two minutes of rest between attempts if multiple trials are desired.

Descriptive Data

The repeated jump test can measure the RSI, but as with the drop jump test, no normative or descriptive data are available. As with other tests without data, coaches and strength and conditioning professionals can perform pre- and posttests to evaluate improvements.

POWER TESTS

The power tests provided in this section allow the coach or strength and conditioning professional to evaluate a basketball athlete's ability to generate force in a short time.

VERTICAL JUMP TEST

Purpose

The purpose of the vertical jump test is to identify sagittal plane vertical power capabilities from a stationary start. The vertical jump is a relevant test in basketball because of the high transfer of skill to common basketball-specific tasks (i.e., jumping to get a rebound). When taken in context of other jump tests, vertical jump capability can provide valuable insight into performance capabilities and aid in talent identification processes.

Equipment

Vertical jump testing can be administered with a variety of equipment. The most common way to administer vertical jump testing employs a vertical target, like a Vertec (figure 3.1). Jump height can be calculated by taking the difference between maximal overhead reach while standing and peak height achieved during jumping. Jump height can also be derived from floor-based timing device like contact mats and photocell mats. When available, motion capture technologies may also be used to collect kinematics and kinetic information during jumping.

Setup

When using a Vertec for vertical jump tests, first establish an athlete's baseline maximal overhead reach by recording the peak height reach with the dominant hand while standing flat-footed. Before testing, position the athlete directly underneath the Vertec to ensure that no wasted movement occurs during jumping. Provide enough space around the testing area to ensure safe takeoff and landing during jumping.

Figure 3.1   Vertec stand.

Testing Protocol

1. After establishing baseline reach height, raise the Vertec to a level appropriate for the athlete based on expected jumping ability. The selected target should be challenging but not unreachable for the athlete.

2. Position the athlete directly underneath the target.

3. Without taking a step but using a countermovement, the athlete performs a maximum-effort jump and touches as high as possible on the Vertec.

4. Take the difference between standing reach height and maximum-effort vertical jump height to determine vertical jump height.

5. Allow at least two minutes of rest between attempts if multiple trials are desired.

Descriptive Data

Table 3.6 provides descriptive data for a vertical jump test for high school basketball athletes. Tables 3.7 and 3.8 provide descriptive data for a vertical jump test for NCAA Division I and II college basketball athletes. Table 3.9 provides descriptive data from the NBA combine.

Table 3.6 Percentile Values of the Vertical Jump for High School Basketball Athletes

	14 years old		15 years old		16 years old		17 years old	
% rank	in.	cm	in.	cm	in.	cm	in.	cm
90	25.6	65.0	27.1	68.8	29.0	73.7	28.3	71.9
80	23.4	59.4	25.0	63.5	27.5	69.9	26.5	67.3
70	22.5	57.2	24.0	61.0	25.7	65.3	24.5	62.2
60	21.6	54.9	23.0	58.4	24.7	62.7	24.0	61.0
50	21.0	53.3	23.0	58.4	24.0	61.0	24.0	61.0
40	20.9	53.1	22.0	55.9	23.0	58.4	23.5	59.7
30	20.3	51.6	21.5	54.6	22.4	56.9	22.9	58.2
20	18.0	45.7	20.5	52.1	20.9	53.1	21.6	54.9
10	15.4	39.1	20.0	50.8	19.5	49.5	21.0	53.3
Average	21.0	53.3	23.1	58.7	24.0	61.0	24.0	61.0
SD	3.1	7.9	3.0	7.6	3.9	9.9	2.3	5.8
n	21		87		58		22	

SD = standard deviation, n = sample size.

Reprinted by permission from J. Hoffman, *Norms for Fitness, Performance, and Health* (Champaign, IL: Human Kinetics, 2006), 61.

Table 3.7 Percentile Values of the Vertical Jump for NCAA Division I College Basketball Athletes

	Men		Women	
Percentile rank	in.	cm	in.	cm
90	30.5	77.5	21.6	54.9
80	30.0	76.2	20.1	51.1
70	28.5	72.4	19.7	50.0
60	28.0	71.1	18.5	47.0
50	27.5	69.9	18.0	45.7
40	26.8	68.1	17.5	44.5
30	26.0	66.0	16.5	41.9
20	25.5	64.8	15.9	40.4
10	24.5	62.2	14.5	36.8
Average	27.7	70.4	18.0	45.7
SD	2.4	6.1	2.5	6.4
n	138		118	

SD = standard deviation, n = sample size.

Reprinted by permission from J. Hoffman, *Norms for Fitness, Performance, and Health* (Champaign, IL: Human Kinetics, 2006), 61.

Table 3.8 Vertical Jump Test Values for NCAA Division II College Women's Basketball Athletes

	All positions		Centers		Forwards		Guards	
	in.	cm	in.	cm	in.	cm	in.	cm
Average	18.1	46	17.68	44.9	17.82	45.3	18.26	46.4
Range	12.5-25	31.8-63.5	14-23	35.6-58.4	13-23	33-58.4	11-25	27.9-63.5
SD	4.4	11.2	2.4	6.1	2.44	6.2	2.58	6.6
n	205		37		65		100	

SD = standard deviation, *n* = sample size.

Data from Schweigert (1996).

Table 3.9 Percentile Values of the Vertical Jump From the NBA Men's Basketball Combine

Percentile rank	in.	cm	Percentile rank	in.	cm
100	39.5	100.3	30	27.5	69.9
90	33.5	85.1	20	27.0	68.6
80	32.0	81.3	10	25.5	64.8
70	31.0	78.7	Average	29.16	74.1
60	30.0	76.2	SD	3.09	7.8
50	29.5	74.9	*n*	1,176	
40	28.5	72.4			

SD = standard deviation, *n* = sample size.

Data from National Basketball Association. https://stats.nba.com/draft/combine-strength-agility/ for the 2000-2020 seasons.

RUNNING VERTICAL JUMP TEST

Purpose

The running vertical jump (called the *maximum vertical leap* test in the NBA) is a common test used in basketball performance testing to identify maximum vertical jumping capability from a running start. In comparison with the vertical jump, the running vertical jump allows the athlete to gain more momentum during jumping and provides additional insight into dynamic power capabilities. The running vertical jump is also a relevant test in basketball given the high transfer of skill to common basketball-specific tasks (i.e., finishing a fast-break layup or dunk). Like the vertical jump, the running vertical jump has been shown to be predictive of basketball talent level (32). When taken in context of other jump tests, running vertical jump capability can provide valuable insight into dynamic power capabilities and aid in talent identification processes.

Equipment

Running vertical jump testing can be administered with a variety of equipment. The most common way to administer vertical jump testing is to use a vertical target, like a Vertec. Jump height can be calculated by taking the difference between maximal overhead reach while standing and peak height achieved during jumping. When available, motion capture technologies can be used to collect kinematics and kinetic information during jumping.

An athlete's maximum vertical jump from a running start is greater than a vertical jump from a stationary start.

Setup

When using a Vertec for vertical jump tests, first establish an athlete's baseline maximal overhead reach by recording the peak height reach with the dominant hand while standing flat-footed. Provide enough space around the testing area to ensure safe takeoff and landing during jumping. To standardize the approach, mark off a 15-foot (4.6 m) arc around the target (i.e., free-throw line extended to the baseline on a basketball court) (32).

Testing Protocol

1. After baseline reach height is established, raise the Vertec to a level appropriate for the athlete based on expected jumping ability. The selected target should be challenging but not unreachable for the athlete.

2. Staying within the 15-foot (4.6 m) arc boundary, the athlete takes as many steps toward the Vertec as necessary to gain momentum for the jump.

3. Take the difference between standing reach height and maximum-effort vertical jump height to determine vertical jump height. Unless otherwise specified, athletes may self-select a single- or double-leg takeoff strategy.

4. Allow at least two minutes of rest between attempts if multiple trials are desired.

Descriptive Data

Table 3.10 provides descriptive data for a running vertical jump test for high school basketball athletes. Table 3.11 provides descriptive data for a running vertical jump test for NCAA Division I college basketball athletes. Table 3.12 provides descriptive data from the NBA combine.

Table 3.10   Running Vertical Jump Test Values Values for High School Basketball Athletes

	Males		Females	
	in.	cm	in.	cm
Maximum	39.0	99.1	24.0	61.0
Average	32.0	81.3	20.0	50.8
Minimum	22.5	57.2	15.0	38.1

Data National Basketball Conditioning Coaches Association (2007).

Table 3.11   Running Vertical Jump Test Values for NCAA Division I College Men's and Women's Basketball Athletes

	Males		Females	
	in.	cm	in.	cm
Average	33.6	85.3	25.4	64.52
SD	4.17	10.59	3.51	8.92
n	14		9	

SD = standard deviation, n = sample size.

Data National Basketball Conditioning Coaches Association (2007).

Table 3.12   Percentile Values of the Maximum Vertical Leap From the NBA Men's Basketball Combine

Percentile rank	in.	cm	Percentile rank	in.	cm
100	45.5	115.6	30	32.5	82.6
90	39.5	100.3	20	31.5	80.0
80	37.5	95.3	10	30.0	76.2
70	36.5	92.7	Average	34.30	87.1
60	35.5	90.2	SD	3.70	9.4
50	34.5	87.6	n	1,180	
40	33.5	85.1			

SD = standard deviation, n = sample size.

Data from National Basketball Association. https://stats.nba.com/draft/combine-strength-agility/ for the 2000-2020 seasons.

ROTATIONAL MEDICINE BALL THROW TEST

Purpose

The purpose of the rotational medicine ball throw (RMBT) is to identify rotational power capabilities (28). Rotational power is highly desirable in basketball because of the high frequency of rotational actions when playing, such as changing direction. In addition, rotational trunk control is an important risk fact for ACL injury (17). In that sense, RMBT testing may help to identify functional rotational asymmetries relevant to basketball performance and injury risk.

Equipment

RMBT testing requires the use of a 6- to 8-pound (3-4 kg) medicine ball and a tape measure. Additionally, test administrators should be certain to pick a testing area that provides enough room for athletes to perform maximum effort during testing. Medicine balls with built-in accelerometers have also been shown to be a valid and reliable tool for assessing upper body power (33).

Setup

Test administrators should set up testing in an area that is long enough for athletes to perform maximum-effort medicine ball throws without risking injury to those around them. Mark the beginning position for athletes to ensure reproducibility between individual trials and athletes. After the beginning position is established, lay a long tape measure flat on the floor so that it runs perpendicular to the starting line.

Testing Protocol

1. Instruct the athlete to approach the starting line so that the feet are positioned perpendicular to the tape measure and parallel to the starting line.
2. Instruct the athlete to "load" into the throw. The loaded position is characterized by triple flexion at the ankles, knees, and hip, along with trunk rotation in the direction opposite the intended trajectory of the ball. The medicine ball should be held with both hands beside the knee farther away from the starting line (i.e., the outside knee; figure 3.2a).
3. Instruct the athlete to rotate and explode up and away while throwing the ball with both hands as far down the line as possible (figure 3.2b).
4. Use the measuring tape to record total distance from the starting line to the point of initial contact.
5. Provide enough rest time (at least two minutes) between trials. Collect at least one successful trial of right-to-left and left-to-right throws. Provide at least two minutes of rest between trials to ensure optimal performance.

Descriptive Data

No normative or descriptive data are available for RMBT testing for high school, college, and professional basketball athletes. Coaches and strength and conditioning professionals can perform pre- and posttesting to monitor improvements in the RMBT.

Figure 3.2 Rotational medicine ball throw: (*a*) start, (*b*) finish.

SPEED AND AGILITY TESTS

The execution of efficient changes in direction is a key determinant of playing performance in basketball athletes (2); therefore, athletes require a combination of perceptual-cognitive factors and strength characteristics to maintain fast directional changes and gain positional advantages during competition (41). During a game, unanticipated directional changes, which require what is termed *agility*, occur more often than planned directional changes. Therefore, athletes should be tested under game-like conditions to assess how they respond from a decision-making and technical proficiency perspective (40).

REACTIVE LANE SHUTTLE TEST

Purpose
The reactive lane shuttle (RLS) is used in the NBA combine to assess an athlete's reactive agility capability from a static start position. Unlike the 5-10-5, a drill that tests nonreactive change-of-direction capability, the RLS challenges change-of-direction, perceptual, and decision-making skills by using an external stimulus to begin testing (18). Previous studies have shown that preplanned and nonplanned agility tests provide important insight when differentiating athlete position and skill level in basketball (38). In that sense, the RLS is an important agility performance test for basketball athletes.

Equipment
Electronic timing gates provide valid and reliable data up to 1/1,000 of a second during RLS testing. If timing gates are unavailable, standard stopwatches or other handheld timing

devices are a reasonable alternative. Companies have integrated wireless, camera-less motion capture systems in reactive testing protocols to provide athlete-specific performance and injury risk insights in addition to the standard time statistics.

Setup

In a standard NBA-sized lane, place three electronic timing gates 8 feet (2.4 m) apart with one at each end of the lane and one at a line added to the center of the key. Ensure that all timing gates are property synchronized to capture total testing time and splits for each portion of the shuttle drill.

Testing Protocol

1. Instruct the athlete to straddle the gate at the center of the key.
2. When the athlete is set, begin testing by cuing the athlete to move to either the right or the left. Some gates may have the reactive stimulus integrated into predetermined testing protocols.
3. After receiving the cue, the athlete should move laterally as quickly as possible until he or she breaks the first gate.
4. After breaking the first gate, the athlete turns 180 degrees and moves as quickly as possible across the entire lane until he or she breaks the far gate.
5. After breaking the far gate, the athlete turns 180 degrees, moves as quickly as possible back across the lane, and finishes through the beginning position.
6. Repeat testing if the athlete moves before receiving the cue or in the wrong direction.
7. Collect two trials in which the athlete begins by moving to the right and two trials in which the athlete begins by moving to the left. Report the lowest scores when recording the performance results.

Descriptive Data

Table 3.13 provides descriptive data from the NBA combine.

Table 3.13 Percentile Values of the Reactive Lane Shuttle Test From the NBA Men's Basketball Combine

Percentile rank	sec	Percentile rank	sec
100	2.64	30	3.20
90	2.88	20	3.26
80	2.95	10	3.32
70	3.02	Average	3.10
60	3.06	SD	0.25
50	3.10	n	336
40	3.15		

SD = standard deviation, n = sample size.

Data from National Basketball Association. https://stats.nba.com/draft/combine-strength-agility/ for the 2000-2020 seasons.

LANE AGILITY TEST

Purpose

The lane agility test examines multidirectional, preplanned change-of-direction capabilities. Although the mean shuffling distance covered by elite basketball athletes (6-7 ft [1.8-2.1 m]) is less than half of the total distance they cover during the lane agility test (16 ft [4.9 m]), the lane agility test has been shown to be a reliable assessment of change-of-direction ability in basketball athletes (6).

Equipment

Four cones, a timing device, and an NBA-sized lane (which is 16 ft [4.9 m] wide, rather than 12 ft [3.7 m] for college or high school) are the only pieces of equipment required for lane agility testing. As with the reactive lane agility test, timing gates may be used when available to get the most reliable and accurate data; otherwise, stopwatches may be used to determine total time during testing.

Setup

Place one cone and a timing gate at each corner of the key (figure 3.3); if a college or high school court is used, the cones would be placed outside the key and lane. If multiple timing gates are not available, only one gate at the beginning position is necessary to measure total time during testing. After all gates are set up, ensure that the system is property synchronized to capture total testing time and splits for each portion of the drill.

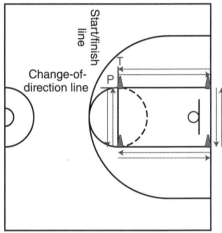

Figure 3.3 Setup for the lane agility test. P = player, T = timer.

Reprinted by permission from National Basketball Conditioning Coaches Association, *Complete Conditioning for Basketball* (Champaign, IL: Human Kinetics, 2007), 6.

Testing Protocol

1. Starting from a stationary two-point stance on the left-hand side of the key while facing the basket, the athlete explodes into a forward sprint until she or he reaches the first turn point.

2. At the first turn point, the athlete cuts to the right and continues into a maximum-effort left-to-right side-shuffle.

3. At the second turn point, the athlete transitions from the side-shuffle to a maximum-effort backpedal.

4. At the third turn point, the athlete transitions from the backpedal to a maximum-effort right-to-left side-shuffle before returning to the beginning position.

5. Without a break, the athlete repeats this process in opposite order until he or she fully completes the rectangle again. When properly synchronized and programmed, testing should end after the athlete breaks the gate at the finish line.

6. Total time is measured as the time the athlete takes to complete the two trips around the key.

7. Collect two trials starting on both the right and left sides (four total). Report the lowest scores when recording the performance results.

Descriptive Data

Table 3.14 provides descriptive data for a lane agility test for high school basketball athletes. Table 3.15 provides descriptive data for a lane agility test for NCAA Division I, II, and III college basketball athletes. Table 3.16 provides descriptive data from the NBA combine.

Table 3.14   Lane Agility Test Values for High School Basketball Athletes

	Males	**Females**
Fastest	10.80 sec	11.34 sec
Average	12.12 sec	12.19 sec
Slowest	13.64 sec	13.80 sec

Data from National Basketball Conditioning Coaches Association (2007).

Table 3.15   Lane Agility Test Values for NCAA Division I, II, and III College Men's and Division I and III College Women's Basketball Athletes

	DI Men*	**DI Women***	**DII Men****	**DIII Men*****	**DIII Women*****
Average	10.24 sec	11.62 sec	11.24 sec	10.38 sec	11.95 sec
SD	0.56 sec	0.43 sec	0.54 sec	0.45 sec	0.58 sec
n	14	9	10	12	12

SD = standard deviation, *n* = sample size.

*Data from reference 29. Data from reference 11. ***Data from reference 6.

Data from National Basketball Conditioning Coaches Association (2007); Dawes, Marshall, and Spiteri (2016); Brown (2012).

Table 3.16   Percentile Values of the Lane Agility Test From the NBA Men's Basketball Combine

Percentile rank	**sec**	**Percentile rank**	**sec**
100	9.97	30	11.70
90	10.73	20	11.89
80	10.95	10	12.25
70	11.10	Average	11.44
60	11.24	SD	0.62
50	11.38	*n*	1,169
40	11.54		

SD = standard deviation, *n* = sample size.

Data from National Basketball Association. https://stats.nba.com/draft/combine-strength-agility/ for the 2000-2020 seasons.

THREE-QUARTER COURT SPRINT TEST

Purpose

The purpose of performing a maximal sprint assessment with athletes is to assess their linear acceleration and speed (22). Sprinting is a key physical requirement because basketball athletes are required to perform multiple short sprinting efforts throughout the game as they transition between offensive and defensive play.

Equipment

Equipment required to administer this assessment includes a tape measure, four cones, and a stopwatch. If timing gates are readily available, they are recommended to obtain a more reliable measurement.

Setup

Place two cones along the baseline as the starting point and place two additional cones at the opposite free-throw line (figure 3.4). Verify that the distance between the two pairs of cones is 75 feet (22.9 m).

Testing Protocol

1. Instruct athletes to start with the front of the foot behind the starting cones.

2. From the beginning position, athletes move in a forward direction in a straight line as fast as they can through the end cones (34).

3. Instruct athletes to keep sprinting all the way through the final cones to record the best time. Allow athletes two attempts. Record the fastest time to the nearest 0.01 seconds.

Descriptive Data

Table 3.17 provides descriptive data for a three-quarter court sprint test for high school basketball athletes. Table 3.18 provides descriptive data for a three-quarter court sprint test for NCAA Division I college basketball athletes. Table 3.19 provides descriptive data from the NBA combine.

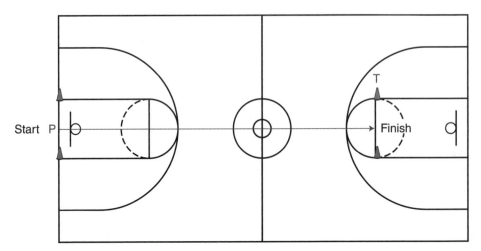

Figure 3.4 Setup for the three-quarter court sprint test. P = player, T = timer.

Table 3.17   Three-Quarter Court Sprint Test Values for High School Basketball Athletes

	Males	**Females**
Fastest	3.06 sec	3.43 sec
Average	3.39 sec	3.71 sec
Slowest	3.91 sec	4.08 sec

Data from National Basketball Conditioning Coaches Association (2007).

Table 3.18   Three-Quarter Court Sprint Test Values for NCAA Division I College Men's and Women's Basketball Athletes

	Men	**Women**
Average	3.36 sec	3.81 sec
SD	0.15 sec	0.14 sec
n	14	9

SD = standard deviation, n = sample size.

Data from National Basketball Conditioning Coaches Association (2007).

Table 3.19   Percentile Values of the Three-Quarter Court Sprint Test From the NBA Men's Basketball Combine

Percentile rank	**sec**	**Percentile rank**	**sec**
100	2.92	30	3.35
90	3.14	20	3.40
80	3.19	10	3.47
70	3.21	Average	3.29
60	3.25	SD	0.13
50	3.28	n	1,171
40	3.31		

SD = standard deviation, n = sample size.

Data from National Basketball Association. https://stats.nba.com/draft/combine-strength-agility/ for the 2000-2020 seasons.

T-TEST

Purpose

The T-test is a commonly used change-of-direction test for basketball athletes. The test assesses how fast an athlete can side-shuffle, backpedal, and forward run, all of which are common movements executed throughout a basketball game (41).

Equipment

Equipment required to administer this assessment includes a tape measure, four cones, and a stopwatch. If timing gates are readily available, they should be used to provide more accurate measurements. Position one set of timing gates at the starting-finishing line to capture the time taken to complete the test.

Setup

Place one cone (cone A) along the base line as the starting point. Place the tape measure on the center of the base line to measure a straight-line distance of 10 yards (9.1 m) and place cone B at this mark. At a 90-degree angle to the left side of this cone, measure a 5-yard (4.6 m) straight line and place cone C at this point. Repeat the same 5-yard (4.6 m) measurement to the right side of cone B to place cone D (figure 3.5).

If a stopwatch or timing gates are being used to time this assessment, timing begins when athletes cross the cones at the starting line and finish when the athletes run back through these same cones, completing the test.

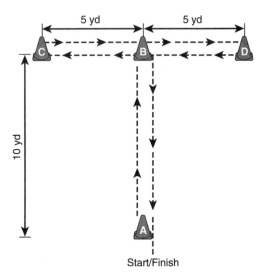

Figure 3.5 Setup for the T-test.

Reprinted by permission from D.H. Fukuda, *Assessments for Sport and Athletic Performance* (Champaign, IL: Human Kinetics, 2019), 111.

Testing Protocol

1. Instruct athletes to start with the front of the foot behind the starting cone A.

2. Instruct athletes to move in a forward direction from the beginning position, running as fast as they can in a straight line toward cone B.

3. Instruct athletes to touch the bottom of cone B with the right hand, before side-shuffling 90 degrees to their left for 5 yards (4.6 m).

4. After athletes reach and touch the bottom of cone C with the left hand, instruct them to change direction and shuffle 10 yards (9.1 m) past cone B to cone D.

5. After athletes reach and touch the bottom of cone D with the right hand, instruct them to change direction and shuffle to the left, back to cone B.

6. After athletes have reached and touched the bottom of cone with the left hand, they must backpedal 10 yards (9.1 m) past cone A to finish the test.

7. Total time is measured as the time the athlete takes to complete the figure-T formation.

8. Perform three trials and report the lowest score when recording the performance results.

Descriptive Data

Table 3.20 provides descriptive data for the T-test.

Table 3.20 T-Test Values for Various Basketball Athletes

Group	Value* (sec)	Reference
12-year-old boys	11.99 ± 0.55	24
14-year-old boys	10.90 ± 0.83	24
Men's NCAA Division I (all)	8.95 ± 0.53	26
Men's NCAA Division I (guards)	8.74 ± 0.41	26
Men's NCAA Division I (forwards)	8.94 ± 0.38	26
Men's NCAA Division I (centers)	9.28 ± 0.81	26
Men's NCAA Division I	9.25 ± 0.46	1
Men's professional	9.49 ± 0.56	12
Men's professional	9.7 ± 0.2	8
Women's professional	11.75 ± 1.15	42
Women's professional	10.45 ± 0.51	13

*Average ± SD.

AEROBIC TESTS

Aerobic tests measure the amount of oxygen that an athlete can take in and use during continuous, rhythmic, repetitive activity.

$\dot{V}O_2$ MAX TEST (BRUCE PROTOCOL)

Purpose

The $\dot{V}O_2$ max test measures aerobic capacity during intense exercise. Although $\dot{V}O_2$ max can be determined through a variety of max and submax protocols, the Bruce protocol is a popular indirect maximal exercise test that estimates $\dot{V}O_2$ max based on an athlete's ability to tolerate progressively increasing workloads on a graded treadmill. Athletes with high $\dot{V}O_2$ max are able to use more oxygen during exercise and are better equipped to sustain higher workloads than athletes with a low $\dot{V}O_2$ max. $\dot{V}O_2$ max scores are commonly measured in milliliters of oxygen used per minute relative to body weight in kilograms ($mL^{-1} \cdot kg^{-1} \cdot min^{-1}$). Formulas used to estimate $\dot{V}O_2$ max are the following (7):

$$\text{Males: } 14.76 - (1.379 \times T) + (0.451 \times T^2) - (0.012 \times T^3)$$

$$\text{Females: } 4.38 \times T - 3.9$$

where T equals the total time on treadmill measured to the fraction of a minute.

Equipment

An incline treadmill, heart rate monitor, and stopwatch are the only necessary pieces of equipment to administer the $\dot{V}O_2$ max Bruce protocol. Metabolic carts, EEG machines, sphygmomanometers, and pulse oximeters are also commonly used pieces of equipment in typical performance lab or clinical settings to provide direct measures of important physiological variables.

Setup Directions

Athletes should wear comfortable clothing and refrain from exercise before testing to minimize the effect of fatigue on performance. Ensure that an RPE chart is readily available near the testing area to provide essential nonverbal communication between the athlete and test administrator regarding fatigue status during testing. Likewise, a heart rate monitor should be worn during testing to monitor heart rate and rhythm during testing. Finally, ensure that the following progression is used during testing procedures:

Stage 1: 1.7 mph (2.7 kph) at 10% grade

Stage 2: 2.5 mph (4.0 kph) at 12% grade

Stage 3: 3.4 mph (5.5 kph) at 14% grade

Stage 4: 4.2 mph (6.8 kph) at 16% grade

Stage 5: 5.0 mph (8.0 kph) at 18% grade

Stage 6: 5.5 mph (8.9 kph) at 20% grade

Stage 7: 6.0 mph (9.7 kph) at 22% grade

Stage 8: 6.5 mph (10.5 kph) at 24% grade

Stage 9: 7.0 mph (11.3 kph) at 26% grade

Testing Protocol

1. Following a standardized warm-up, the athlete comes to a ready position on the treadmill at stage 1 incline specifications (10%).

2. After receiving verbal confirmation from the athlete, start the treadmill belt at stage 1 speed specifications (1.7 mph [2.7 kph]). Instruct the athlete to maintain a steady pace for three minutes.

3. Ten to 20 seconds before the completion of stage 1, ensure that the athlete is ready to continue using a nonverbal form of communication (e.g., RPE scale).

4. Increase treadmill speed and incline grade to stage 2 specification following verbal consent from the athlete.

5. Instruct the athlete to hold a comfortable pace at this stage for three minutes.

6. Repeat this process until the athlete is exhausted. Total time during testing is considered the total time from the beginning of stage 1 until exhaustion. Record total treadmill time as a fractional score (i.e., 10 minutes and 30 seconds is recorded as 10.5).

7. Provide steady state cool-down for at least two minutes follow completion of testing.

8. Input the total time on the treadmill to calculate $\dot{V}O_2$ max.

Normative Data

Average scores for nontrained adult males and females typically range from 35 to 40 mL^{-1} · kg^{-1} · min^{-1} and 27 to 30 mL^{-1} · kg^{-1} · min^{-1}, respectively (7). Table 3.21 provides normative data for $\dot{V}O_2$ max for men and women.

Table 3.21 Aerobic Capacity Classifications (mL^{-1} · kg^{-1} · min^{-1})

Age (yr)	Poor	Fair	Good	Excellent	Superior
Women					
20-29	≤33	34-39	40-45	46-51	≥52
30-39	≤27	28-31	32-36	37-40	≥41
40-49	≤24	25-28	29-32	33-38	≥39
50-59	≤21	22-24	25-28	29-32	≥33
60-69	≤18	19-21	22-24	25-27	≥28
Men					
20-29	≤44	45-49	50-56	57-62	≥63
30-39	≤39	40-44	45-49	50-57	≥58
40-49	≤35	36-39	40-45	46-52	≥53
50-59	≤30	31-34	35-40	41-46	≥47
60-69	≤26	27-29	30-35	36-40	≥41

Reprinted by permission from A.L. Gibson, D.R. Wagner, and V.H. Heyward, *Advanced Fitness Assessment and Exercise Prescription*, 8th ed. (Champaign, IL: Human Kinetics, 2019), 81; Adapted from Kaminsky, Arena, and Myers (2015).

SHUTTLE RUN (BEEP) TEST

Purpose
The shuttle run, or beep test, is a popular field test used to measure aerobic fitness (27, 39). Several studies demonstrate that aerobic fitness assessments, like the beep test, are useful not only for predicting an athlete's maximum oxygen uptake but also for evaluating the effectiveness of training programs and monitoring long-term athlete performance (30). Aerobic capacity is an important quality for basketball athletes because it allows them to maintain and produce high levels of intermittent activity for the duration of a game (35).

Equipment
Equipment required to administer this assessment includes a tape measure, four cones, a stopwatch, and an audio device to play the pacesetting beeps used for the test.

Setup
Place two cones along the base line as the starting point. Place the tape measure on the center of the base line and measure a straight-line distance of 20 meters (22 yd). Place two cones along the 20-meter (22 yd) mark in line with the cones on the starting (boundary) line.

Testing Protocol
This test involves continuous running between two lines 20 meters (22 yd) apart in time to recorded beeps.

1. Instruct athletes to start standing behind the cones on the base line facing the second line and to begin running to the second line of cones when instructed by the recording.
2. The speed at the start is quite slow; the velocity is set at 5.3 mph (8.5 km/h) for the first minute. But the velocity increases by 0.3 mph (0.5 km/h) every minute (or level) thereafter.
3. Instruct athletes to continue running between the two lines, turning when signaled by the recorded beeps.
4. If the athlete reaches the line before the beep sounds, she or he must wait until the beep sounds before continuing.
5. If the athlete does not reach the line before the beep sounds, she or he is given a warning and must continue to run to the line, turn, and try to catch up with the pace within two more beeps.
6. The test is stopped if the athlete fails to reach the line (within 2 m [6.6 ft]) for two consecutive ends after a warning, or if the athlete voluntarily withdraws from the test.

The athlete's score is the level and number of shuttles reached before he or she is unable to keep up with the recording. This level score can be converted to a $\dot{V}O_2$ max equivalent score using the following formula (27), in which velocity (in km/h, not mph) is determined using the distance covered in 30 seconds during the last stage of the test:

$$\dot{V}O_2 \text{ max} = 31.025 + (3.238 \times velocity) - (3.248 \times age) + (0.1536 \times age \times velocity)$$

Normative Data
Table 3.21 provides normative data for $\dot{V}O_2$ max for men and women.

CONCLUSION

The tests described in this chapter highlight some of the key tests for basketball athletes. Recommendations and conclusions derived from holistic testing procedures set up teams and organizations for success by providing objective measures related to athlete development, roster management, talent scouting, and injury rehabilitation. As basketball and sport science continue to develop, so too will an understanding of the variables most important to optimal health and performance for basketball athletes. In that sense, strength and conditioning professionals should make every effort to become comfortable administering and interpreting the performance and agility tests described in this chapter to help optimize athlete performance and create long-term organization success.

4

SPORT-SPECIFIC PROGRAM DESIGN GUIDELINES

KATIE FOWLER AND AMANDA D. KIMBALL

Basketball is a multifaceted sport that requires consideration of a wide range of physical and physiological traits. This chapter outlines basic training concepts and principles that can be used as guidelines when developing a year-round training program for basketball athletes. A well-planned, well-executed resistance training program will help them maximize their physical abilities and stay healthy throughout their playing season.

GOALS OF A BASKETBALL-SPECIFIC RESISTANCE TRAINING PROGRAM

One particularly important physiological trait for basketball athletes is power, because it is a key determinant of performance. **Power** is the product of force and velocity (power = force × velocity). Therefore, improving either of these components can lead to increased power production and improve the explosiveness of the athlete.

The **force-velocity relationship** is a basic principle that all strength and conditioning professionals should understand and use as a reference for any training program they prescribe. The force-velocity curve has an x- and y-axis (figure 4.1). The y-axis is the vertical axis that denotes velocity, and the x-axis is the horizontal axis that denotes force. The curve itself is hyperbolic and shows an inverse relationship between force and velocity. For example, heavier loads will move slower; conversely, lighter loads can be moved faster. Different types of training occur on different parts of the force-velocity curve. The primary objective of strength and power training is to shift the force-velocity curve to the right, which should result in the athlete being able to produce more force at higher speeds, thereby becoming more explosive. Improving the **rate of force development** (RFD) may also improve power production, because it reflects the ability to produce large forces in short periods (42).

When training on the force-velocity curve, the entire curve should be trained, not just one component of it. Five zones make up the curve (figure 4.2).

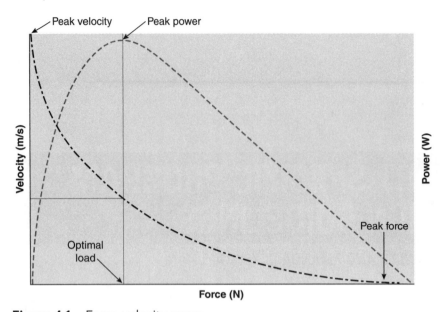

Figure 4.1 Force-velocity curve.

Reprinted by permission from G.G. Haff and S. Nimphius, "Training principles for power," *Strength and Conditioning Journal* 34, no. 6 (2012): 2-12.

1. Maximum strength—The primary objective in this zone is strength. Training at loads greater than 90% of the 1RM is typically prescribed.

2. Strength–speed—This zone is an intermediate zone because it does not allow peak power or peak force production. But because the loads prescribed are typically 80% to 90% of the 1RM, strength (rather than velocity) is emphasized.

3. Peak power—This zone results in peak power output and sits in the middle of the curve at training intensities between 30% and 80% of the 1RM.

4. Speed–strength—This zone is another intermediate zone because it allows greater velocities of movement but lower forces and power than the peak power zone, and greater forces and power but lower velocities than the max velocity zone. When training in this zone, intensities of 30% to 60% of the 1RM should be prescribed.

5. Max velocity—This zone enables the athletes to produce maximal movement velocity because training loads are generally less than 30% of the 1RM.

Based on need, training may be prescribed in specific training zones (or sections of the force-velocity curve) to maximize the desired physiological adaptations in the athlete. For example, a center on a basketball team might be extremely strong but perform poorly on speed tests. For this athlete, a resistance training program focusing on maximum strength might not be as beneficial as one that focuses on maximal velocity or speed–strength. Inversely, a point guard who excels at speed and agility but lacks strength and is consistently injured might benefit from improving strength deficits. In this case, spending most of the resistance training time in the maximum strength and strength–speed zones might have a greater benefit and help develop a stronger foundation. Athletes love to perform tasks that they are good at. Coaches, however, need to expose athletes to their weaknesses so that they can develop those attributes as well.

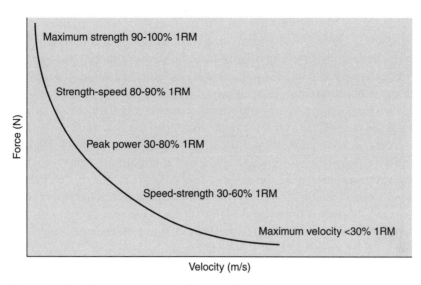

Figure 4.2 Five zones of the force-velocity curve.

Adapted by permission from NSCA, Advanced Power Techniques, by D.N. French, in *Developing Power*, edited by M. McGuigan (Champaign, IL: Human Kinetics, 2017), 191.

RESISTANCE TRAINING PRINCIPLES

The **SAID principle** is one of the most important basic concepts in strength and conditioning; it stands for *specific adaptations to imposed demands*. These adaptations occur when the body is placed under stress. After being exposed to a stressor, the body adapts and becomes more capable of handling the same stressor in the future (19). In resistance training, mechanical stress is placed on the body, and muscles, tendons, and ligaments strengthen and thicken, making them more capable of handling that stress in the future. Basically, after practicing a task, the body gets better at executing that task.

Specificity, periodization, and the size principle are important, fundamental concepts that should be considered when designing a resistance training program. The principle of **specificity** states that the mode, frequency, and duration of exercise are highly related to the training response or adaptation made (19). Specificity refers to the general observation that the closer the training is to the desired outcome, the better the outcome is. Therefore, the more specific the exercises used in the resistance training program are to the movements and speeds found in a sport (i.e., the actual speed of movement, type of muscle action, joint angles, and so on), in theory, the better the adaptations made will transfer to the sport (19). Further, most training-induced adaptations occur only to those muscles that have been recruited during the exercise program; little or no adaptive changes occur to the untrained musculature (19).

When training a basketball athlete, a coach needs to be especially aware of the demands of the sport to prescribe effective training. A basketball athlete should not train in the same way that a marathon runner trains. Each of these athletes requires a different training regime and different training goals. The most important thing about training for a certain sport is making sure that the body makes adaptations to withstand the specific stress it encounters while doing that sport. An athlete who wants to get better at a certain skill must train as specific to that skill as possible. Ultimately, if an athlete needs to get into a better condition to play basketball, then he or she needs to play more basketball. Many strength and conditioning professionals "cross-train" for basketball by putting athletes on a bike to mimic the physiological demands of a basketball game. Basketball requires locomotion in the form of running, cutting, and jumping, all of which are complex activities that rely on a much greater degree of skill and coordination than riding a stationary bike and have different bioenergetic requirements. Riding a stationary bike is a much simpler skill, so carryover to the basketball court is limited.

The key components to any resistance training program are the volume, intensity, and frequency of exercise. Specificity is tightly coupled with the volume, intensity, and frequency of exercise. Together, these determine the magnitude of adaptive responses that either enhance or decrease exercise capacity (19). There is a threshold at which additional stimuli do not induce further increases in functional capacity. Many elite athletes need to train on a fine line of chronic intensive training and inadequate recovery that, if not navigated carefully, can result in performance decrements.

Periodization is the systematic approach to organizing resistance training programs in cyclical periods, around specific training variables, to maximize performance while minimizing overtraining (18, 41). Periodization is highly dependent on changes in frequency, intensity, and volume. Within a year-long **macrocycle** are four basic **mesocycles**: postseason, off-season, preseason, and in-season. **Microcycles** within each mesocycle provide further detail in the process of progressive exercise modification or the sequencing and structuring of overall workloads and intensities to achieve peak performance of various strength attributes, at appropriate points in time throughout the macrocycle. Progressive exercise integration, modifications to the frequency of practice, stress application (force or velocity), and total workload placed on the muscles will be carefully planned to promote continual, positive adaptations.

Several models of periodization have been studied. **Linear periodization** refers to a gradual movement from high-volume, low-intensity exercise to low-volume, high-intensity exercise (18) over the course of a macrocycle. Over time, strength is gained by a gradual increase in load while volume decreases. **Block periodization** is a more concentrated form of linear periodization in that a periodic sequencing of one physical quality after another occurs (i.e., hypertrophy, strength, power). These adaptations still occur sequentially, one after the other, in linear fashion, but a macrocycle is broken down into mesocycles, and sometimes even further into microcycles. **Undulating periodization** varies workload in microcyclic fashion. In this nonlinear approach, volume and intensity are modified more frequently (daily or weekly) to address various strength qualities simultaneously. Although all three styles of periodization have been proved effective, choosing one over the others might be up to the discretion of the coach and depend on what is most conducive to the training time and environment that each athlete is subject to. Although younger or untrained athletes might respond to any stimuli, block and undulating periodization models are often used in collegiate and professional settings when highly trained athletes need to peak at various times of the year and over the course of a competitive season.

Another model, perhaps more applicable to the basketball athlete, involves concurrent training practices. **Concurrent periodization** refers to the strategy of training several competing qualities, such as aerobic endurance and strength, simultaneously within the same microcycle. Resistance training aims to improve a muscle's maximal contractile force by enhancing muscle fiber activation and hypertrophy, whereas aerobic endurance training increases mitochondrial density and oxidative capacity (14). Although basketball athletes require strength and power, increased aerobic capacity and resistance to fatigue are also necessary. In many cases an athlete will be involved in an off-season resistance training program focused on maximal strength, while still taking part in a high volume of basketball-related activity. In this circumstance, what is referred to as the **interference effect** may come into play; aerobic endurance training may inhibit hypertrophy-, strength-, and power-related adaptations to resistance training (14, 20). Research has shown that **high-intensity interval training** (HIIT) and resistance training can coexist to a certain extent. In a review, Sabag and colleagues concluded that HIIT with resistance training resulted in similar gains in upper body strength and hypertrophy (34). But when compared with resistance training alone, HIIT with resistance training resulted in lower increases in lower body strength. One way to combat interference when strength development is the priority is to ensure that resistance exercise occurs before aerobic endurance-related activities. These tactics might be best explored during extra conditioning events, when basketball-related activities remain a primary focus and a high volume of running is already taking place. Ultimately, if lower body strength and power are the goal, as is often the case with a basketball athlete, resistance training should remain a major focus and take priority in the absence of aerobic endurance training at specific times throughout the off-season. Basketball activities can still coincide with resistance training but perhaps be more focused on individual skill work rather than live play and conditioning-related drills.

The **size principle** is the concept that motor units are recruited in an orderly fashion based on the size of their motor neuron from smallest to largest (29). In addition, muscle fibers associated with smaller, lower-threshold motor units are rich in mitochondrial ATP-ase and more fatigue resistant (e.g., type I muscle fibers), whereas fibers associated with larger, higher-threshold motor units produce greater forces but are less fatigue resistant (e.g., type II fibers) (29). Thus, low-force, fatigue-resistant, slow-twitch muscle fibers are activated before high-force, less fatigue-resistant, fast-twitch muscle fibers (29). This order of motor recruitment progresses in the same manner regardless of the type of muscle action performed (29). In resistance training, factors such as the load, rate of acceleration, and the number of repetitions completed all likely play a major role in dictating how many motor units are activated and, therefore, which fibers are stimulated.

In the book *Transfer of Training*, Dr. Anatoliy Bondarchuk opens the first chapter with this statement: "The transfer of training is one of the central problems in the theory and practice of physical education." He goes on to explain that the complexity of the systems of the human body and the interpretation of the research devoted to the area of transfer and physical activity have led to many different theories on the subject (4). The complexity of it all is easy to see when considering that basketball strength and conditioning professionals around the world are all trying to prepare their athletes to succeed on the court, all while using varying training strategies and techniques.

When developing a resistance training program for basketball athletes, strength and conditioning professionals must consider what program and exercises will have the most transfer to enhance the athlete's on-court performance, as well as put in place the plan to execute that program properly. Coaches must have a firm grasp on the physical, mental, and tactical requirements of the game of basketball. Coaches must also be equipped with the tools to determine what exercise to prescribe (exercise selection), how often to prescribe that particular exercise (frequency), how much of the exercise to prescribe (volume), what level of difficulty of the exercise to prescribe (intensity), and how and when to modulate those variables to maximize adaptation (periodization). For both short- and long-term program planning, coaches must understand those factors of influence to achieve an optimal training environment.

Bondarchuk outlines three types of training transfer: positive, negative, and neutral (4). Positive training transfer pertains to an exercise or exercise program that has a positive effect on the athlete's performance. A negative training transfer pertains to an exercise or exercise program that has a negative effect on the athlete's performance (4). Finally, a neutral transfer of training has no effect, positive or negative, on an athlete's performance. A simple question to ask when navigating around a resistance training program is, "Is this particular exercise, placed in this particular part of the workout, on this particular workout day, within the context of this athlete's training schedule having a positive, negative, or neutral effect on his or her development?" After asking that question the coach must then go even further to find the answer with proper athlete monitoring and testing procedures. How does the coach know whether the exercise program is working without strategically scheduling testing opportunities? Coaches should always remember that using assessments and tests to establish baseline numbers for their athletes and revisiting those tests after completion of a workout program or training phase will help determine the training effect.

A goal for coaches should be to create a positive workout environment designed to help athletes progress from year to year. Whether the athlete is an elite professional athlete or a first-year junior varsity athlete on a high school team, coaches should strive to create a space where physical, mental, and tactical progression are the goals. When planning workouts, coaches should remember these fundamental principles of progression: simple to complex, slow to fast, easy to difficult, and general to specific. **Progressive overload** describes a training principle that describes gradual increases in the stress imposed during resistance training workouts (12). Gradual increases are key, because the progression principle is often violated in a "too much, too soon" training style. Coaches need to start simple with their athletes, teaching them proper movement mechanics, and allow them to learn before advancing them to more complex exercises or periodization schemes.

Examples of variants in resistance training that might create a new stress for an athlete are weight lifted, speed of weight lifted, range of motion of weight lifted, number of repetitions lifted at a specified load, rest between exercises, rest between sets of an exercise, additional sets, additional exercises, and the form or execution of the exercise. Altering one or more of these variables during a workout session and throughout a training cycle can lead to acute changes in how the athlete responds to the workout stimulus, which in turn may facilitate long-term adaptation (24).

An important feature of progressive overload is the ability of the coach to identify where each athlete falls on the performance spectrum. Executing proper testing of performance markers and evaluating movement throughout the training process cannot be overemphasized in terms of creating a proper plan and adjusting plans to meet the needs of each athlete. Later in this section, the long-term athlete development (LTAD) model will be identified and discussed. It can serve as a tool that strength and conditioning professionals can use to design a plan not only for the athlete's biological age but also for the athlete's training age when developing long-term workout programs.

For proper progression when designing a resistance training program, the National Strength and Conditioning Association has outlined these seven variables to consider (12).

Needs analysis: Considers the physical requirements of the sport and includes an assessment of the athlete. A sport like basketball requires frequent changes of speed and direction; acceleration and deceleration are common features of high-level competition. Athletes must be able to jump and land safely on one or two feet. They must also be able to maintain certain postures on the offensive, defensive, and transition aspects of the game. These positional postures require the athlete to have core strength, leg strength, and spatial awareness. The coaching staff should individually screen each athlete to determine any prior injuries sustained, movement capacity and ability, and specific goals that the athlete might have for her or his training program. Common questions to ask each athlete before beginning a training program are the following:

- Have you ever resistance trained before?
- How long was the previous training program?
- What types of exercises were prescribed in the previous training program?
- Have you ever been injured? If so, list injuries including site of injury, date of injury, and mechanism of injury.
- Are you medically cleared for participation in a resistance training program? If you were previously injured, what type of rehabilitation program did you do?

Coaches should take copious notes on their athletes throughout the training process and create a profile of all the information they collect. They should use this information to tailor their training plans further for each athlete.

Exercise selection: Considers the movement demands of the sport, muscular demands of the sport, resistance training experience of the athlete, equipment available, and amount of training time available. Coaches should use the needs analysis of the sport to choose exercises that will help each athlete excel at that sport. Basketball requires high levels of acceleration and deceleration; therefore, coaches should consider implementing single- and double-leg exercises such as squatting, lunging, and glute bridging. Ground-based movements such as Olympic lifts and their derivatives that teach the athlete how to generate force and extend the body while moving a load are also great selections and have a high transfer to the court. Coaches should also consider plyometric progressions that teach athletes proper landing mechanics because jumping for rebounds, blocks, and offensive moves is common in the sport. Proper plyometric progressions should be implemented in programming to ensure that athletes can safely perform these movements during practices and games. The training space available to the coach and the number of athletes in the given training space will also affect each workout. Coaches need to make sure that the exercises they are prescribing in workouts can be executed properly and safely in the workout space and that the workout can adequately flow in the space provided. If the training space provided has only one barbell and the workout group consists of 15 athletes, prescribing barbell complexes to the group might not be the most efficient approach.

Training frequency: Considers the amount of training exposures that the athlete will participate in during each training microcycle. Training frequency may change from athlete to athlete, as well as throughout the calendar year. The better that coaches can understand the athlete's current state of wellness, both physically and mentally, the better they will be able to determine how frequently to schedule training exposures. Throughout the calendar year, basketball strength and conditioning professionals often run into variables such as court workouts, practices, game schedules, travel schedules, and academic demands that may affect the number of workouts each week and the time available to complete these workouts. A consistent schedule of training exposures throughout the year, even during in-season, will help athletes maintain muscle mass and strength. Taking large breaks in training can result in performance drops because of loss of strength and power, as well as increased soreness when returning to resistance training. Coaches working with basketball athletes need to make sure they monitor their team members, especially during the in-season training microcycles, because athletes who play more in competitions will need a different workout prescription than those who do not play. Those who do not see as much action in games might need additional attention given to energy system development and are able to handle a greater training load in the weight room.

Exercise order: Considers the workout design, flow, and sequence of exercises. Coaches can choose from infinite combinations of exercise pairings and progressions in training sessions, but the key takeaway for most is finding the best option for each athlete at any given time. Resources commonly recommend that exercises that require maximal force production and technical proficiency should be placed near the beginning of a workout to ensure that the athlete is physically and mentally prepared to execute the movement (3, 12, 42). Examples of such exercises are Olympic lifts and their derivatives such as the snatch, power clean, hang clean, and push jerk. These exercises are designed to promote power development in athletes and are highly technical; therefore, high-repetition programming and placement of such exercises at the end of a workout may have a negative training effect on the athlete. Other drills that need to be executed when athletes are mentally and physically fresh are speed drills, in which improvements are highly influenced by close attention and sharp execution. If speed drills are placed at the end of workouts, when athletes are physically tired and less focused, they will no longer enhance speed. Following explosive movements, coaches should program movements that involve multiple joints (multijoint) and large-muscle groups. Examples of these movements include deadlifts, squats, chin-ups, bench press, and overhead pressing. Lastly, coaches should program assistance or accessory exercises that complement the current workout being performed or set the movement table for workout sessions in the future. Some common and basic exercise ordering in strength and conditioning include pairing of a pushing movement and a pulling movement, pairing of an upper body movement and a lower body movement, super-setting similar movements to elicit a desired response, and compound sets that pair movements that stress the same muscle group.

Training load and repetitions: Considers the amount of weight lifted for each exercise and the number of times that the weight is lifted. After completing the thorough needs analysis, evaluating each athlete, and deciding what the training goal should be, coaches should begin to decide what exercises, loads, and repetition assignments should be used in the resistance training program. Coaches should monitor athletes throughout the training program, tracking training loads and repetition changes. As the athlete adapts to the training stimulus, coaches must make tweaks to the training program to continue to get positive training results.

Volume: Considers the total amount of work done in a training session. Coaches need to consider the volume completed per exercise and muscle group and know that varying degrees of volume will elicit different training results. Basketball strength and conditioning professionals need to frame volume within the resistance training program with what activity the athlete is doing outside the weight room. The athlete's training load and the intensity of activities performed on the court in both individual workouts and team practice can have an effect on the total workload of the athlete and may affect the volume that the athlete can handle in the resistance training routine. Communication with the sport coaches and athletic training staff, as well as the athlete, can be invaluable to the strength and conditioning professional when planning workouts for each athlete. Note that more-trained athletes typically handle higher workloads better than their less-trained counterparts (12). Training volume may fluctuate throughout the calendar year as coaches begin to consider periodization, court time, travel schedules, game schedules, in-game performance, and other factors that could affect an athlete's training session. Off-season workouts typically provide wide enough training windows to fit higher volume workouts into an athlete's training program. In contrast, after playoffs begin, resistance training volume decreases because the primary focus between games will be recovery. Strength and conditioning professionals should be aware that the volume they prescribe is program and athlete dependent, and therefore they should use personal discretion in how they prescribe it throughout the season.

Rest periods: Considers the time taken between sets, exercises, and training sessions. Oftentimes overlooked or completely ignored, rest can be one of the most powerful tools in a strength and conditioning professional's repertoire. Rest can be considered during the workout (between exercises and sets of exercises), between workout sessions, and during training mesocycles (between training microcycles). The length of a rest period during workout sessions can be affected by the goal of training (different training goals such as hypertrophy and power require varying rest intervals), load being lifted (heavier loads lifted often require more rest), and training status of the athlete (athletes in poor physical shape may require more rest during workouts than their more physically fit peers). Recovery time during microcycles and between mesocycles of training allows the athletes' minds and bodies to recover from the previous training session as well as prepare for the next training session. Coaches should use discretion when planning their training schedules and understand the influential role that rest time and recovery play in programming.

LONG-TERM ATHLETIC DEVELOPMENT

The holistic plan for athletic development that considers the various physical and psychological changes that athletes will experience throughout their active lives is termed **long-term athletic development** (LTAD) (1). Long-term athletic development has gained more attention in recent years as athletes, parents, and coaches have become more invested in sport performance and training at earlier ages. By using a properly designed LTAD model, coaches can better identify their athletes' current physical ability as well as design a plan to help them improve over the course of their athletic careers. In the book *Long-Term Athletic Development*, the authors described a seven-part model for LTAD that coaches and parents can use when planning developmental progressions for athletes (1). Here are the seven parts:

1. Active start—encourage activity in the form of free play. This stage typically lasts until age 6.

2. FUNdamentals—encourage movement in the form of more structured activity by introducing fundamental movements such as crawling, skipping, shuffling, running, and jumping. These fundamental movements will help develop not only movement and motor skills but also agility, coordination, and balance. This stage typically lasts from age 6 to 8 in girls and age 6 to 9 in boys.

3. Learn to train—in this stage, sport skills can be introduced to children. Coaches and parents should encourage proper skill and game instruction and encourage children to participate in a wide variety of sports that will continue to build on their fundamental movements and grow their movement vocabulary. Coaches and parents should refrain from encouraging children to pick one sport to specialize in during this stage of development, because early specialization hinders future stages of the LTAD model. This stage typically lasts from age 8 to 11 in girls and age 9 to 12 in boys. A growth spurt can cause a jump in this part of the LTAD model.

4. Train to train—in this stage of development, typically following a growth spurt, children reach the physical and mental maturity necessary to begin a more focused physical training program. Coaches should create programs that challenge their athletes to master bodyweight exercises first, focusing on simple exercise execution that will lay a solid foundation for more advanced training in the future. This stage typically last from age 11 to 15 in girls and from age 12 to 16 in boys.

5. Train to compete—at this stage of development, athletes begin to refine their training program to help them meet the demands and excel at their sport of choice. At this stage, athletes also may decide to move from a competitive arena to a recreational level of involvement in their sport or vice versa. Training during this stage is more intense and focused as athletes begin to shift their focus from participating in sport to participate to participating in sport to compete. Coaches should continue to build on the fundamental movements introduced earlier in development to more advanced training models and exercises. The age range for this stage can vary based on sport, and coaches should use discretion when advancing athletes into a more intense training environment.

6. Train to win—this stage of development is reserved for elite or full-time athletes. Athletes have reached a stage in their development where they are competing at high levels of their sport and training to meet the demands of their sport. Training programs are athlete specific and year-round. In the United States this level of training can be found at most collegiate sport programs and professional sport organizations in which athletes and teams train and compete year-round. These teams and athletes are surrounded by sport coaches, strength and conditioning professionals, and sports medicine professionals who are dedicated to ensuring proper development and peak performance during this time.

7. Active for life—at this stage, athletes enter into a long-term relationship with movement and activity. Following the LTAD model, active children become active adolescents who become active adults, embracing a healthy lifestyle throughout the duration of their lifetimes. Elite athletes enter this stage of development following the end of their athletic careers and can continue to participate in the sport that they competed in or choose to be active in other ways (1).

After reviewing the seven-part model, coaches and parents can begin to analyze and improve on the current structure of the resistance training programs they have in place for the youth athletes they are working alongside. Note that in the LTAD model, children initiate activity in the form of play at an early age. Unfortunately, in today's youth sports culture it has become increasingly common for coaches and parents to push young, aspiring athletes into an intense, focused, year-long sport practice before they are physically and mentally prepared. **Early specialization** is the term used to describe the process of young athletes focusing on one sport at a young age. Experts have turned to early specialization as a cause for burnout later in athletic careers (6).

So, we might pose the question, why are parents and athletes themselves devoting all their time and attention to one sport at a young age? Some believe that their motives include aspirations to gain college scholarships or become elite Olympic or professional athletes in their sport of choice.

Note that only 1% of high school athletes will receive an NCAA athletic scholarship and 0.03% to 0.5% of high school athletes will make it to the professional level (6). For a 2017 study by the *American Journal of Sports Medicine*, high school athletic trainers in Wisconsin were asked to track injury occurrences in practices and games over the course of a season for high school athletes from 29 high schools (28). Of the 1,500 athletes tracked that year, 235 sustained injuries that were serious enough to hold them out of competition for at least a week, an astonishingly high number. Organizations such as the American Orthopedic Society for Sports Medicine and the American Academy of Pediatrics have released studies and statements that encourage young athletes and parents to avoid early specialization (28).

The American Academy of Pediatrics outlines these nine guidelines when dealing with early specialization for medical professionals, coaches, parents, and athletes (6):

- The primary focus of sports for young athletes should be to have fun and learn lifelong physical activity skills.
- Participating in multiple sports, at least until puberty, decreases the chances of injuries, stress, and burnout in young athletes.
- For most sports, specializing in a sport later (i.e., late adolescence) may lead to a higher chance that the young athlete will accomplish his or her athletic goals.
- Early diversification and later specialization provide a greater chance of lifetime sport involvement, lifetime physical fitness, and possibly elite participation.
- If a young athlete has decided to specialize in a single sport, discussing his or her goals to determine whether they are appropriate and realistic is important. This discussion may involve helping the young athlete distinguish these goals from those of the parents or coaches.
- Parents must closely monitor the training and coaching environment of "elite" youth sport programs and be aware of best practices for their children's sports.
- Having a total of at least three months off throughout the year, in increments of one month, from their sport of interest will allow athletes to recover physically and psychologically. Young athletes can remain active in other activities to meet physical activity guidelines during the time off.
- Having at least one to two days off per week from their sport of interest can decrease the chance for injuries in young athletes.
- Closely monitoring young athletes who pursue intensive training for physical and psychological growth and maturation as well as nutritional status is an important parameter for health and well-being (28).

These nine guidelines coupled with the seven-part model for LTAD are useful educational resources for parents and athletes and can serve as decision-making guidelines concerning sport participation. As participation rates in youth sport continue to rise, coaches and athletes need to spend time evaluating where they are in the developmental process and how much time they should dedicate to their sport. In any event, parents, coaches, and athletes need to maintain realistic expectations and understand the value of participating in multiple sports to develop well-rounded athleticism.

ADAPTATION (GENERAL ADAPTATION SYNDROME)

Hans Selye was a Hungarian endocrinologist who, in the 1930s, was the first to explain how the body responds to stress. His three-part model became known as the **general adaptation syndrome** (GAS) and has become an inspiration for strength and conditioning professionals in their pursuit of proper exercise and training load prescriptions throughout each training cycle. A proper understanding of stress and the body's subsequent hormonal and neural response to stress within Selye's model can serve as a valuable tool for coaches (12, 16).

When most people hear the word *stress*, they think of something negative. So how does stress serve as a valuable tool to strength and conditioning professionals? Selye's three-part model (alarm, resistance, exhaustion) within GAS help make the connection that stress is a good thing in a training environment if applied appropriately (37).

A **stressor** or **stress** can be considered anything that knocks the body out of homeostasis (35). The body's subsequent response—alarm, resistance, and exhaustion—serve as safeguards to ensure that the body safely responds to the stress, adapts to the stress, and returns to a place where it is prepared to maintain a dynamic balance. The **alarm phase** is the initial phase of the stress response system, whereby the body notes that the stress is occurring and begins the process of releasing a cavalry of hormones and other substances to help respond to the impending threat. In a resistance training environment, triggers to the stress response system can include exercise selection, frequency, intensity, volume, load, and so on. Athletes and coaches should be aware of fatigue, muscle soreness, muscle stiffness, and cognitive changes during the alarm phase. Note also that athletes may experience a drop in performance. Therefore, coaches should monitor each athlete individually and keep track of how long the alarm phase lasts because it can vary among athletes even if the same exercise protocol is prescribed (9, 35).

Following the alarm phase, the next step in the body's response to stress is the **resistance phase**. The resistance phase is also known as the adaptation phase, rightfully so, because the body begins to adapt to the stress stimulus and return to normal function. For strength and conditioning professionals, the resistance phase is critical to the success of any training program because of the opportunity to help improve the athlete's function as he or she adapts to the stressor and becomes more resilient from a biomechanical, chemical, and structural standpoint (12). A coach's goal when developing a resistance training program should be to choose an adequate stressor for each athlete that will drive him or her to elevate above the baseline level of performance (9).

Supercompensation is a term used to describe athletes' response to training when, after the stress is applied, they not only return to their original baseline level of function but also recover above their original baseline level of function. Simply put, when supercompensation occurs, an athlete can handle a greater training load than before she or he started the training program (12, 31). Note that the supercompensation principle is specific to each individual athlete; factors such as health, training age, biological age, volume, intensity, frequency, exercise selection, and so on affect training results. College freshman basketball athletes with little training experience might have significant training gains within the first six months of a training program because of their novice training status, whereas a college senior who has been in the training program for several years could do the same program as the freshman and have no results (33). In summary, the stimulus applied must be specifically designed for each athlete. A resistance training program that is not challenging enough will not cause a stress response and therefore will not change an athlete's baseline level of function. On the other hand, a resistance training program that is too stressful could potentially cause injury and not allow the athlete to return to baseline levels of function (16).

If stress is good, then why not keep applying it over months and months of training? Herein lies an important feature of the GAS model that coaches and athletes must pay close attention to: overtraining and overreaching. **Overtraining** occurs when numerous bouts of exercise, typically for months on end, are performed with little or no time for the athletes to recover. Essentially, the athletes become trapped in the alarm phase with no time for the body to recover from the previous exercise session and thus never fully enters the resistance phase. Instead of making positive adaptations to the workout stimulus, athletes instead slip into a state of negative adaptation and become susceptible not only to drops in performance but also to illness, extreme fatigue, and injury. Athletes and coaches can prevent overtraining with proper planning of workout sessions, rest and recovery periods, and nutritional interventions (9, 12).

Overreaching is a milder form of overtraining and results from excessive training that leads to short-term performance drops (9). Unlike overtraining, overreaching can be resolved or recovered from within several days to up to two weeks of rest for the athlete. In turn, rest leads to a compensatory supercompensation improvement in performance (9). Coaches often use overreaching during periods of training when they know that rest periods for their athletes are built into the training schedule.

Coaches should always be aware that adequate amounts of rest and regeneration are appropriate to prevent overtraining. Some college strength and conditioning professionals working with basketball athletes may use the summer training session to drive some of their athletes to a place of overreaching, knowing that they will have a one- to two-week break at the end of the summer training cycle to recover before beginning their preseason resistance training program. Research supports this notion, because strength and power gains have been shown to occur when an adequate tapering period follows a short-term period of overreaching (12).

Resistance training is critical to the overall development and advancement of basketball athletes. Strength and conditioning professionals need to remember this point as they choose what exercises to include in their resistance training sessions as well as what drills to place in movement and resistance training to obtain the appropriate training effect.

To create a resistance training program that is specific to basketball athletes, coaches need to go through their sport analysis, conduct their personnel analysis, and finally incorporate their own training knowledge. Strength and conditioning professionals should not fall into the trap of thinking that they only need to include movements that look similar to basketball skills in the resistance training menu for basketball athletes. Instead, programs should include movements and exercises that have been proved to improve strength, speed, and power, as well as drills and movement sessions that develop linear, lateral, and multidirectional acceleration and deceleration. Athletes will respond differently to the same stimulus and therefore will progress and regress at different rates. As a result, a blanket approach to resistance training applied to the team will not result in positive transfer for all athletes.

PHYSICAL DEMANDS OF THE SPORT

The physical demands of basketball for strength and power depend on the style of play and physical characteristics of the athletes. A 2013 study by Boone (5) showed that the physiological profile of elite athletes in the Belgian first division differs by athlete position. More specifically, guards were characterized by high aerobic endurance, speed, and agility, whereas centers and power forwards had higher muscular strength than other positions (5). Another study (22) showed similar findings with Turkish professional basketball athletes. The study indicated that physical performance of professional basketball athletes differed among guards, forwards, and centers. Guards scored higher on the speed, agility, and aerobic endurance tests, and the centers scored higher on the strength test. These results suggest that strength and conditioning professionals should tailor resistance training programs according to specific positions on the court (22).

Wearable technology is becoming increasingly prevalent in college and professional sport. This technology monitors and quantifies the physical demands of athletes during training and competition. Defining exactly what the athlete's stress is and where it comes from makes it easier for practitioners to manage. Stress is best defined using heart rate, which measures the internal load or effort that the athlete is putting forth, and work, which is the actual speed and distance covered in training. These two variables combined are referred to as **training load**. Training load is based on the intensity and duration of a training session. The intensity of a session is measured using heart rate, and the calculation is further affected by the athlete's personal information, such as age, sex, weight, $\dot{V}O_2max$, and training history.

More teams are increasingly leaning on objective measures to inform their decision making, from advanced analytics used by front offices and coaching staffs to sport science techniques that empower teams to make smarter and more informed medical decisions with their athletes. These data are also important to coaches, who can better plan and deliver training strategies appropriate to the needs of their athletes. Coaches can use this information to help manage fatigue and implement an injury risk management plan.

The competition and training demands for a collegiate and professional athlete are extensive. The NBA has one of the longest seasons, which consists of 82 games played over six months (about 3.4 games per week). If teams are successful and make the playoffs, they may play up to an additional 28 games over a two-month period (up to 110 total games). In the collegiate setting, the season lasts about five months with 30 regular-season games. In addition to the game-related demands, athletes may travel all over the country for approximately half of their games. The physiological stress placed on the athlete accumulates over the course of the season and causes signs of fatigue, which can lead to decreased performance or injury (38). With the use of technology, coaches can get a global picture of the athlete in training, practice, and competition to quantify strength, power, and workload as well as identify fatigue early on. Having such data can give coaches information to make informed decisions and gain insight on actual physical status instead of perceived state. For example, the position played by a basketball athlete needs to be factored in when planning and prescribing workout volume and intensity. A recent study revealed that workloads in practice obtained by accelerometry are greatest in point guards, irrespective of the drill (36). This high workload may be because of the tactical requirements of the position as a point guard, who typically covers more distance per possession. Another reason could be that guards typically have lower body mass and can accelerate quicker than larger forwards and centers (36). Another study investigated the practice and competition demands of semiprofessional basketball athletes and reported significantly higher workloads during five-on-five-based training than in actual competition (13). This finding shows that the training drills in practice adequately simulate game demands and potentially prepare the athletes for competition. Technology can help manage position-specific conditioning, improve training periodization, and provide a more accurate drill classification (13). Sprint speed is an important attribute for basketball athletes. Being able to monitor an athlete's high-end accelerations may be an appropriate method to identify decrements in game-time physical performance.

As mentioned earlier, because of the physical demands of the sport and the length of the season, managing fatigue and stress in basketball athletes is essential when attempting to program in-season strength maintenance programs. Being able to forecast potential unhealthy situations for athletes can give teams who use this technology an edge over their competition.

Another popular piece of technology that strength and conditioning professionals use to monitor their athletes is a force plate. Measuring vertical jump ability has been a popular fatigue-monitoring method used in high-performance sports to assess lower body strength and power and the integrity of musculotendinous prestretch, or countermovement stretch-shortening cycle (23). Basketball requires athletes to accelerate, decelerate, and change direction rapidly, which relies on their ability to transition from eccentric to concentric contraction. Measuring various types of jumps like the countermovement jump, the drop jump, and the static squat jump can reveal information about the athlete's neuromuscular function and assist in making decisions on how to progress the resistance training program.

ATHLETE-SPECIFIC CONSIDERATIONS

When planning a resistance training program, coaches should consider each individual athlete they are training during the needs analysis portion of the planning process. As touched on earlier, coaches should consider certain factors that might affect the athlete's training status, such as biological age, resistance training experience, injury history, and position on the court. All these factors could cause minor or sometimes major deviations in the resistance training plans that are developed for each athlete. Although making individual adjustments to workout programs for each athlete may be difficult in certain situations, keeping those factors in mind is still critical when planning workouts.

Rich von Biberstein/Icon Sportswire via Getty Images

When possible, resistance training programs should reflect the unique aspects of each individual athlete.

Biological age is an important consideration in programming because athletes of varying ages will be at different points of maturation, both physically and mentally. A 14-year-old male should not necessarily perform the same workout prescription as an 18-year-old male. Performing the same resistance training program could have a negative training effect for either athlete. The 18-year-old may have already gone through puberty and have a firm handle on his body awareness and control, as well as the mental maturity to complete a higher intensity workout. The 14-year-old athlete who is a freshman in high school might have the skill set to compete with varsity-level athletes on the basketball court, but the same training program should not necessarily be administered to both athletes in the weight room.

Training age is the amount of time that the athlete has spent training for her or his sport. This consideration is important because athletes of the same biological age walking into a weight room have likely had varying experiences in resistance training in the past. In planning resistance training programs, this point is critical because although athletes may have similar athletic ability on the basketball court, they may be at two different levels in terms of physical development or resistance training experience. For example, a 15-year-old basketball athlete who has been involved in a resistance training program since she was 12 years old (training age of 3) will require a different resistance training program than another 15-year-old who has no training experience (training age of 0). The athlete older in training age may be able to handle complex exercise prescription under load, whereas the newborn athlete may need a basic program that emphasizes learning proper movement execution. In the needs analysis portion of the planning process, coaches need to determine where their athletes fall on the training-age spectrum.

Injury history refers to the past injuries that the athlete may have experienced before beginning a resistance training program. Collecting this information from each athlete is critical, because a well-cited risk factor for injuries in sport is a previous injury (26). Obtaining this information from athletes can be helpful in the planning process because coaches may be able to make individualized changes to help bolster the athlete's durability in hopes of protecting him or her from reinjury or sustaining a new injury.

Coaches should be aware that recall bias happens with some athletes in regard to remembering their past injuries. Asking clear and concise questions during the evaluation process such as, "Have you ever missed a competition or training session because of an injury?" can help clear up the injury history picture. Coaches should ask detailed questions about the exact location of the injury, the mechanism of the injury, and whether subsequent surgery or rehabilitation was required following the injury. If the athlete has sustained an injury, coaches can be even more thorough in their information gathering by contacting the athlete's rehabilitation provider to gain more insight into the details of the injury as well as where the athlete falls on the return-to-play continuum (15).

Body type, including biomechanical considerations, is another important factor that deserves attention when developing resistance training programs. Before beginning a training program, coaches can take anthropometrical measurements of their athletes such as height, weight, wingspan, shoe size, hand size, and body composition. This information can be helpful in guiding the coach in exercise selection as well as monitoring the effects of the training program.

Body composition may play a critical role in planning the resistance training program because it can serve as another evaluation tool of the program's effectiveness. Rather than look simply at body weight, coaches can analyze body fat measurements to gain deeper insight into lean muscle mass and fat mass. An increase in lean muscle mass will allow the athlete to develop further strength and power. A decrease in fat mass may contribute to greater range of motion, better aerobic endurance, and greater movement capacity. Resistance training improves body composition by helping to reduce fat mass (12).

In his book *The Sports Gene*, David Epstein takes anthropometric measurements from the National Basketball Association in hopes of painting a better picture of the ideal body type for a professional basketball athlete. Although less than 5% of the American male population is over 6 feet, 3 inches tall (190 cm), the average height of an NBA athlete was 6 feet, 7 inches (201 cm) tall. Although some athletes under 6 feet (183 cm) tall have achieved success in the NBA, for the most part the highest level of play is a taller person's game (11).

Coaches working with basketball athletes need to be aware of this circumstance because of the implications involved with training longer-limbed, taller athletes, such as postural considerations, limb control considerations, and range-of-motion implications. If basketball athletes are taller and live in a world designed for relatively smaller people, what effect might that have on their physical structure? Strength and conditioning professionals might observe from a postural standpoint that their athletes may structurally adapt to meet those conditions. Implications may be kyphosis in the spinal column, internal rotation at the shoulder joint, and various muscle imbalances. Coaches need to be aware that those issues may arise, and they may have to work diligently to design a program that works to help counterbalance those issues (16).

Limb control for taller athletes may also be a training implication that coaches need to consider when planning workouts for basketball athletes. Athletes with longer limbs may have a more difficult time controlling their bodies throughout a full range of motion because of their longer levers (arms, legs, and spine). Coaches may notice that taller athletes struggle initially with lower body movements such as two-leg squats and single-leg squats and upper body movements such as chin-ups and push-ups. In those exercises, taller athletes not only have a much larger range of motion to complete compared with their shorter counterparts but also must spend more time controlling their bodies through that longer range of motion. Full range of motion and total body control through the full range of motion through the movement should be the coach's first concerns when working with taller athletes. After full range of motion and control is established, coaches can begin to add load and varying velocities to those movements.

In general, the annual resistance training program should include exercises that focus on various strength components; address total body, lower body, upper body, and core strengthening; and offer bilateral and unilateral, as well as multiplanar, variance. Regardless of position, here are some general suggestions to exercise selection.

Explosive Movements:

- Olympic lifts and derivatives: snatch, power clean, hang clean, push jerk
- Kettlebell swings
- Medicine ball throws
- Plyometrics: vertical and horizontal, jumps, hops, bounds

Lower Body Movements:

- Squat patterns: bodyweight squat, weight vest squat, goblet squat, back squat, front squat, single-leg bodyweight squat
- Deadlifts: dumbbell RDL, barbell deadlift, single-leg RDL
- Lunges: directional bodyweight lunge, directional weight vest lunge, directional dumbbell lunge
- Bridging: glute bridge, barbell loaded hip thrust

Upper Body Movements:

- Pressing: bodyweight push-up, weight vest push-up, bodyweight dip, weight vest dip, dumbbell bench press, dumbbell incline bench press, barbell bench press, barbell incline bench press, dumbbell overhead press (single arm, two arm), barbell overhead press
- Pulling: lat pulldown, chin-up progressions, one-arm dumbbell row, barbell bent-over row

Core Development:

- Carrying variations: farmer carry, waiter walk, rack carry
- Planking progressions: short-lever plank, long-lever plank, forward plank, side plank
- Crawling progressions: linear in-sync, linear out-of-sync, lateral in-sync, lateral out-of-sync

POSITION-SPECIFIC CONSIDERATIONS

According to Bompa and Buzzichelli, guards can be broken down into two main groups: point guards and shooting guards. Both spend most of the game on the perimeter on offense and defense and, for the majority of offensive possessions, are facing the basket. Offensively, guards must be able to handle and pass the ball, read defenses, and be fast and quick on their feet. Guards must be able to execute the skills and tactics of the game, all while moving at an extremely fast pace. Training to prepare guards to compete at a high level should include a resistance training program focused on strength, speed, and power development, a conditioning program designed to develop the anaerobic and aerobic energy systems, and a movement and plyometric program that emphasizes linear, lateral, and multidirectional acceleration and deceleration movements (39).

Forwards can also be broken down into two main groups: small and power. Small forwards are typically more dynamic athletes who can be moved into a guard position if need be. While on offense, they spend part of the game facing the basket and the other part of the game with their backs to the basket. Power forwards spend most of the game both offensively and defensively inside the perimeter. They are likely to play a more physical style of basketball with body-to-body contact happening frequently in rebounding opportunities and positional ownership situations. Both small forwards and power forwards must be able to cover large segments of the floor, oftentimes baseline to baseline, defend perimeter and interior athletes, and be able to pass and handle the ball on offense. Forwards must be able to jump and safely land to secure rebounds, but they also need to have great timing on those rebounding attempts. Training to prepare forwards to compete at a high level should include a resistance training program focused on strength, speed, and power development; a conditioning program designed to develop the anaerobic and aerobic energy systems; and a movement and plyometric program that emphasizes linear, lateral, and multidirectional acceleration and deceleration movements (39).

Centers are often the tallest athletes on the court and typically spend more time close to the basket than the other positions. Centers must be able to move quickly in tight spaces and have sufficient strength to gain optimal position in those tight spaces. They spend the majority of offensive possessions with their backs to the basket or in screening plays. Both situations requiring great footwork and strength to be successful. Centers must be able to jump and land safely to secure rebounds, but they also need to have great timing on those rebounding attempts. Training to prepare centers to compete at a high level should include a resistance training program focused on strength, speed, and power development; a conditioning program designed to develop the anaerobic and aerobic energy systems; and a movement and plyometric program that emphasizes linear, lateral, and multidirectional acceleration and deceleration movements. Coaches should be aware of body types when training centers, knowing that taller athletes may require differing exercise progressions than shorter athletes (39).

GENERAL PERIODIZATION MODEL

"A long-term training plan is an essential component of the training process because it guides the athlete's development over many years of athletic activities. A major goal of long-term planning is to facilitate the progressive and continual development of the athlete's motor potential, skills, and performance" (3, page 117).

Creating an annual plan allows each athlete to improve consistently over time to achieve short-term and long-term goals. An example of an annual plan (macrocycle) is seen in table 4.1. In general, it includes the postseason, off-season, preseason, in-season, and extended competitive phases. Each of these separate phases, known as mesocycles, typically has a different emphasis to achieve the goals for that point in the annual training plan. Mesocycles are a good place to start with a collegiate or professional basketball athlete because they have only one competitive season.

Transitional periods after each phase, when loading schemes are lower and overall volume is lessened, can be programmed into the macrocycle to serve as an active recovery to promote tissue regeneration. In high school and college, transitional phases are valuable when properly timed and programmed into the macrocycle during instances when athletes are returning to school, are at the end of semesters during exams, or have extended breaks. This period is an attempt to promote recovery from the cumulative stress of the previous mesocycle or to prepare athletes for the upcoming mesocycle. An extended recovery and regeneration period can be granted for teams that do not make the playoffs or for athletes who are injured. The length of this period will vary and largely depends on individual needs.

The postseason phase typically lasts anywhere between 2 and 6 weeks depending on the level of play. Postseason programming largely depends on the physical and mental wellness of the athletes. In this phase the athletes start to recover and regenerate from the in-season mesocycle. Sometimes, athletes may need medical attention in the form of surgery and continued rehabilitation from injuries sustained during the season. Athletes who do not need any continued medical attention can begin training. The goal of this phase is to rebuild gradually and identify areas of weakness. A lifting schedule of two to three times per week with low intensities, low volumes, and increased rest periods is appropriate during this short phase. The off-season phase typically lasts between 8 and 16 weeks, depending on level of play. The focus of this phase is strength and power development, and it is during this mesocycle that athletes usually spend the most time in the weight room. Participating in resistance training four or

Table 4.1 Example of an Annual Plan for Basketball

Month	Apr		May	Jun	July	Aug		Sept	Oct		Nov	Dec	Jan	Feb	Mar
Mesocycle	Postseason		T	Off-season			T		Preseason		In-season				T
Microcycle	Re	GPP	Rg	GPP	Strength	Power	Rg		Reactive strength and velocity	Competitive phase I	Competitive phase II			Playoffs	Rg

T = transition phase; GPP = general preparation phase; Re = recovery phase; Rg = regeneration phase.

more days per week is common in this phase. Generally, exercise order is organized by demand. Multijoint exercises are first in the exercise order because they require the most effort from the athlete. Having the athletes perform the more advanced technical exercises first is a safe and effective approach. Volumes, intensities, and rest periods in this phase vary widely depending on the athletes' goals. Eccentric training is popular during this phase because it emphasis a unique external load methodology by slowing the lowering, or eccentric-loading, phase of an exercise. This training stimulus may elicit changes in the muscles that improve their strength, function, and size (25). In fact, recent research indicates that longer times under tension increase the metabolic processes that promote muscle protein synthesis, which has been observed for 24 to 30 hours after the muscle experiences the training stimulus (25). This type of training is intense, and if used properly during this phase of training, it can prove to be especially beneficial.

The preseason phase occurs right before the regular season and typically last four to six weeks. Based on NCAA rules and regulations, the start date for the first practice depends on the first competition date, so preseason lengths may vary. The major objective in preseason resistance training is to prepare the athlete to endure the higher speed, intensity, and volume of work that basketball practice and games will demand in the upcoming weeks. Resistance training will emphasize high-quality, high-speed movement, performing exercises explosively. This phase is a good time to implement velocity-based training in which the focus switches from load to movement velocity. The objective is to move the resistance as fast as possible while maintaining control. This type of training will help prepare the athletes for more basketball-specific demands as they approach the season.

Although beyond the scope of this chapter, it must be mentioned that plyometric progressions will be a focal point of this phase, although at a lesser volume because basketball-specific work will likely have increased by this time. The concept of concurrent training will take great effect during this phase with the increased volume of on-court basketball workouts, combined with the additional conditioning that the strength and conditioning professional will administer. The preseason phase should include the onset and continuation of organized practice and exhibition games before the first official game. This mode of training prepares the athlete for the regular season and should be seen by the strength and conditioning professional as part of the process that helps the athlete maximize basketball performance in conjunction with the resistance training program. Initially, one of the preseason goals should be to have the athletes ready to sustain the rigors of the first few weeks of practice or preseason games. As training progressions reach these demands, the focus should turn to maximizing performance for the start of the competitive season.

The in-season phase typically lasts anywhere between 16 and 30 weeks, depending on the level of play. This time can be broken up into additional competitive phases. Because of the length of the basketball season, the optimal approach is to split the in-season mesocycle into two or three microcycles. Breaking up the mesocycle gives the strength and conditioning professional freedom in the planning process and the ability to manage the ebbs and flows of the season appropriately and, ideally, gear up for a strong playoff push. To achieve a proper training effect in this concurrent environment, the volume and intensities in resistance training sessions need to be adjusted. The second microcycle might be time to start gradually picking up the intensity in the weight room in a continual effort to maintain strength and power. For the coach and the athlete, planning and implementing remains a balancing act of knowing when to push forward and when to pull back. In-season training is more of an art than a science at times because many variables need to be accounted for when making decisions about the athletes' wellness and ability to perform at their highest level. Needs differ from athlete to athlete, so recognizing signs of both growth and regression is especially important. Special provisions must also be made around travel schedule and recovery status for each athlete.

As the season winds down, a winning team needs to begin focusing on preparing for the playoffs. The resistance training program within the in-season phase should be fine-tuned to help athletes realize peak performance levels again during this time. This is not necessarily a good time to overhaul the resistance training program, but anticipation and proper planning can allow the introduction of slight tweaks and, as in the preseason, help athletes regain any losses in strength and power that might have occurred over the course of the long season. After the playoffs begin, resistance training volumes and intensities should be reduced. The frequency at which the athletes train can remain the same as it has all season, but the primary focus during this time and between games is recovery.

When designing training programs for each phase of the season, consider these principles to help guide the process:

- Frequency of training—number of workouts performed per week highly dependent on competition and travel schedule, individual playing time, and individual athlete load and recovery status
- Exercise order—multijoint movements before single-joint movements (large- to small-muscle groups)
- Intensity—training percentage of the 1RM or velocity-based training
- Volume—sets and repetition ranges
- Rest periods—dependent on training goals

Athletic performance depends on the athlete's adaptation, psychological adjustment to training and competitions, and the development of skills and abilities. Training to enhance performance requires a special approach that involves periodization and planning. All the training factors need to be integrated to manage the training stress of the athletes. To achieve success and promote growth, strength and conditioning professionals must work closely with coaching staffs and medical staffs.

CONCLUSION

When developing an all-encompassing training system designed to enhance the performance of basketball athletes, coaches need to have a thorough understanding of general training principles. This chapter outlined basic training concepts and principles that can be used as guidelines when developing a training strategy specifically for the performance enhancements of basketball athletes and teams. Understanding the athletes being trained, the sport being prepared for, and the training concepts outlined in this section will be valuable tools to strength and conditioning professionals of all sports and disciplines, not just basketball. The ability of strength and conditioning professionals to take these concepts and frame them with the game of basketball, the movements involved and the energy systems required, and the athletes they are training will help them have a positive effect on their athletes and teams.

PART II

EXERCISE TECHNIQUE

5

TOTAL BODY EXERCISE TECHNIQUE

BILL FORAN AND ERIC FORAN

Total body exercises are an essential part of any training program to enhance performance for basketball athletes. Exercises that involve both the lower and upper body together in integration should be included to optimize movement and the expression of power throughout the entire kinetic chain. Basketball requires strength, power, speed, quickness, agility, and coordination, and performing resistance training exercises that involve the total body can enhance all these qualities (2, 3, 4).

On the basketball court, athletes must be able to coordinate lower body and upper body movements so that they can make plays and optimize performance. Athletes will be exposed to a variety of movements in all planes of motion: forward, backward, lateral, rotational, and vertical, so including exercises that work the body in all planes is important.

A group of the total body exercises covered in this chapter are called **Olympic lifts** (only in this context is the term *lifts* used instead of *exercises*) because two of these exercises, the clean and jerk and the snatch, are performed in competition in the Olympic sport of weightlifting. Research has shown that Olympic lifts improve power, strength, speed, agility, coordination, and flexibility (1). Olympic lifts are traditionally performed from the floor, but they can be adapted to a "hang" position, in which the bar starts just above knee height. The hang position closely simulates an athletic, vertical jump position, so it is applicable to basketball performance.

SPOTTING GUIDELINES

Spotters should not be used when coaching the Olympic lifts; doing so is dangerous for both the athlete and the spotter, and spotting is unnecessary because athletes can drop the weight (in a controlled manner) if they need to.

BREATHING GUIDELINES

Breathing is an important, but often overlooked, aspect of total body exercises. Breathing to increase abdominal pressure and stability is important when lifting heavy loads. Most exercises use similar breathing guidelines: Before each repetition, take a big breath in, expanding the abdominal cavity, and then exhale at the end of the exertion phase of each repetition. Make sure that the athlete does not hold his or her breath throughout the set.

COACHING TIPS

Specific coaching tips or cues are included for each exercise in this chapter, but some general coaching recommendations apply to all the total body exercises: Stay focused, stay balanced, and maintain proper posture.

POWER CLEAN

Primary Muscles Trained

Gluteus maximus, biceps femoris, semitendinosus, semimembranosus, vastus lateralis, vastus intermedius, vastus medialis, rectus femoris, soleus, gastrocnemius, trapezius

Beginning Position

- Stand with the feet slightly turned out, hip-width apart, holding the bar near the shins.
- Grip the bar with a closed **pronated grip** (palms facing the body) and the elbows fully extended (a).
- Hands should be shoulder-width apart or slightly wider than shoulder-width apart.

Movement Phases

1. Under control, lift the bar from the floor, keeping the shoulders over the bar and the back flat (neutral spine). Keep the bar close to the body and the hips down. While lifting the bar, raise the hips a little to prepare for the second pulling phase *(b)*.

2. Start the second pull by explosively extending the hips, legs, and ankles while keeping the elbows fully extended. Thrust the shoulders up and slightly back and the hips slightly forward and up *(c)*. Extend up on to the toes before the arms begin pulling. Keep the bar close to the body.

3. As the lower body becomes fully extended, rapidly shrug the shoulders and start the pull with the arms *(d)*. Lower to a quarter squat and prepare to rack the bar on the front of the shoulders. Rotate the wrists under the bar while raising the elbows through in front, so that the upper arm is parallel with the floor *(e)*. With the bar racked on the shoulders, stand up straight *(f)*.

4. Under control, lower the bar to the thighs, keeping it close to the body. Then lower the bar to the floor by flexing the hips and knees, keeping the shoulders over the bar and the back flat.

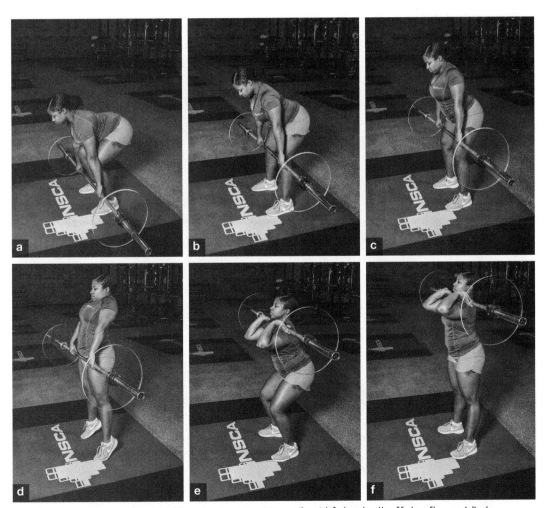

Figure 5.1   Power clean: *(a)* beginning position; *(b-c)* lift barbell off the floor; *(d)* shrug shoulders; *(e)* catch; *(f)* end position.

Breathing Guidelines

Take a deep breath before initiating the first pull off the floor. Exhale during the aggressive, explosive jumping action of the second pull.

Exercise Modifications and Variations

Lateral Clean

Hold a dumbbell in the right hand with a pronated grip and a fully extended elbow. Get into the same stance and posture as described with the power clean or the hang clean and position the dumbbell in between the legs. Perform the upward movement of the power or hang clean but instead of jumping straight up, laterally drive to the right with both legs while pulling the dumbbell toward the shoulders. When the feet land back on the floor, drop the hips and catch the dumbbell in an underhanded (supinated) position at shoulder level. Return to the beginning position by jumping to the left and lowering the dumbbell back across the body toward the floor (for the power clean version) or the knees (for the hang clean version). Repeat on the same side for the desired amount of repetitions then hold the dumbbell in the left hand and laterally drive to the left for the next set.

Coaching Tips

- Do not yank the bar from the floor.
- After the initial pull, be explosive.

To mimic the unilateral nature of basketball, it is important to perform one-arm (and single-leg) total body resistance training exercises.

Tim Warner/Getty Images

HANG CLEAN

Primary Muscles Trained

Gluteus maximus, biceps femoris, semitendinosus, semimembranosus, vastus lateralis, vastus intermedius, vastus medialis, rectus femoris, soleus, gastrocnemius, trapezius

Beginning Position

- Stand with the feet hip- or shoulder-width apart, the bar near the shins, and the toes turned out slightly.
- Grip the bar with a closed pronated grip and the elbows fully extended.
- Hands should be shoulder-width apart or slightly wider than shoulder-width apart.
- Under control, lift the bar from the floor, keeping the shoulders over the bar and the back flat (neutral spine).
- Keep the bar close to the body.
- From the upright position, lower the bar along the thighs to just above the knees (a).

Movement Phases

1. Start the pull by explosively extending the hips, legs, and ankles while keeping the elbows fully extended. Thrust the shoulders up and slightly back and the hips slightly forward and up. Extend up on to the toes before the arms begin pulling. Keep the bar close to the body (b).
2. As the lower body becomes fully extended, rapidly shrug the shoulders and start the pull with the arms. Lower to a quarter squat and prepare to rack the bar on the front of the shoulders. Rotate the wrists under the bar while raising the elbows through in front, so that the upper arms are parallel with the floor (c). With the bar racked on the shoulders, stand up straight (d).
3. Under control, lower the bar to the thighs, keeping it close to the body, and then lower the bar to just above the knees for the next repetition. After the last repetition, slowly lower the bar to the floor.

Breathing Guidelines

Take a deep breath before initiating the pull from the hang position. Exhale during the aggressive, explosive jumping action.

Exercise Modifications and Variations

- The beginning position can be off blocks or a rack.
- The exercise can be performed by catching the bar in a deep squat position or in a taller position.

Coaching Tip

Be explosive.

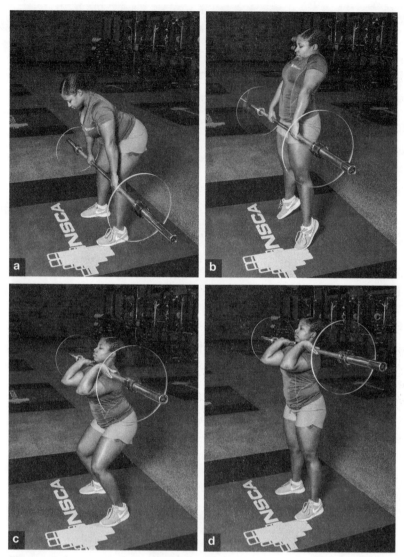

Figure 5.2 Hang clean: *(a)* beginning position; *(b)* shrug shoulders; *(c)* catch; *(d)* end position.

POWER SNATCH

Primary Muscles Trained

Gluteus maximus, biceps femoris, semitendinosus, semimembranosus, vastus lateralis, vastus intermedius, vastus medialis, rectus femoris, soleus, gastrocnemius, deltoids, trapezius

Beginning Position

- Stand with the feet hip- or shoulder-width apart, the bar near the shins, and the toes turned out slightly.

- Grip the bar with a closed pronated grip and the elbows fully extended (a).
- Hands should be about 6 to 8 inches (15-20 cm) wider than for the power clean grip.

Movement Phases

1. Under control, lift the bar from the floor, keeping the shoulders over the bar and the back flat (neutral spine). Keep the bar close to the body and the hips down. While lifting the bar, raise the hips a little to prepare for the second pulling phase (b).

2. Start the second pull by explosively extending the hips, legs, and ankles while keeping the elbows fully extended (c). Thrust the shoulders up and slightly back and the hips slightly forward and up. Extend up on to the toes before the arms begin pulling (d). Keep the bar close to the body.

Figure 5.3 Power snatch: (a) beginning position; (b) lift barbell off the floor; (c) shift weight back; (d) shrug; (e) catch; (f) end position.

3. As the lower body becomes fully extended, rapidly shrug the shoulders and start the pull with the arms. Pull the body under the bar and rotate the hands under the bar while dropping to a quarter squat. Catch the bar overhead with the elbows fully extended *(e)* and then stand up to an upright position *(f)*.

4. Under control, lower the bar to the thighs, keeping it close to the body. Then lower the bar to the floor by flexing the hips and knees, keeping the shoulders over the bar and the back flat.

Breathing Guidelines

Take a deep breath before initiating the first pull off the floor. Exhale during the aggressive, explosive jumping action of the second pull.

Exercise Modifications and Variations

The exercise can be performed by catching the bar in a deep squat position or in a taller position.

Coaching Tips

- The exercise should be one fluid movement from the floor to overhead.
- After the initial pull, be explosive.

ONE-ARM DUMBBELL SNATCH

Primary Muscles Trained

Gluteus maximus, biceps femoris, semitendinosus, semimembranosus, vastus lateralis, vastus intermedius, vastus medialis, rectus femoris, soleus, gastrocnemius, deltoids, trapezius

Beginning Position

- Hold a dumbbell in one hand, assuming the same beginning position and posture as described for the power snatch.
- Instead of beginning on the floor (unlike what is shown in *[a]*), lower the dumbbell between the legs to a position 3 to 4 inches (8-10 cm) below knee level.

Movement Phases

1. Perform an explosive jumping action in the same manner as the second pull of the power snatch *(b)*.
2. At the top of the jump, turn the wrist over to receive the dumbbell at arm's length overhead *(c)*.
3. Stand up to an upright position *(d)*. The dumbbell should be in line with the body's center of gravity, even with or slightly back over the shoulder.

Breathing Guidelines

Take a deep breath before initiating the first pull off the floor. Exhale during the aggressive, explosive jumping action of the second pull.

Figure 5.4   One-arm dumbbell snatch: *(a)* beginning position; *(b)* lift dumbbell and shrug; *(c)* catch; *(d)* end position.

Exercise Modifications and Variations

The exercise can be performed by catching the dumbbell in a deep squat position or in a taller position with knees and hips slightly flexed.

Coaching Tip

A set can be performed all with the same hand holding the dumbbell or by switching the dumbbell between the hands before beginning each repetition.

HANG SNATCH

Primary Muscles Trained

Gluteus maximus, biceps femoris, semitendinosus, semimembranosus, vastus lateralis, vastus intermedius, vastus medialis, rectus femoris, soleus, gastrocnemius, deltoids, trapezius

Beginning Position

- Stand with the feet hip- or shoulder-width apart, the bar near the shins, and the toes turned out slightly.
- Grip the bar with a closed pronated grip and the elbows fully extended.
- Hands should be about 6 to 8 inches (15-20 cm) wider than for the power clean grip.
- Under control, lift the bar from the floor, keeping the shoulders over the bar and the back flat (neutral spine).
- Keep the bar close to the body.
- From the upright position, lower the bar along the thighs to mid-thigh, at the knees, or just above the knees (a).

Movement Phases

1. Start the pull by explosively extending the hips, legs, and ankles while keeping the elbows fully extended. Thrust the shoulders up and slightly back and the hips slightly forward and up. Extend up on to the toes before the arms begin pulling (b). Keep the bar close to the body.
2. As the lower body becomes fully extended, rapidly shrug the shoulders and start the pull with the arms. Pull the body under the bar and rotate the hands under the bar while dropping to a quarter squat. Catch the bar overhead with the elbows fully extended (c) and then stand up to an upright position.
3. Under control, lower the bar to the thighs, keeping it close to the body, and then lower the bar to mid-thigh, at the knees, or just above the knees for the next repetition. After the last repetition, lower the bar to the floor.

Breathing Guidelines

Take a deep breath before initiating the pull from the hang position. Exhale during the aggressive, explosive jumping action.

Exercise Modifications and Variations

The exercise can be performed by catching the bar in a deep squat position or in a taller position.

Coaching Tips

- The exercise should be one fluid movement from mid-thigh, at the knees, or just above the knees to overhead.
- Be explosive.

Figure 5.5   Hang snatch: *(a)* beginning position; *(b)* lift barbell and shrug; *(c)* catch.

HANG PULL

Primary Muscles Trained

Gluteus maximus, biceps femoris, semitendinosus, semimembranosus, vastus lateralis, vastus intermedius, vastus medialis, rectus femoris, soleus, gastrocnemius, deltoids, trapezius

Beginning Position

- Stand with the feet hip- or shoulder-width apart, the bar near the shins, and toes turned out slightly. Grip the bar with a closed pronated grip and the elbows fully extended. The grip should be slightly wider than for the power clean grip.
- Under control, lift the bar from the floor, keeping the shoulders over the bar and the back flat (neutral spine). Keep the bar close to the body.
- From the upright position, lower the bar along the thighs to mid-thigh, at the knees, or just above the knees *(a)*.

Movement Phases

1. Start the pull by explosively extending the hips, legs, and ankles while keeping the elbows fully extended. Thrust the shoulders up and slightly back and the hips slightly forward and up. Extend up on the toes before the arms begin pulling. Keep the bar close to the body.
2. As the lower body becomes fully extended, rapidly shrug the shoulders and pull the bar up to chest height, keeping it close to the body, with the elbows above the bar *(b)*.
3. Under control, lower the bar to the thighs. Then lower the bar to mid-thigh, at the knees, or just above the knees for the next repetition. After the last repetition, lower the bar to the floor.

Figure 5.6 Hang pull: *(a)* beginning position; *(b)* highest bar position.

Breathing Guidelines

Take a deep breath before initiating the pull from the hang position. Exhale during the aggressive, explosive jumping action.

Exercise Modifications and Variations

The beginning position can be off blocks or a rack.

Coaching Tip

Be explosive.

PUSH PRESS

Primary Muscles Trained

Gluteus maximus, biceps femoris, semitendinosus, semimembranosus, vastus lateralis, vastus intermedius, vastus medialis, rectus femoris, deltoids, trapezius, triceps brachii

Beginning Position

- Start with the bar at shoulder height on the outside supports of a power rack (not shown in figure 5.7a).
- Grip the bar with a closed pronated grip (palms facing away from the body).
- The hands should be slightly wider than shoulder-width apart.

Movement Phases

1. Step under the bar with the feet hip-width apart. With the bar across the front of the shoulders, lift the bar out of the rack and step back. Lower to a quarter squat or slightly higher while maintaining a tight flat back (neutral spine); this phase is called the *dip (b)*.

Figure 5.7 Push press: *(a)* beginning position; *(b)* controlled dip; *(c)* upward drive; *(d)* press overhead.

2. Start the press *(c)* by explosively extending the hips, legs, and ankles and then fully extend the arms to press the weight overhead *(d)*; this phase is called the *drive*.

3. Lower the bar under control back to the front of the shoulders. After the last repetition, step forward and place the bar back on the supports.

Breathing Guidelines
Take a deep breath before initiating the dip and exhale during the drive.

Exercise Modifications and Variations

The exercise can be performed by using dumbbells or kettlebells rather than a barbell.

Coaching Tips

- Keep the torso erect during the dip; do not lean forward.
- Drive the bar straight overhead.

SPLIT JERK

Primary Muscles Trained

Gluteus maximus, biceps femoris, semitendinosus, semimembranosus, vastus lateralis, vastus intermedius, vastus medialis, rectus femoris, gastrocnemius, soleus, deltoids, trapezius

Beginning Position

- Start with the bar at shoulder height on the outside supports of a power rack (not shown in figure 5.8a).
- Grip the bar with a closed pronated grip (palms facing away from the body).
- The hands should be slightly wider than shoulder-width apart.

Movement Phases

1. Step under the bar with your feet hip-width apart. With the bar across the front of the shoulders, lift the bar out of the rack and step back. Lower (dip) to a quarter squat or slightly higher while maintaining a tight flat back (neutral spine) (b).
2. Start the jerk (c) by explosively extending the hips, legs, and ankles. As the bar passes in front of the face, quickly extend the arms overhead and split the feet (d). The feet should be shoulder-width apart and evenly split with the back heel raised off the floor (e).
3. From the overhead locked-out split position, return the feet to the beginning position (f).
4. Lower the bar under control back to the front of the shoulders. After the last repetition, step forward and place the bar back on the supports.

Breathing Guidelines

Take a deep breath before initiating the dip and exhale during the jerk.

Exercise Modifications and Variations

The exercise can be performed by using dumbbells or kettlebells rather than a barbell.

Coaching Tips

- Keep the torso erect during the dip; do not lean forward.
- Drive the bar straight overhead.

Figure 5.8 Split jerk: *(a)* beginning position; *(b)* controlled dip; *(c)* upward drive; *(d)* split feet and lunge; *(e)* extend hips and knees; *(f)* bring feet together to a fully standing position.

TRAP BAR POWER UP

This exercise is a safe, triple-extension alternative to the Olympic lifts.

Primary Muscles Trained

Gluteus maximus, biceps femoris, semitendinosus, semimembranosus, vastus lateralis, vastus intermedius, vastus medialis, rectus femoris, gastrocnemius, soleus, deltoids, trapezius

Beginning Position

- Set up a trap bar on blocks at an appropriate height, with the handles at approximately knee height or slightly higher.
- Grip the handles, ensuring that the grip is centered and not too far forward or backward.
- Stand in an athletic stance, with the feet hip-width apart, back flat, and head neutral (a).

Movement Phases

1. Start the movement by explosively extending the hips, legs, and ankles.
2. Shrug the shoulders at the top while keeping the elbows fully extended (b) and then return the bar back to the blocks.

Breathing Guidelines

Take a deep breath before initiating the first pull off the floor. Exhale during the aggressive, explosive jumping action of the second pull.

Exercise Modifications and Variations

Block height can be altered to accommodate athletes of different heights as well as specific ranges of motion.

Coaching Tips

- Make sure that the hands are centered on the handles to avoid angling the bar forward or backward.
- Be explosive.

Figure 5.9   Trap bar power up: (a) beginning position; (b) maximal jump.

TURKISH GET-UP

Primary Muscles Trained

Gluteals (maximus, medius, and minimus), biceps femoris, semitendinosus, semimembranosus, vastus lateralis, vastus intermedius, vastus medialis, rectus femoris, rectus abdominis, transverse abdominis, external and internal oblique, deltoids, rhomboids

Beginning Position

- Lie supine on the floor with a kettlebell near the left shoulder.
- Grasp the kettlebell with the left hand in a closed, pronated grip.
- Flex the left hip and knee to place the left foot flat on the floor.
- Lift the kettlebell to a position over the face with the left elbow fully extended.
- Place the right arm flat on the floor (a).

Movement Phases

1. Simultaneously push the left foot into the floor to rotate the hips and torso so that the body is balanced on the right forearm and right hip (b).
2. Continue the movement to transition from the right forearm to the right hand on the floor (c).
3. Extend the left hip until the left knee is at a 90-degree flexed position (d).
4. Continue to hold the kettlebell overhead with the eyes focused on the kettlebell.
5. Keeping the left leg in the same position, sweep the right leg underneath and behind the body to place the right knee and foot on the floor behind the hips (e).
6. Extend the right hip to lift the right hand off the floor and bring the torso to a fully upright position with the lower body in a lunged position (f).
7. Step forward with the right foot and stand up with the kettlebell held directly over the left shoulder (g).
8. Balance for a moment before reversing the steps back to the beginning position.
9. After the last repetition, begin with the kettlebell held in the right hand with the right foot flat on the floor.

Breathing Guidelines

If the exercise will be performed in stages or steps, exhale during each active movement and inhale during the pause after each stage or step. If the exercise will be performed as a flow, breathe naturally without holding the breath at any point or without timing an exhale or inhale at any specific point in the movement.

Exercise Modifications and Variations

The kettlebell can be held "bottoms up" with the large part of the kettlebell on top. A dumbbell or a small medicine ball may also be used.

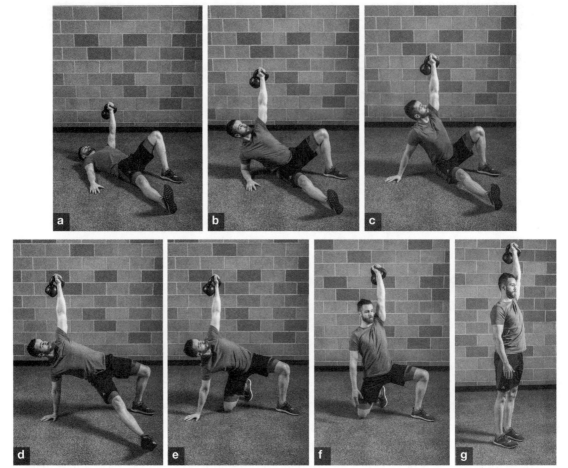

Figure 5.10 Turkish get-up: *(a)* beginning position; *(b)* support on forearm; *(c)* support on hand; *(d)* lift hips and maximally extend them; *(e)* move right leg back and kneel under the hips; *(f)* lift hand off floor and extend torso upright; *(g)* shift weight to left leg and push into the floor to stand up in a balanced stance.

Kneeling Turkish Get-Up

Set up on the floor in a tall kneeling position and a kettlebell overhead in the left arm, with the arm extended overhead. While maintaining a tall posture, step the left leg forward into a lunge position. From this position, stand up on the left leg, continuing to hold the kettlebell overhead, and drive the right leg up. Fully stand up and balance for a moment before reversing the steps back to the original kneeling position. After the last repetition, begin with the kettlebell held in the right hand and step the right leg forward into a lunge position.

Coaching Tips

- When learning the exercise, move through the steps one at a time, pausing if needed. As technique improves, the athlete can flow through the steps more seamlessly.
- Make sure that the front foot is far enough forward that the athlete can sit back while keeping the heel on the floor.

TWO-ARM KETTLEBELL SWING

Primary Muscles Trained

Gluteus maximus, semimembranosus, semitendinosus, biceps femoris, vastus lateralis, vastus intermedius, vastus medialis, and rectus femoris

Beginning Position

- Straddle a kettlebell with the feet placed between hip- and shoulder-width apart and the toes pointed straight ahead.
- Squat down with the arms between the legs and grasp the kettlebell with both hands using a closed, pronated grip *(a)*.
- Position the body with a flat back, head neutral, shoulders down, chest out, and feet flat on the floor in a quarter-squat position.
- Allow the kettlebell to hang off the floor at arm's length between the thighs.

Movement Phases

1. Begin the exercise by flexing the hips to swing the kettlebell down and backward.
2. Keep the knees in a moderately flexed position with the back flat and elbows extended.
3. Keep swinging the kettlebell backward until the torso is nearly parallel to the floor *(b)*.
4. Reverse the movement by extending the hips and knees to swing the kettlebell forward and up *(c)*.
5. Keep the elbows extended throughout the exercise.
6. Allow momentum to raise the kettlebell up to eye level (farther up than what is shown in figure 5.11c).
7. After reaching its highest position, allow the kettlebell to move down and backward and flex the hips and knees to absorb the weight.

Figure 5.11   Two-arm kettlebell swing: *(a)* beginning position (when the kettlebell is still on the floor); *(b)* swing kettlebell backward; *(c)* swing kettlebell forward.

Breathing Guidelines

Inhale during the downward, backward movement and exhale during the upward, forward movement.

Coaching Tip

Focus on a hip extension "pop" to propel the kettlebell forward and up rather than rely on lumbar extension or shoulder flexion.

SIDE LUNGE TO OVERHEAD PRESS

Primary Muscles Trained

Gluteus maximus, semimembranosus, semitendinosus, biceps femoris, vastus lateralis, vastus intermedius, vastus medialis, rectus femoris, iliopsoas, soleus, gastrocnemius, deltoids, trapezius, triceps brachii

Beginning Position

- Stand with the feet about hip-width apart, holding a dumbbell in each hand, with the hands in front of the shoulders (a).

Movement Phases

1. Step to the right, pushing the buttocks back, keeping the left leg extended, and keeping weight on the right heel (b).
2. Drive the right leg back up to the original standing position (c) and press both arms overhead (d).
3. Under control, return the dumbbells back to the beginning position.
4. After the last repetition, repeat on the left side.

Breathing Guidelines

Take a deep breath before the lunge and exhale during the overhead press.

Exercise Modifications and Variations

- Kettlebells can be used rather than dumbbells.
- The athlete may press one arm at a time.
- The athlete may alternate between lunging right and lunging left.

Coaching Tips

- Keep the nonmoving leg extended while lunging.
- During the press, keep the torso erect and push the dumbbells straight overhead.

Figure 5.12   Side lunge to overhead press: *(a)* beginning position; *(b)* lunge to the right; *(c)* drive right leg to return to standing position; *(d)* press dumbbells overhead.

ONE-ARM CLEAN TO PRESS

Primary Muscles Trained

Gluteus maximus, biceps femoris, semitendinosus, semimembranosus, vastus lateralis, vastus intermedius, vastus medialis, rectus femoris, soleus, gastrocnemius, deltoids, trapezius, triceps brachii

Beginning Position

- Stand with the feet hip- or shoulder-width apart, holding a dumbbell in the right hand, hanging it centered to the front of the body.
- From the upright position, lower the dumbbell to mid-thigh, at the knees, or just above the knees (a).

Movement Phases

1. Start the pull by explosively extending the hips, legs, and ankles while keeping the right arm extended. Thrust the shoulders up and back and the hips slightly forward and up. Extend up on to the toes (b) before pulling with the right arm. Keep the dumbbell close to the body.
2. As the lower body becomes fully extended, rapidly shrug the right shoulder and start the pull with the right arm. Lower to a quarter squat and prepare to rack the dumbbell on the front of the right shoulder. Rotate the right wrist under the dumbbell while getting the elbow through in front (c).
3. Press the dumbbell straight overhead (d).
4. Under control, lower the weight back to shoulder height and then down to the beginning position.
5. After the last repetition, repeat on the left side.

Breathing Guidelines

Take a deep breath before the clean and exhale during the dumbbell press.

Exercise Modifications and Variations

A kettlebell or sandbag can be used in place of a dumbbell.

Coaching Tip

Do not arch the back while pressing.

Figure 5.13 One-arm clean to press: *(a)* beginning position; *(b)* lift the dumbbell and shrug; *(c)* catch; *(d)* stand and press the dumbbell overhead.

LANDMINE REVERSE LUNGE TO PRESS

Primary Muscles Trained

Gluteus maximus, semimembranosus, semitendinosus, biceps femoris, vastus lateralis, vastus intermedius, vastus medialis, rectus femoris, iliopsoas, soleus, gastrocnemius, deltoids, trapezius, triceps brachii

Beginning Position

- Stand facing a landmine with the end of the bar at shoulder height, gripping the bar in the right hand *(a)*.

Movement Phases

1. Take a large step backward into a lunge position with the right leg, keeping the right arm just in front of the shoulder (b).
2. Drive back up, keeping most of the weight on the left foot, and press the arm up overhead while stepping forward (c).
3. Under control, lower the right hand back to shoulder height.
4. After the last repetition, repeat on the left side.

Figure 5.14 Landmine reverse lunge to press: (a) beginning position; (b) lunge; (c) drive and press.

Breathing Guidelines

Take a deep breath before the backward step and exhale during the drive and press.

Exercise Modifications and Variations

The landmine can be pressed while lunging back and then lowered either while standing back up or at the top of the repetition.

Coaching Tip

- Make sure that the backward step is far enough that the athlete can sit back while keeping the heel of the front foot on the floor.

LANDMINE SQUAT TO ROTATIONAL PRESS

Primary Muscles Trained

Gluteus maximus, semimembranosus, semitendinosus, biceps femoris, vastus lateralis, vastus intermedius, vastus medialis, rectus femoris, iliopsoas, soleus, gastrocnemius, rectus abdominis, obliques, deltoids, trapezius, triceps brachii

Beginning Position

- Stand perpendicular to a landmine with the base of the landmine to the left.
- With the right hand, hold the end of the bar in front of the right shoulder using a closed supinated grip (palms facing the body) (a).

Figure 5.15 Landmine squat to rotational press: *(a)* beginning position; *(b)* squat; *(c)* drive, rotate, and press.

Movement Phases

1. Sit back into a squat position, pushing the hips back with the chest up *(b)*.
2. Drive back up and, at the top of the squat, press the landmine up and across the body to the left, rotating the torso to face the landmine *(c)*.
3. Under control, return to the beginning position.
4. After the last repetition, repeat on the left side.

Breathing Guidelines

Take a deep breath before the squat and exhale during the landmine press.

Coaching Tip

Form a straight line from the rear foot to the hand that is holding the bar at the top of the press.

CABLE LUNGE WITH ROTATIONAL ROW

Primary Muscles Trained

Gluteus maximus, biceps femoris, semitendinosus, semimembranosus, vastus lateralis, vastus intermedius, vastus medialis, rectus femoris, soleus, gastrocnemius, rectus abdominis, obliques, rhomboids, latissimus dorsi, teres major, posterior deltoid

Beginning Position

- Stand facing a cable unit, making sure that there is enough space in front to step forward.
- Adjust the cable handle to approximately knee height.
- Grip the handle with the left hand, keeping the arm extended *(a)*.

Movement Phases

1. With the left arm extended, take a large step forward into a lunge position with the right leg *(b)*.
2. Drive back up, pushing off the right foot, while pulling the left arm into the side of the chest and rotating the upper body and shoulders to the left *(c)*.
3. Under control, return to the beginning position with the arm extended in front and shoulders square to the cable unit.
4. After the last repetition, repeat on the right side.

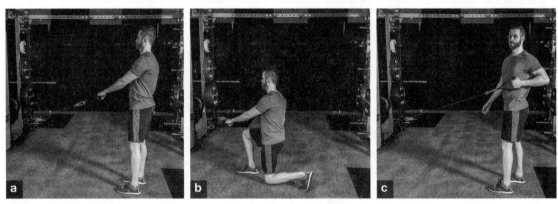

Figure 5.16 Cable lunge with rotational row: *(a)* beginning position; *(b)* lunge; *(c)* drive, pull, and rotate.

Breathing Guidelines

Take a deep breath before the lunge and exhale during the foot push-off and row.

Exercise Modifications and Variations

The height of the cable units can be adjusted to change the angle of the row.

Coaching Tip

Make sure that the forward step is far enough that the athlete can sit back while keeping the heel of the front foot on the floor.

CABLE SQUAT TO ROW

Primary Muscles Trained

Gluteus maximus, biceps femoris, semitendinosus, semimembranosus, vastus lateralis, vastus intermedius, vastus medialis, rectus femoris, soleus, gastrocnemius, rectus abdominis, rhomboids, latissimus dorsi, teres major, posterior deltoid

Beginning Position

- Stand facing a dual cable unit, with the cable handles at approximately chest height.
- Stand with the feet shoulder-width apart, the toes pointed out slightly, and the arms extended straight out in front, holding the handles *(a)*.

Movement Phases

1. With the arms extended and palms facing each other, sit back into a squat position, keeping the heels on the floor and the chest and head up *(b)*.
2. Stand up, pulling both arms in to the sides of the chest *(c)*.

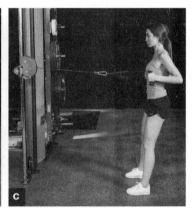

Figure 5.17   Cable squat to row: *(a)* beginning position; *(b)* squat; *(c)* stand and pull.

Breathing Guidelines

Take a deep breath before the squat and exhale during the row.

Exercise Modifications and Variations

- The height of the cable units can be adjusted to change the angle of the row.
- Rows can be performed one arm at a time or together.

Coaching Tips

- Squeeze the shoulder blades down and back while pulling.
- Sit deep.

ISOMETRIC MID-THIGH PULL

The exercise is performed in a rack, with the safety catches at midthigh height and the barbell under the catches (i.e., safety crossbars) so that the athlete can pull with maximal force. The exercise may also be performed on a device built specifically for isometric mid-thigh pulls, which includes a bar that can be pulled without moving.

Primary Muscles Trained

Gluteus maximus, biceps femoris, semitendinosus, semimembranosus, vastus lateralis, vastus intermedius, vastus medialis, rectus femoris, erector spinae, deltoids, trapezius

Beginning Position

- Stand with the feet hip-width apart and the bar near the midthigh.
- Grip the bar with a closed pronated grip and the elbows fully extended.
- Hands should be shoulder-width apart.

Movement Phases

1. With the chest up and the elbows fully extended, attempt to extend the legs and hips while pulling as hard as possible into the bar.
2. Exert maximal effort for about 5 seconds, relax, and return to the beginning position.

Breathing Guidelines

Take a deep breath before initiating the pull and exhale during the attempt to extend the legs and hips.

Exercise Modifications and Variations

- Can be performed with a trap bar rather than a barbell.
- Can be performed as a single-leg exercise.
- Can be performed on a force plate to quantify and assess maximal strength.

Coaching Tips

- Pull as hard as possible.
- Push the feet into the floor.

6

LOWER BODY EXERCISE TECHNIQUE

MUBARAK MALIK

Lower body strength and power is essential in a game that requires repeated bouts of intense activity. Primary movements that are common in basketball include sprinting, jumping, shuffling, cutting, and crossover stepping. Basketball athletes need strength derived from resistance training exercises to maintain proper lower body mechanics and generate high levels of power output to reduce the risk of injury and maximize and maintain performance. Power may even be the main essential quality for running and jumping high (2). A well-balanced resistance training program must accommodate a highly lateral and reactive sport with multiplanar bilateral and unilateral lower body exercises (3).

FUNDAMENTALS OF TECHNIQUE

With any sporting activity, some degree of risk is always involved when engaging in resistance training. Basketball is a game played in all planes of motion—sagittal, frontal, and transverse—so all lower body exercises selected must involve similar movements around the same joints. Many commonalities are found among resistance training exercises for the lower body. Most of the lower body exercises in this chapter require some sort of handgrip on a barbell or weighted implement as well as optimal limb position, movement range and speed, and methods of breathing (1). In addition, all exercises must be performed and, when appropriate, spotted correctly.

Hand Grips and Width

The main types of hand grips are the following:

- **Pronated grip**, with palms down and knuckles up, also called the **overhand grip**.
- **Supinated grip**, with palms up and knuckles down, also known as the **underhand grip**.
- **Neutral grip**, with the knuckles pointing laterally as in a handshake.
- **Alternating grip**, in which one hand is in a pronated grip and the other is in a supinated grip.
- **Hook grip**, similar to the pronated grip, except that the thumb is positioned under the index and middle fingers.

Establishing the proper grip in an exercise involves placing the hands at the correct distance from each other, from the center of the bar. The grip widths that are most common are shoulder width and hip width. A wide grip is farther apart than shoulder width or hip width, and a narrow grip is closer together.

Body Positioning

Whether an exercise requires lifting a barbell or dumbbell from the floor, establishing a stable position is critical for safety and optimal performance. A stable position is described as *feet flat on the floor, neutral spine, chest up,* and *shoulders back.* This position enables the athlete to maintain proper body alignment during an exercise, which in turn places an appropriate stress on muscle and joints. Body positioning is critical because basketball athletes need large amounts of proximal stability to maintain neutral alignment of the spine and distal stability to maintain proper contact with the floor (3).

Movement Range and Speed

All exercises should be performed in the full range of motion of the exercise, and the speed of the movement is determined by the type of exercise being performed. Exercises performed in a slow, controlled manner increase the likelihood that the full range of motion can be reached. For the power exercises covered in chapter 5, however, effort should be made to accelerate the bar to a maximal speed while maintaining control and form throughout. The non-power lower body resistance exercises included in this chapter help improve a basketball athlete's muscle function and enable effective control of joint movements through a full range of motion.

BREATHING GUIDELINES

Strength and conditioning professionals should typically instruct athletes to exhale through the **sticking point,** which is the most strenuous portion of a repetition (typically soon after the transition from the eccentric phase to the concentric phase) and to inhale during the less stressful phase of the repetition (1). The most important technique for breathing during exercise is to use the muscle that extends across the bottom of the chest cavity, also known as the **diaphragm**. Breathing from the diaphragm instead of the chest allows the athlete to get deep, full breaths that fill the lungs with air and oxygen that the body needs for exercise. For exercises using heavier loads, the **Valsalva maneuver** can be used for maintaining vertebral alignment and support. The Valsalva maneuver involves expiring against a closed glottis,

Sam Wasson/Getty Images

Performing exercises through a full range of motion has direct carryover to the basketball athlete.

which when combined with the contracting abdominal and rib cage muscles, creates rigid compartments of fluid in the lower torso and air in the upper torso (1). When using this method of breathing, however, be aware that there may be side effects of dizziness, disorientation, excessively high blood pressure, and blackouts. This type of breathing should be used only with experienced resistance trained athletes. The benefits of proper breathing techniques include exercising more safely, preventing injuries such as hernias, minimizing spikes in blood pressure and strain on blood vessels, reducing incidence of back pain, increasing blood flow throughout the body, increasing the athlete's ability to relax, and helping the athlete stay focused on the exercise with minimal distraction. (In the descriptions of the exercises, the Valsalva maneuver is not included.)

SPOTTING GUIDELINES

A **spotter** is someone who assists in the execution of an exercise. The sole responsibility of the spotter is to help ensure the safety of the athlete being spotted. For exercises that involve a bar being placed on the back or front of the shoulders, spotting should be performed inside the rack with the safety bars placed at the appropriate position. Because loads can be high in some exercises, to provide sufficient leverage to the athlete, the spotter should be at least as strong as the athlete lifting. The number of spotters needed is largely determined by the load being lifted, the experience and ability of the athlete and spotters, and the physical strength of the spotters (1). When using a spotter, communication between the spotter and athlete is critical. The spotter should know when the bar will be initially handled, how many repetitions will be performed, and when the athlete is ready to move the bar into position. Knowing how much and when to help an athlete is an important aspect of spotting, so the spotter needs to be experienced in proper spotting techniques (1). Spotting needs may vary from athlete to athlete.

Exercise Finder

(continued)

DEADLIFT

Primary Muscles Trained

Gluteus maximus, semimembranosus, semitendinosus, biceps femoris, vastus lateralis, vastus intermedius, vastus medialis, rectus femoris, erector spinae

Beginning Position

- Stand with feet hip-width apart.
- Set the bar over the middle of the feet with the toes slightly pointing out.
- Grip the bar with a closed, pronated, or alternating grip about shoulder-width apart.
- Arms should be vertical to the floor with the elbows fully extended.
- Lower the hips by flexing the hips and knees to get into the beginning position with the shins near the bar *(a)*.
- Keep the bar over midfoot and raise the chest.
- Maintain a neutral spine.

Movement Phases

1. With the chest held out, shoulders held back, and elbows fully extended, extend the hips and knees to stand up with the weight *(b)*.
2. Keep the bar in contact with the front of the thighs as it is lifted.
3. Fully extend the hips and knees *(c)*.
4. Lower the bar under control to the floor.
5. The bar should be lowered in a straight line over the midfoot.

Breathing Guidelines

Inhale during the downward movement and exhale after the sticking point of the upward movement.

Figure 6.1 *(a)* beginning position; *(b)* lift the barbell off the floor; *(c)* extend to standing position.

Coaching Tips

- The barbell should be on the floor, over the midfoot, at the start of each repetition.
- Feet should be hip-width apart, narrower than for the squat.
- Keep the chest up to avoid rounding the back.
- The head should be in neutral position.
- Do not shrug or lean back at the top of the movement.

FRONT SQUAT

Primary Muscles Trained

Gluteus maximus, semimembranosus, semitendinosus, biceps femoris, vastus lateralis, vastus intermedius, vastus medialis, rectus femoris

Beginning Position: Athlete

- Set the bar on a rack at shoulder height (not seen in figure 6.2).
- Grasp the bar and position it on the front of the shoulders and close to the neck, using one of these arm positions:

  1. Crossed-arm position (figure 6.2)

  - Cross the arms in front, step up to and under the bar to get in position, and place the hands on the top of the barbell at the opposite shoulders.
  - Drive the elbows up so that the upper arms are parallel to the floor.

Figure 6.2 Front squat (crossed-arm position): *(a)* beginning position; *(b)* squat.

2. Parallel-arm position (figure 6.3)

- With the barbell in position, grasp the bar with a closed, pronated grip just outside the shoulders.

- Step up to and under the bar to get in position with the arms parallel to each other.

- Drive the elbows up so that the upper arms are parallel to the floor.

- Lift the bar off the rack by extending the hips and knees.

- Take a few small steps back from the rack and position the feet in a shoulder-width stance with the toes slightly pointed out. This is the beginning position for all repetitions (figure 6.2a).

Figure 6.3 Front squat (parallel-arm position).

Beginning Position: Two Spotters

- Stand at the ends of the bar and hold it with an underhand grip.

- When the athlete is ready, help lift the bar off the rack, let go of the bar, and hold the hands under the end as the athlete walks back into the position to do the exercise.

- Before the athlete begins the set, stand erect with a shoulder-width stance and the knees slightly flexed in the ready position to spot (figure 6.2a).

Movement Phases: Athlete

1. Flex the hips and knees in unison so that the torso-to-floor angle remains approximately constant throughout the movement.
2. Maintain a neutral spine with the elbows and chest up.
3. Continue the downward movement until the top of the thighs is approximately parallel to the floor (figure 6.2b).
4. Reverse the movement by pressing through the feet and extending the hips and knees at the same rate to maintain a consistent torso-to-floor angle.
5. Continue the upward movement to return to the beginning position.

Movement Phases: Two Spotters

1. Keep the hands under the bar and follow it down by mimicking the athlete's squatting movements (figure 6.2b).
2. When the athlete's set is completed, follow the athlete back to the rack, grasp the ends of the bar, and help to return the bar to the rack.

Breathing Guidelines

Inhale during the downward movement and exhale after the sticking point of the upward movement.

Exercise Modifications and Variations

One or two kettlebells can be used instead of a barbell (and then a spotter would not be needed). The version in which the athlete holds the kettlebell or kettlebells at the front of the chest is often called a *goblet squat*.

Coaching Tips

- Before lowering into the squat, pick a point on the wall and focus on it.
- Keep looking at this point during the descent and then drive back up.
- Keep the chest up throughout the movement.
- Keep the weight over the heels and midfoot throughout the exercise.

BACK SQUAT

Primary Muscles Trained

Gluteus maximus, semimembranosus, semitendinosus, biceps femoris, vastus lateralis, vastus intermedius, vastus medialis, rectus femoris

Beginning Position: Athlete

- Set the bar on a rack at shoulder height (not seen in figure 6.4).
- Grasp the bar and position it on the upper back and shoulders in one of these positions:
  - High bar position: The bar rests at the base of the neck on the back of the shoulders, sitting on the shirt collar (a).

- Low bar position: The bar sits 2 to 3 inches (5-8 cm) below the high bar position (across the posterior deltoids at the middle of the trapezius).

- In either bar position, lift the elbows to "set" the bar in place on the upper back and shoulders.

- Take a few small steps back from the rack and position the feet in a shoulder-width stance with the toes slightly pointed out (a). This is the beginning position for all repetitions.

Beginning Position: Two Spotters

- Stand at the ends of the bar and hold it with an underhand grip.

- When the athlete is ready, help lift the bar off the rack, let go of the bar, and hold the hands under the end as the athlete walks back into the position to do the exercise.

- Before the athlete begins the set, stand erect with a shoulder-width stance and the knees slightly flexed in the ready position to spot (a).

Movement Phases: Athlete

1. Flex the hips and knees in unison so that the torso-to-floor angle remains approximately constant throughout the movement.

2. Maintain a neutral spine with the elbows and chest up.

3. Continue the downward movement until the top of the thighs is approximately parallel to the floor (b).

4. Reverse movement by pressing through the feet and extending the hips and knees at the same rate to maintain a consistent torso-to-floor angle.

5. Continue the upward movement to return to the beginning position (c).

Movement Phases: Two Spotters

1. Keep the hands under the bar and follow it down by mimicking the athlete's squatting movements (b and c).

2. When the athlete's set is completed, follow the athlete back to the rack, grasp the ends of the bar, and help to return the bar to the rack (d).

Breathing Guidelines

Inhale during the downward movement and exhale after the sticking point of the upward movement.

Figure 6.4 Back squat: *(a)* beginning position; *(b)* squat; *(c)* return to standing; *(d)* racking the bar.

Exercise Modifications and Variations

Box Squat

A box or a cubed pad can be placed behind the athlete as a guide for the range of motion (i.e., squatting depth). The athlete should be coached to touch the glutes lightly to the top surface of the box or pad (figure 6.5). The torso remains braced at the moment of contact; the athlete does not actually sit on top of the box or pad.

Hatfield Squat

A barbell with padded parallel arms that drape over the shoulders with handles held in a neutral grip is an alternative to a standard barbell (figure 6.6). Taller athletes with longer arms often find they can keep the bar more firmly anchored on the upper back than they can with a barbell.

Figure 6.5 Box squat cubed pad.

Figure 6.6 Hatfield squat bar.

Courtesy of the NSCA.

Coaching Tips

- Before lowering into the squat, pick a point on the wall and focus on it.
- Keep looking at this point during the descent and then drive back up.
- Keep the chest up throughout the movement.
- Keep the weight over the heels and midfoot throughout the exercise.

BARBELL HIP THRUST

Primary Muscles Trained

Gluteus maximus, semimembranosus, semitendinosus, biceps femoris

Beginning Position

- Begin sitting on the floor with the legs extended and the torso leaning against the long side of a bench directly behind the back. (Be sure the bench will not move during the exercise.)
- Roll the bar over and directly above the hips and then flex the hips and knees so that the feet are flat on the floor *(a)*.
- Adjust the torso so that the shoulder blades are resting on the top edge of the bench.
- Hold the bar with a closed, overhand grip outside the hips.

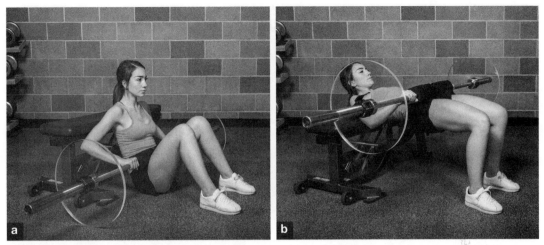

Figure 6.7 Barbell hip thrust: *(a)* beginning position; *(b)* full thrust.

Movement Phases

1. Brace the core, drive through the heels, and extend the hips by contracting the glutes to lift the bar off the floor.
2. Continue to extend the hips and knees until the lower legs are approximately perpendicular to the floor *(b)*.
3. Return the barbell to the beginning position.

Breathing Guidelines

Exhale after the sticking point of the upward movement and inhale during the downward movement.

Exercise Modifications and Variations

Single-Leg Hip Thrust

To perform a single-legged variation of the exercise, keep one leg up (i.e., keep the knee of the free leg fully extended) during the exercise.

Coaching Tips

- Push through the heels.
- Be sure to reach full hip extension.
- Maintain forward eye gaze.

ROMANIAN DEADLIFT

Primary Muscles Trained

Gluteus maximus, semimembranosus, semitendinosus, biceps femoris, erector spinae

Beginning Position

- Hold the barbell at hip level with a pronated grip.
- Keep the chest up and shoulders back.
- Slightly flex the knees (more than what is shown in figure 6.8a).

Movement Phases

1. Lower the bar by flexing the hips and pushing the hips back.
2. Keep the bar in touch with the thighs as the torso moves forward while maintaining a rigid torso and neutral back position.
3. Lower the bar until the torso is parallel with the floor and the barbell is aligned with the patella, or until reaching maximum range of motion according to the body's flexibility (b).
4. Return to the beginning position by extending the hips and standing tall.

Breathing Guidelines

Inhale during the downward movement and exhale after the sticking point of the upward movement.

Exercise Modifications and Variations

One or two dumbbells or kettlebells can be used instead of a barbell.

Figure 6.8 Romanian deadlift: (a) beginning position (but with a greater degree of knee flexion); (b) end position.

Coaching Tips

- Begin with a loaded stretch on the hamstrings by performing the exercise from top down to lower the bar to the floor.
- Avoid excessive extension in the lumbar spine during all phases of the exercise.
- Keep the bar close to the body at all times and keep the shoulders over the bar.

HAMSTRING SLIDE

Primary Muscles Trained

Gluteus maximus, semimembranosus, semitendinosus, biceps femoris

Beginning Position

- Lie on the floor in a supine position with the lower legs perpendicular to the floor.
- Heels should be on the center of the slide board.
- Arms should be out to the sides to stabilize the body during the movement *(a)*.

Movement Phases

1. Slide the feet forward until the legs are fully extended *(b)*.
2. Keep the hips up as the body is lowered.
3. Squeeze the glutes and pull the heels back to return to the beginning position *(c)*.

Breathing Guidelines

Inhale during the forward movement and exhale after the sticking point of the backward movement.

Exercise Modifications and Variations

To perform a single-legged variation of the exercise, keep one leg up (i.e., keep the knee of the free leg fully extended) during the exercise.

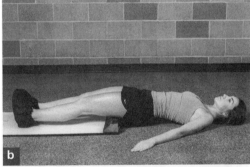

Coaching Tips

- Start with the hips up in a bridge position by focusing on squeezing the glutes at the top.
- Keep the toes up as the knees extend and flex.
- Focus on driving the heels into the floor when returning to the beginning position.

Figure 6.9 Hamstring slide: *(a)* beginning position; *(b)* forward slide; *(c)* backward slide.

BARBELL JUMP SQUAT

Primary Muscles Trained

Gluteus maximus, semimembranosus, semitendinosus, biceps femoris, vastus lateralis, vastus intermedius, vastus medialis, rectus femoris

Beginning Position

- Follow the instructions for the high bar back squat exercise to get into the correct beginning position for this exercise (*a*).

Movement Phases

1. Using a countermovement, partially squat (to approximately a quarter-squat position) (*b*) and then immediately reverse direction to explode off the floor.
2. Fully extend the hips, knees, and ankles (*c*).
3. Maintain good posture throughout the jump.
4. When landing back on the floor, absorb the impact through the legs by slightly flexing the hips and knees.

Breathing Guidelines

- Inhale right before the descent into a partial squat.
- Exhale during the transition up out of the squat into the air.

Coaching Tips

- Using an appropriate load for this exercise is important. If the load is too heavy, the athlete's speed will be too slow and the rate of force development will be reduced (see figure 4.1).

Figure 6.10 Barbell jump squat: (*a*) beginning position; (*b*) countermovement squat; (*c*) maximal jump.

- Be sure that space is adequate to do this exercise safely (e.g., on an Olympic platform).
- For safety reasons, this exercise should not be spotted because athletes can drop the weight (in a controlled manner) if they need to.
- Do not let the knees cave inward on the ascent or during landing.

GLUTE-HAM RAISE

Primary Muscles Trained
Gluteus maximus, semimembranosus, semitendinosus, biceps femoris, erector spinae

Beginning Position
- Start on a glute-ham bench with the roller pad positioned at the mid to lower thigh and the torso parallel to the floor with the ear, hip, knee, and ankle forming a straight line *(a)*.
- Feet should be firmly on the platform (although some athletes may not reach it as shown in figure 6.11).

Movement Phases
1. Push the feet into the foot plate (when possible) and raise the torso *(b)* by contracting the hamstrings while maintaining hip extension. The result is that the knees will flex to lift the body into a vertical position *(c)*.
2. Keeping the hamstrings engaged, allow the knees to extend and the torso to lower back to the beginning position.
3. Be sure that the ear, hip, knee, and ankle remain in a straight line.

Breathing Guidelines
Exhale after the sticking point of the upward movement and inhale during the downward movement.

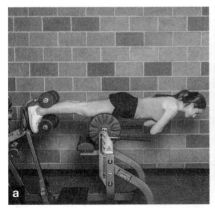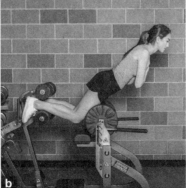

Figure 6.11 Glute-ham raise: *(a)* beginning position; *(b)* midway through the upward phase; *(c)* end position.

Coaching Tips

- Do not hyperextend the lower back.
- Control the speed of the upward and downward movements.

NORDIC HAMSTRING CURL

Primary Muscles Trained
Semimembranosus, semitendinosus, biceps femoris

Beginning Position

- Set up in a Nordic hamstring machine with the hips extended and torso upright.
- If a Nordic hamstring machine is not available, consider the partner-assisted version (as shown in figure 6.12). If a partner is not available to hold the ankles in place, consider a setup with a power rack in which the ankles are positioned underneath the squat pad or weighted barbell.
- The beginning position is with the torso upright with the hips extended, gluteals contracted, and knees flexed to approximately 90 degrees (a).

Movement Phases

1. Keeping the torso rigid and hips extended, allow the knees to extend to lower the torso (b) as slowly as possible until the descent is no longer under control.
2. Allow the body to fall to the floor in a controlled fashion and "catch" it with the hands in a push-up position (c).
3. Give just enough of a push off the floor with the hands to get the torso back to where the hamstrings can pull the body back to the beginning position.

Breathing Guidelines
Inhale during the downward movement and exhale after the sticking point of the upward movement.

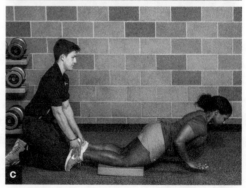

Figure 6.12 Nordic hamstring curl: (a) beginning position; (b) midway through the downward phase; (c) (nearly the) catch.

Coaching Tips

- Keep the torso rigid throughout the movement.
- Keep the hips extended throughout the duration of the set; do not allow them to flex and take tension off the hamstrings.
- When extending the glutes, no pressure or contraction should be felt in the lower back.

FORWARD STEP LUNGE

Primary Muscles Trained

Gluteus maximus, semimembranosus, semitendinosus, biceps femoris, vastus lateralis, vastus intermedius, vastus medialis, rectus femoris, iliopsoas

Beginning Position

- Position a barbell across the shoulders using the high bar position of the back squat.
- Position the feet approximately shoulder-width apart (a).

Movement Phases

1. Take one large step forward with either leg (b).
2. Flex the knee of the lead leg until the front thigh approaches parallel to the floor.
3. As front thigh approaches parallel, keep pressure on the front foot and use the rear foot to help maintain balance.
4. Keep the torso erect; do not lean forward.
5. As the front knee flexes, the heel of the rear foot lifts off the floor and the rear knee flexes.
6. Lunge to a position where the front knee is over the front foot and the rear knee is 1 to 2 inches (3-5 cm) off the floor (c).
7. Push the front foot off the floor to bring it back to be next to the rear foot (d).
8. Keep the torso erect; do not lean backward.
9. Pause and repeat with the other leg.

Breathing Guidelines

Inhale during the downward and forward movement and exhale after the sticking point of the upward and backward movement.

Spotting Guidelines

- When the athlete is ready, position the hands near the athlete's hips, waist, or torso.
- Stand 12 to 18 inches (30-46 cm) behind the athlete with the knees slightly flexed (a).
- Step forward with the same foot as the athlete; shadow the movement and be prepared to assist if the athlete staggers (b-d).

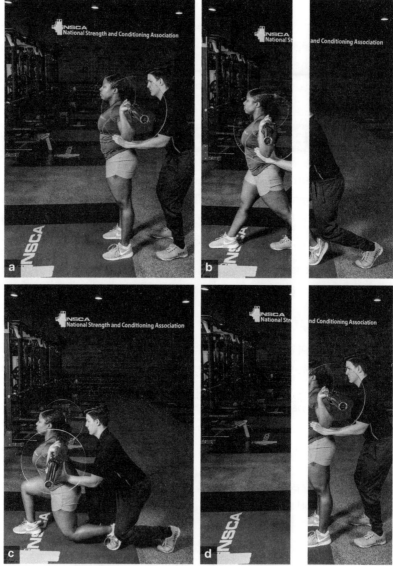

Figure 6.13 Forward step lunge: *(a)* beginning p⸱ tion; *(b)* forward step; *(c)* bottom lunged position; *(d)* retur⸱ ⸱ beginning position.

Coaching Tips

- Adjust the width of the stance to find the right distance⸱ ⸱tay in balance.
- The back knee should be in line with the body and point⸱ at the floor at the bottom of the lunge.
- If there is not sufficient room around the athlete to perfor⸱ ⸱he exercise with a barbell, two dumbbells can be used. Instruct the athlete to hol⸱ ⸱e dumbbells in a neutral grip with the arms at the sides and hanging perpendic⸱ ⸱r to floor throughout the exercise (i.e., the arms should not swing forward and bac⸱ ⸱ard with each repetition).

WALKING LUNGE

Primary Muscles Trained

Gluteus maximus, semimembranosus, semitendinosus, biceps femoris, vastus lateralis, vastus intermedius, vastus medialis, rectus femoris, iliopsoas

Beginning Position

- Stand with a dumbbell in each hand.
- Hang the arms at the sides, holding the dumbbells in a neutral grip.
- Position the feet slightly narrower than shoulder-width apart (a).

Movement Phases

1. Take one large step forward with either leg.
2. Flex the knee of the lead leg until the front thigh approaches parallel to the floor.
3. As front thigh approaches parallel, keep pressure on the front foot and use the rear foot to help maintain balance.
4. As the front knee flexes, the heel of the rear foot lifts off the floor and the rear knee flexes.
5. Lunge to a position where the front knee is over the front foot and the rear knee is 1 to 2 inches (3-5 cm) off the floor (b).
6. Instead of pushing back with the lead leg to get back to the beginning position (as in the forward step lunge exercise), push through the front foot to step the rear foot forward (c).
7. Alternate steps to lunge-walk forward.

Breathing Guidelines

Inhale during the downward movement and exhale after the sticking point of the upward movement.

Figure 6.14   Walking lunge: (a) beginning position; (b) bottom lunged position; (c) stepped-forward end position.

Coaching Tips

- Keep the torso erect; do not lean forward or backward.
- Adjust the width of the stance to find the right distance to stay in balance.
- The back knee should be in line with the body and pointed at the floor at the bottom of the lunge.
- Do not make the mistake of taking a step that is too long or too short.

REVERSE LUNGE

Primary Muscles Trained

Gluteus maximus, semimembranosus, semitendinosus, biceps femoris, vastus lateralis, vastus intermedius, vastus medialis, rectus femoris, iliopsoas

Beginning Position

- Stand with a dumbbell in each hand.
- Hang the arms at the sides, holding the dumbbells in a neutral grip.
- Position the feet slightly narrower than shoulder-width apart (a).

Movement Phases

1. Take one large step backward with either leg and land on the ball of the rear foot with the heel off the floor.
2. Lower into a lunge in which the front knee is over the front foot and the rear knee is 1 to 2 inches (3-5 cm) off the floor (b).
3. Push with the rear foot and extend the hip and knee of the front leg to bring the rear foot back to be next to the front foot.
4. Pause and repeat with the other leg.

Figure 6.15 Reverse lunge: (a) beginning position; (b) stepped-backward end position.

Breathing Guidelines

Inhale during the downward and backward movement and exhale after the sticking point of the upward and forward movement.

Coaching Tips

- Keep most of the weight on the front leg.
- Keep the knee of the front leg over the front foot when stepping back with the rear foot.

SIDE LUNGE

Primary Muscles Trained

Gluteus maximus, rectus femoris, vastus lateralis, vastus medialis, hip abductors (gluteus medius, gluteus minimus, tensor fascia latae), hip adductors (gracilis, obturator externus, adductor brevis, adductor longus, and adductor magnus)

Beginning Position

- Stand with a dumbbell in each hand. Alternatively, a single dumbbell or a kettlebell can be used instead; hold it between the legs with both hands.
- Hang the arms at the sides, holding the dumbbells in a neutral grip.
- Position the feet approximately shoulder-width apart (a).

Movement Phases

1. Take one large step to one side with either leg.
2. After the lead foot is fully planted, push the hips back and flex the knee of the lead leg (with the knee of the trailing leg remaining extended). The lead knee should point in the same direction as the lead foot.
3. Side-lunge to a position where the lead knee is over the lead foot and the lead thigh is approximately parallel to the floor (b).
4. Push the lead foot off the floor to bring it back to the beginning position.
5. Pause and repeat by stepping to the other side with the other leg.

Breathing Guidelines

Inhale during the downward movement and exhale after the sticking point of the upward movement.

Coaching Tips

- The lead knee should not travel forward beyond the line of the toes.
- Do not let the back collapse while lowering into the lunge.
- Keep the chest and head up throughout the exercise.

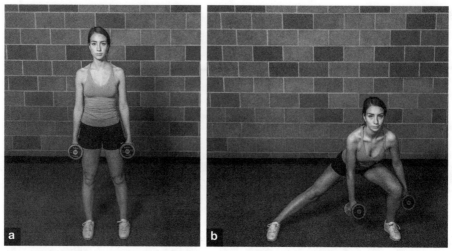

Figure 6.16 Side lunge: *(a)* beginning position; *(b)* side-lunged end position.

PISTOL SQUAT

Primary Muscles Trained

Gluteus maximus, semimembranosus, semitendinosus, biceps femoris, vastus lateralis, vastus intermedius, vastus medialis, rectus femoris

Beginning Position

- Stand with one foot on the edge of a 12- to 24-inch (30-61 cm) plyometric box and the other leg held suspended off the box *(a)*.

Movement Phases

1. Squat down by pushing the hips back and flexing the supporting knee.
2. Extend the arms forward to maintain balance.
3. Lower the hips until the top of the supporting thigh is parallel to the floor *(b)*.
4. Extend the supporting knee and hip to return to the beginning position.
5. At the end of the set, repeat with the other leg.

Breathing Guidelines

Inhale during the lowering phase and exhale during the upward phase of the movement.

Exercise Modifications and Variations

- The exercise can be also performed on the floor.
- The athlete can hold on to one or two dumbbells or kettlebells for a counterweight or as a means to increase intensity. This version is sometimes called a *single-leg squat* (*with a reach*).

Figure 6.17 Pistol squat: *(a)* beginning position; *(b)* lowest squat position.

Coaching Tips

- Make sure that the supporting knee does not move beyond the toes of the supporting foot when squatting down.
- Minimize the movement at the supporting ankle.
- Do not let the knee of the supporting leg move inward; make sure it tracks over the second and third toe of the supporting foot.

SINGLE-LEG ROMANIAN DEADLIFT

Primary Muscles Trained

Gluteus maximus, semimembranosus, semitendinosus, biceps femoris, erector spinae

Beginning Position

- Using the hand opposite the supporting leg, hold a kettlebell with an overhand grip in front of the hip on that side of the body.
- Hold the chest up and shoulders back.
- Slightly flex the knee of the supporting leg (more than what is shown in figure 6.18*a*).

Movement Phases

1. Lower the kettlebell by flexing the hip of the supporting leg; the movement is called a *hinge* (of the hip of the supporting leg), rather than simply flexing the torso forward.

2. Keep the knee and hip of the other leg extended; as the torso flexes forward, that leg becomes the rear leg.

3. Maintain a rigid torso and neutral back position as the torso flexes forward and the hip of the supporting leg hinges.

4. Allow the knee of the supporting leg to flex slightly.

5. Continue flexing the hip of the supporting leg until the kettlebell is about midshin height *(b)* and then reverse the movement to return to the beginning position.

6. At the end of the set, repeat with the other leg.

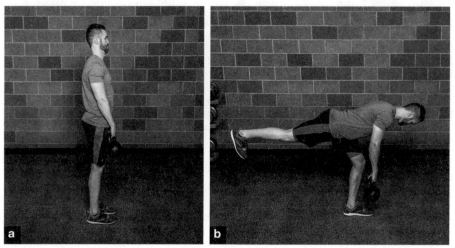

Figure 6.18 Single-leg Romanian deadlift: *(a)* beginning position; *(b)* end hinged position.

Breathing Guidelines

Inhale during the lowering phase and exhale during the upward phase of the movement.

Exercise Modifications and Variations

If a dumbbell or kettlebell is used, it can be held in the hand on the same side **(ipsilateral)** as the supporting leg or in the hand opposite **(contralateral)** the supporting leg.

Coaching Tips

- Cue the athlete to feel as if he or she is being pulled backward by a rope placed around the waist.
- Keep the spine neutrally aligned throughout the entire exercise.

SINGLE-LEG SQUAT (BULGARIAN)

This exercise has many names such as *Bulgarian squat*, *Bulgarian split squat*, *rear-foot elevated split squat*, and *rear-foot elevated single leg squat*. Further, *single-leg squat* can imply a *loaded pistol squat*.

Primary Muscles Trained

Gluteus maximus, semimembranosus, semitendinosus, biceps femoris, vastus lateralis, vastus intermedius, vastus medialis, rectus femoris, iliopsoas

Beginning Position

- Position a barbell across the shoulders using the high bar position of the back squat.
- Stand in front of a bench or box that is approximately knee height.
- Take a moderate step forward with one leg and place the instep of the rear foot on top of the bench or box.
- Allow both knees to be slightly flexed in this balanced beginning position *(a)*. The torso should be fully erect.

Movement Phases

1. Allow the hip and knee of the front leg and the knee of the rear leg to flex at the same rate so that the body lowers down rather than forward.
2. Keep the instep of the rear foot flat on top of the bench or box.
3. Continue the descent until the top of the front thigh is parallel to the floor *(b)*.
4. Extend the hip and knee of the front leg to return to the beginning position.
5. At the end of the set, repeat with the other leg.

Figure 6.19   Single-leg squat (Bulgarian): *(a)* beginning position; *(b)* squat down (not lunge forward).

Breathing Guidelines

Inhale during the lowering phase and exhale during the upward phase of the movement.

Exercise Modifications and Variations

- Two dumbbells or two kettlebells can be used instead of a barbell.
- One dumbbell or kettlebell can be used; if only one is used, it can be held in the hand of the same side (ipsilateral) as the supporting leg or in the hand opposite (contralateral) the supporting leg.

Coaching Tips

- Keep the front knee in line with the front foot; do not let the front knee extend beyond the toes.
- Both feet and knees should be pointing in the same direction.

STEP-UP

Primary Muscles Trained

Gluteus maximus, semimembranosus, semitendinosus, biceps femoris, vastus lateralis, vastus intermedius, vastus medialis, rectus femoris

Beginning Position

- Position a barbell across the shoulders using the high bar position of the back squat.
- Stand in front of a bench or box that is approximately knee height.
- The torso should be fully erect (a).

Movement Phases

1. Flex one hip and knee to place the lead foot up on top of the bench (b).
2. Press through the lead foot and extend the hip and knee of the lead leg to step up onto the bench.
3. Carry the trailing leg to place that foot on the top of the bench next to the lead foot (c).
4. Pause and then reverse the movement to step down with the same trailing leg.
5. Return to the beginning position by carrying the lead foot to place that foot on the floor next to the trailing foot.
6. Pause and switch to the other leg as the lead leg.

Breathing Guidelines

Exhale during the upward phase and inhale during the lowering phase of the movement.

Exercise Modifications and Variations

- Two dumbbells or kettlebells can be used instead of a barbell.
- One dumbbell or kettlebell can be used; if only one is used, it can be held at the front of the chest or held in the hand at the same side of the body at the lead leg (therefore, the dumbbell or kettlebell would need to alternate hands as the lead leg alternates).

Figure 6.20 Step-up: *(a)* step onto box; *(b)* press into box to lift body; *(c)* stand on top of box.

Coaching Tips

- As the athlete progresses, the height of the bench or box can be increased so that the lead hip and knee flex and extend farther during the step.
- Keep most of the weight over the midfoot to heel of the trailing leg rather than the ball of the foot.
- Do not hop or jump up with the trailing leg or foot.

DROP STEP SQUAT

Primary Muscles Trained

Gluteus maximus, semimembranosus, semitendinosus, biceps femoris, vastus lateralis, vastus intermedius, vastus medialis, rectus femoris, hip abductors (gluteus medius, gluteus minimus, tensor fascia latae)

Beginning Position

- Stand in the ready position with the feet hip-width apart.
- Make sure that the toes are pointing outward *(a)*.

Movement Phases

1. Flex the left hip to lift the left leg and then open the left hip to move the left leg horizontally away from the beginning position. This movement is caused by active hip flexion and abduction, thereby transversely turning the body to the left approximately 90 degrees.
2. Place the left foot on the floor roughly shoulder-width apart from the right foot; keep the right foot in its original position. Both feet should be (and remain) externally rotated

approximately 45 degrees to mimic a sumo squat stance.

3. Descend in a squat until the thighs are parallel to the floor.

4. Maintain a position with a neutral spine, high elbows, and the chest up and out *(b)*.

5. Extend the hips and knees at the same rate (to keep the torso-to-floor angle constant) back to the standing position.

6. Flex the left hip to lift the left leg, close the left hip to move the left leg horizontally, and place the left foot back on the floor in the beginning position *(c)*.

7. At the end of the set, repeat with the other leg.

Breathing Guidelines

Inhale during the lowering phase and exhale during the upward phase of the movement.

Exercise Modifications and Variations

Instead of placing the foot of the stepping leg back on the floor in the beginning position at the end of repetition, the hip of the stepping leg can be kept flexed (so that the thigh remains parallel to the floor with the foot off the floor) as the leg moves back to the beginning position, pauses, and then begins the next repetition.

Coaching Tips

- Keep the torso tall and erect.
- Keep the foot of the supporting leg in its original position as the stepping leg moves out, contacts the floor, lifts back up, and moves back into the beginning position.
- Grip the floor with the foot of the supporting leg, thereby preventing pronation or collapse during flexion and extension of the lower extremities.
- Do not let the knees sway in.
- Sit the hips back during the descent, as when squatting down to sit on a chair.

Figure 6.21 Drop step squat: *(a)* beginning position; *(b)* step out and drop down; *(c)* return back to the beginning position.

SINGLE-LEG CABLE HIP ABDUCTION

Primary Muscles Trained

Hip abductors (gluteus medius, gluteus minimus, tensor fascia latae)

Beginning Position

- Stand on one leg with the ankle cable of the low-pulley machine attached to the other anklebone (leg farther from the pulley).
- Stand perpendicular to the pulley.
- Place the hand closer to the cable machine on the machine handle.
- Stand far enough from the machine to ensure tension on the cable.
- Raise the exercising leg 1 to 2 inches (3-5 cm) off the floor (a).
- Make sure to keep proper posture.

Movement Phases

1. Slowly and with control, abduct the hip to move the outer leg laterally away from the body.
2. Continue until the hip position can no longer be maintained or is beginning to be compromised (b).
3. Pause and then slowly lower the leg.
4. At the end of the set, repeat with the other leg.

Figure 6.22   Single-leg cable hip abduction: (a) beginning position;
(b) abduct.

Breathing Guidelines

Inhale during the outward movement and exhale during the return to the beginning position.

Coaching Tips

- Use a light weight and focus on the contraction.
- Keep the hips centered over the vertical line of the body.
- The exercising leg should move directly away from the body in an arc to the side and up.
- Keep the feet parallel during the movement.
- Avoid allowing the thigh of the exercising leg to rotate externally or the hips to twist while lifting the leg.
- Maintain a neutral spine.

7

UPPER BODY EXERCISE TECHNIQUE

BRYAN D. DOO

Many actions performed on the basketball court require upper body strength. Developing upper body muscular strength and endurance has been proved to help the athlete become more proficient in tasks like dribbling and shooting (1). Muscle fatigue can reduce shooting accuracy, negatively affecting shoulder and wrist kinematics (2). Additional neuromuscular adaptations acquired through upper body resistance training can help to combat the effects of peripheral fatigue. With that said, both the overall goals and benefits of upper body resistance training for the basketball athlete are to improve proprioception and joint stability, as well as enhance upper body muscle architecture. In the acts of shooting and dribbling, improved proprioception helps to stabilize the shoulder joint dynamically and transfer forces distally. Other examples of applied upper body strength in basketball pertain to, but are not limited to, gaining good position while boxing out, meeting an opponent at the rim for a block or rebound, and creating separation from a defender to receive a pass. These abilities help create success on the court. Developing upper body strength allows the athlete to be more proficient in many of the physical tasks involved in a contact sport and helps create a well-rounded basketball athlete.

All upper body exercises need to be performed with proper technique, so begin with lower loads that can be controlled throughout the optimal range of motion of the exercise. A lower load would be considered a weight or resistance that the athlete can control with optimal technique for the designated number of repetitions. Performance intensity will vary from exercise to exercise and will depend on the experience of the athlete, his or her goals, and the season or phase of training. Ultimately, basketball is a sport that places a large demand on the muscles and joints of the upper body, so the athlete must include applicable exercises to improve performance.

EQUIPMENT

Upper body exercises can be performed with many pieces of equipment to obtain the desired effects of resistance training. For this chapter, the minimum equipment needed is dumbbells of various weights, a loaded pulley system, and an adjustable bench.

Exercise variations require other equipment that might include a stability ball, suspension trainer, medicine balls, or resistance bands.

TEMPO GUIDELINES

When exercising, **tempo** refers to the rate or speed of the activity or exercise being performed. The speed can vary from slow to fast for both concentric and eccentric actions of the upper body exercise and does not need to be the same speed for the two phases (4). For example, when performing a bench press, tempo of the eccentric and concentric actions does not have to match and may have a different effect on the body if performed slower or faster. Isometric exercise should also be considered. Tempo needs to be thought about and matched to the goals and experience of the athlete.

SPOTTING GUIDELINES

Spotters should realize where the athlete is most at risk for injury during an exercise. For instance, during a dumbbell chest press, the risk is highest in two positions. The first is at the top when the dumbbells are over the head and face and could fall or even slip out of the hand or hands and on to the athlete. Therefore, when using dumbbells, the spotter should place his or her hands around the athlete's wrists. If an athlete is using a barbell, the spotter should use an alternating grip between the athlete's hand placement on the bar. The alternating grip provides leverage and prevents the bar from slipping from the spotter's grip.

The second position of increased risk for a failed attempt or injury occurs when the muscles are lengthened and the athlete begins to initiate the concentric phase. In this moment, motion stops, making it more difficult to change direction and move the resistance. Improper execution or a failed attempt could lead to injury. Therefore, a spotter's responsibility is to find the optimal position to help if the athlete loses control. When using dumbbells, the spotter again positions the hands around the wrists. When a barbell is being used, the spotter again uses an alternating grip between the athlete's hands and, if need be, assists by helping move the barbell back to the beginning position. Spotting positions and techniques will change based on the athlete's experience level, strength, and the exercise and equipment being used. Some exercises do not require a spotter. In any case, the spotter should take time to think about when and where a spot is needed and make sure to maintain focus.

BREATHING GUIDELINES

Breathing technique should not be overlooked when performing upper body resistance training. Learning to breathe properly and stay relaxed while training with external loads takes practice. Proper breathing technique is necessary to create intraabdominal pressure that helps the body stabilize itself under increased loads. For most of the exercises in this chapter, inhaling should take place during the eccentric phase, and exhaling should be performed through the sticking point during the concentric phase. Exhaling with some force during the concentric phase helps the body stay relaxed while also providing support (3).

COACHING TIPS OR CUES

Each upper body exercise has its own set of coaching cues. Make sure that the equipment is safe and is being used for its designed purpose. Learn what the correct posture position is for each exercise and try to maintain that position. An **athletic stance** pertains to a standing posture in which the feet are flat on the floor and hip- to shoulder-width apart, the knees are slightly flexed, the hips are neutral, the spine is upright, and the shoulders are rolled back with the chest out. A good setup gives the best chance of successfully completing exercises the correct way.

Ethan Miller/Getty Images

Similar to cues used to reinforce sport skills such as dribbling while changing directions, coaches can give athletes cues to help them properly perform resistance training exercises.

Exercise Finder

DUMBBELL BENCH PRESS

Primary Muscles Trained
Pectoralis major, anterior deltoids, triceps brachii

Beginning Position
- Lie down in a supine position on a bench with feet flat on the floor, shoulders flat on the bench, and arms pronated and extended straight above the nipple line with a dumbbell in each hand (closed grip).
- Shoulders should be relaxed and not elevated, and the wrists should be above the elbows *(a)*.

Movement Phases
1. Lower the dumbbells from over the chest to the nipple line at the chest level. The dumbbells will separate on the way down so that they are a little wider than shoulder-width apart *(b)*.
2. Brace the body by contracting the muscles of the abdomen and push the dumbbells away from the body to the beginning position *(a)*. The hands should trace the shape of a triangle, wide at the bottom of the exercise and close together at the top.

Spotting Guidelines
The spotter should be stationed at the head of the athlete in an athletic stance, with the hands ready to support the wrists (not the elbows). The spotter follows the path of the wrists, ready to brace the wrists at any point and take the weight away when appropriate.

Exercise Modifications and Variations
- Perform the standard barbell bench press.
- Use only one dumbbell.

Figure 7.1 Dumbbell bench press: *(a)* beginning position; (b) lower dumbbells.

- Alternate arms (hold both dumbbells at the top or at the bottom).
- Perform lying on the floor instead of a bench to limit the range of motion.
- Perform lying on an incline or decline bench instead of a flat bench.

Coaching Tips

- Maintain control of the dumbbells at all times.
- Wrists should be stiff and directly above the elbows, and the abdominal muscles should be held tight.
- Do not let the arms come too close to the body or let the wrists stray from being above the elbows.

ONE-ARM CABLE CHEST PRESS

Primary Muscles Trained
Pectoralis major, anterior deltoids, triceps brachii (plus anatomical core muscles as stabilizers)

Beginning Position

- Stand in front of the cable machine with one foot forward and the other foot back with flexed knees. Attach a handle attachment to the cable and position it at chest level. Grasp the handle with a neutral grip using the hand that is on the same side as the rear foot.
- The cable will be underneath the armpit with the hand positioned at the chest holding onto the handle.
- The elbow should be behind the wrist, and the wrist should be stopped before reaching the chest line, to protect the shoulder (a).

Movement Phases

1. Maintaining a rigid, upright upper body position throughout the movement, push the handle forward until the elbow is extended out to a straight, but not locked, position (b).
2. Keeping the rest of the body still, slowly reverse direction and retreat the hand with the handle back toward the chest, keeping the elbow behind the wrist.

Exercise Modifications and Variations

- Kneel on one knee and place the other leg in front at a 90-degree angle at the hip and knee. Start with cable a little above the shoulder and over the top of the shoulder, not under the armpit.
- In this position, the cable will be above the shoulder, not under the armpit.
- Add a rotation when pressing the cable forward (like a boxer). This version will actively involve the anatomical core muscles.

Coaching Tips

- Maintain an athletic stance.
- Keep the handle in front of the elbow.
- Do not allow the wrist to flex during the exercise; keep it in a straight, locked position.

Figure 7.2 One-arm cable chest press: *(a)* beginning position; *(b)* press forward.

ONE-ARM CABLE ROW

Primary Muscles Trained

Latissimus dorsi, teres major, middle trapezius, rhomboids, posterior deltoids

Beginning Position

- Stand facing the cable machine in a split stance with one foot forward and the other foot about 2 to 3 feet (61-91 cm) behind *(a)*.
- Slightly flex the knees and hold the handle in the hand that is on the same side of the body as the rear foot.
- Maintain an upright, athletic stance with the scapulae pulled back slightly and the shoulder relaxed and not elevated.

Movement Phases

1. Maintaining a rigid, upright upper body position throughout the movement, pull the handle back to the torso. The elbow should drive directly backward, and the wrist should fall right in line with the elbow while remaining close to the body *(b)*.
2. Reverse direction by allowing the handle to move forward in a controlled manner.

Exercise Modifications and Variations

- Use a rope, V-bar, or bar, or place a towel around the handle to improve grip strength.
- Kneel on one knee and place the other leg out in front at a 90-degree angle at the hip and knee.
- Attach a cable basketball attachment to the cable and work on pulls.
- Change the tempo of the concentric or eccentric actions or add pauses before or after the pull.

Figure 7.3 One-arm cable row: (a) beginning position; (b) pull backward.

Coaching Tips

- Make sure that the pulling action is initiated by the muscles of the back, not the torso or midsection.
- Make sure that the wrist involved in the movement is not higher or lower than the elbow, but directly in line with it.
- Control the weight being moved and keep the upper body erect.

LAT PULLDOWN (MACHINE)

Primary Muscles Trained

Latissimus dorsi, teres major, middle trapezius, rhomboids, posterior deltoids

Beginning Position

- Sit down facing the machine with the thighs under the pad and feet flat on the floor.
- Grab the bar wider than shoulder-width apart with a closed, pronated grip (a).
- Fully extend the arms, draw the shoulders back and down slightly, and lean the torso back slightly.
- Look slightly up and maintain a fixed eye position to help maintain proper posture and keep the neck relaxed.

Movement Phases

1. Pull the bar down toward the upper chest in a smooth, controlled manner while maintaining proper posture.
2. Touch the bar to the upper portion of the chest, keeping the wrists stiff and the shoulders back and down (b).
3. Slowly return to the beginning position by allowing the elbows to extend while maintaining torso position.

Figure 7.4 Lat pulldown (machine): *(a)* beginning position; *(b)* pull down to upper chest.

Exercise Modifications and Variations

- Change the bar to a handle, rope, towel, or other attachment.
- Change the tempo of the concentric or eccentric actions or add pauses before or after the pull.

Coaching Tips

- Do not pull the bar below the nipple line.
- Relax the neck and do not let the shoulders shrug up.
- Do not round the back when trying to touch the bar to the chest.
- Do not use the torso to jerk the weight.

PULL-UP

Primary Muscles Trained

Latissimus dorsi, teres major, middle trapezius, rhomboids, posterior deltoids

Beginning Position

- Grasp the bar with a pronated grip at or slighter wider than shoulder-width apart.
- Begin from a full hang with the elbows extended and the feet off the floor *(a)*.
- Look straight ahead.

Movement Phases

1. Maintaining a rigid, upright upper body position throughout the movement, squeeze the shoulders back together and pull the body upward until the upper chest meets the bar (or the shoulders near the handles as shown in figure 7.5b).

Figure 7.5 Pull-up: *(a)* beginning position; *(b)* pull the body up to handles.

2. Pause at the top and then allow the elbows to extend to lower the body back toward the floor in a controlled manner.

3. Lower until the elbows are fully extended.

Spotting Guideline

A spotter can assist the athlete by pushing on the middle back (or lift up under the shins or ankles if the athlete has flexed knees).

Exercise Modifications and Variations

- Change the grip to a supinated position (commonly called a *chin-up*), a neutral grip, or an alternated grip.
- Flex the hips to bring the knees into the chest during the upward movement or for the entire movement.
- Add an extended pause at the top or bottom of the pull-up.
- Wrap a towel around the bar to make it thicker.
- Use a band for assistance.

Coaching Tips

- Make sure that the elbows extend at the bottom of the movement.
- Avoid swinging (also called *kipping*) to complete the movement.
- Brace the muscles of the core to protect the back and prevent any flexing through the midsection.

BENT-OVER ROW

Primary Muscles Trained

Latissimus dorsi, teres major, middle trapezius, rhomboids, posterior deltoids

Beginning Position

- Stand with the feet shoulder-width apart, toes pointed straight ahead, knees slightly flexed, and the shins close to the bar.
- Grip the bar with a pronated, closed grip wider than shoulder-width apart.
- Hinge at the hips, so that the torso is almost parallel to the floor with a flat back and neutral spine (a).
- Eyes should look toward the floor.
- Chin should remain tucked so that the neck is in a neutral position.
- Alternatively, perform the deadlift exercise (see chapter 6) to lift the bar from the floor and then hinge at the hips to get into the beginning position of this exercise.

Movement Phases

1. Pull the bar toward the torso.
2. Control the movement of the bar and keep the torso rigid, back neutral, and knees slightly flexed.
3. Touch the bar to the lower chest or upper abdomen (not happening in figure 7.6b).
4. Lower the bar back toward the floor in a controlled manner, maintaining the neutral spine and torso and knee positions.

Exercise Modifications and Variations

- Use two dumbbells or one dumbbell.
- Reverse the grip to a supinated hand position.
- Lie on a tall bench and place the bar under the bench.
- Perform while standing on one leg with a dumbbell.

Figure 7.6 Bent-over row: (a) beginning position; (b) pull bar toward torso.

Coaching Tips

- Hinge at the hips. This technique allows the torso to move forward while helping to protect the back.
- Flex the knees more if the hamstrings are tight.
- Maintain a stationary, rigid torso position throughout the movement.

FACE PULL

Primary Muscles Trained

Latissimus dorsi, teres major, middle trapezius, rhomboids

Beginning Position

- Stand facing a high-pulley cable machine and grasp a rope handle with a closed, pronated grip and the palms facing the floor.
- Step back so that the cable is taut with the arms fully extended way out in front of the face.
- Point the elbows out to the sides.
- Place the head in line with the spine and be sure that the torso is fully erect (a).

Movement Phases

1. Squeeze the shoulder blades together and then pull the handle toward the face.
2. When the upper arms are aligned with the shoulders, continue the backward movement (in one smooth motion, not two separate movements) by pulling only with the hands (keeping the upper arms stationary) until the hands finish close to the ears and the center of the handle finishes close to the forehead (b).
3. Return to the beginning position.

Exercise Modifications and Variations

Perform the exercise while in a seated position on a bench placed perpendicular to the machine.

Figure 7.7 Face pull: (a) beginning position; (b) pull toward face.

Coaching Tips

- Do not round the upper back, especially when the arms are all the way out in front of the face.
- Keep the head, torso, and body in the same position throughout the exercise.

LATERAL SHOULDER RAISE

Primary Muscles Trained

Deltoids

Beginning Position

- Stand in an athletic stance with two dumbbells in front of the thighs with a neutral, closed grip.
- Flex the elbows slightly but keep them stiff when the movement begins.
- Keep the eyes fixed straight ahead (a).

Movement Phases

1. Raise the dumbbells up and away from the body until the arms are approximately parallel to the floor. The elbows and wrists should move up together at the same time and ahead of the forearms, hands, and dumbbells (more than what is shown in figure 7.8b).
2. Keep the head neutral.
3. Pause at the top and control the movement back down toward the beginning position (eccentric movement).
4. Maintain a slightly flexed elbow position throughout the exercise.

Figure 7.8 Lateral shoulder raise: (a) beginning position; (b) raise.

Exercise Modifications and Variations

- Use kettlebells to change where the weight is positioned.
- Perform the exercise while seated.
- Use a cable machine instead of dumbbells.

Coaching Tips

- Think about moving the elbows and wrists at the same time, not one before the other.
- Do not let the torso or head fall forward.
- Control the weight; do not let it swing.

PLATE FRONT SHOULDER RAISE

Primary Muscles Trained

Anterior deltoids

Beginning Position

- Standing in an athletic stance, hold a weight plate in front of the body with both hands.
- Flex the elbows slightly but keep them stiff when the movement begins.
- Hold the plate perpendicular to the arms with the wrists stiff.
- Keep the eyes fixed straight ahead (a).

Movement Phases

1. Raise the plate in an arc in front of the body up to shoulder height. Think about moving the elbows and wrists at the same time, not one before the other. The arms should remain near full extension throughout the movement.
2. Contract the abdominal muscles to maintain good posture, keep a neutral spine, and control the movement of the weight plate.
3. Pause when the hands reach shoulder height (b) and then lower the plate back to the beginning position at the top of the thighs.

Exercise Modifications and Variations

- Use dumbbells, a medicine ball, or a barbell.
- Stand on an uneven surface.
- Place the back flat against a wall.
- Use a cable machine.

Coaching Tips

- Make sure that the upper torso does not lean back as the arms elevate.
- Find a weight that can be lifted without shrugging the shoulders.
- Prevent rocking of the body or rounding of the back.
- Do not lock the elbows fully straight.

Figure 7.9 Plate front shoulder raise: *(a)* beginning position; *(b)* raise to shoulder height.

STANDING DUMBBELL SHOULDER PRESS

Primary Muscles Trained
Deltoids, triceps brachii

Beginning Position
- Stand in an athletic stance.
- Hold a dumbbell in each hand with the palms facing each other.
- Position the hands approximately shoulder-width apart and directly over the elbows.
- Keep the eyes fixed straight ahead *(a)*.

Movement Phases
1. Push the dumbbells upward until the elbows are fully extended *(b)*.
2. Keep a firm grip on the dumbbells and keep the wrists rigid (do not allow them to flex).
3. Lower the dumbbells back to the beginning position under control, making sure that the wrists and dumbbells remain over the elbows.

Spotting Guidelines
If a spotter is used, the athlete should sit on a bench so that the spotter can stand behind the athlete in an athletic stance, with the hands ready to support the wrists (not the elbows). The spotter follows the path of the wrists, ready to brace the wrists at any point and take the weight away if needed.

Figure 7.10 Standing dumbbell shoulder press: *(a)* beginning position; *(b)* press to full elbow extension.

Exercise Modifications and Variations

- Perform the standard barbell shoulder press.
- Use a split stance or perform the exercise in a seated or kneeling (on one or two knees) position.
- Rotate the hands to a pronated grip.
- Hold a kettlebell in an inverted ("bottom-up") position to work on grip strength.
- Alternate arms to press the dumbbells overhead.
- Only use one arm.

Coaching Tips

- Do not allow excessive back arching or the torso to fall backward.
- Allow the dumbbells to move from wide to narrow naturally through the concentric phase.
- Do not lock out the knees if performing the exercise while standing.

PRONE Y'S, T'S, I'S

Primary Muscles Trained

Infraspinatus, teres minor and major, trapezius, rhomboids, posterior deltoids

Beginning Position

- Lie in the prone position on a stability ball or a bench that is inclined 20 to 35 degrees.
- Keep the head face down in a neutral position.
- Hang the arms straight down, holding the dumbbells using a closed, neutral grip *(a)*.

Movement Phases

1. Rotate the hands so that the palms face each other with the thumbs pointing up.
2. Squeeze the shoulder blades together and raise the arms by flexing the shoulders at a 45-degree angle to create the letter *Y* *(b, top)*.
3. Return the arms to the beginning position and then raise them at a 90-degree angle from the body to create the letter *T* *(b, middle)*.
4. Return the arms to the beginning position and then raise them directly above the shoulders to create the letter *I* *(b, bottom)*.
5. Return the arms to the beginning position.

Exercise Modifications and Variations

- Perform the exercise on the floor (although this technique reduces the range of motion of the exercise).
- Use a cable machine and perform the movements while standing.
- Lie on a table and perform the exercise with one arm at a time.

Coaching Tips

- Do not let the chest lift throughout the exercise. Keep it stationary.
- Do not squeeze the neck and shoulders forward but draw the shoulder blades back and down.
- Keep the thumbs pointing up throughout the exercise.

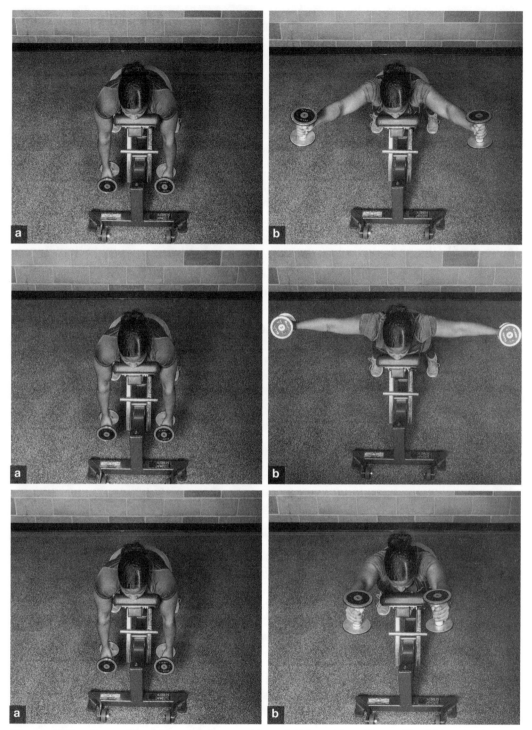

Figure 7.11 Prone Y's: *(a)* beginning position; *(b)* Y position. Prone T's: *(a)* beginning position; *(b)* T position. Prone I's: *(a)* beginning position; *(b)* I position.

TRICEPS PUSHDOWN (MACHINE)

Primary Muscle Trained

Triceps brachii

Beginning Position

- Attach a short bar to a cable machine.
- Stand facing a cable machine and grab each end of the bar with one hand.
- Keep the arms close to side of the body and flex the torso forward slightly at the same angle as the cable (a).

Movement Phases

1. Keeping the upper arms next to the torso, extend the elbows and push through the wrists until the elbows are fully extended (b).
2. Allow the elbows to flex back up to at least 90 degrees while attempting to move through the greatest range of motion possible without allowing the elbows to leave the side of the body.

Exercise Modifications and Variations

- Use various attachments like a rope or triangle handle or drape a hand towel around the bar and hold the ends.
- Lean against a wall with the cable straight up and down.
- Use one arm at a time with a single-grip rope or handle.

Coaching Tips

- Maintain an athletic stance throughout the exercise.
- Be aware of the elbows leaving the side of the body; instead, they should remain by the side of the body throughout the movement.
- Keep the core tight to prevent forward flexion or the use of momentum.

Figure 7.12 Triceps pushdown (machine): (a) beginning position; (b) extend elbows.

BARBELL BICEPS CURL

Primary Muscles Trained

Biceps brachii, brachialis, brachioradialis

Beginning Position

- Start in an athletic stance. Hold a bar about shoulder-width apart with a supinated grip.
- Stand up tall and keep the knees slightly flexed.
- The bar should rest on the thighs (a).

Movement Phases

1. Curl the bar by flexing the elbows and moving the hands toward the front of the shoulders.
2. The bar should travel in an arc.
3. The elbows should remain at the side of the body.
4. After reaching the top (b), lower the bar back toward the thighs in a steady, controlled manner until the elbows are extended.

Exercise Modifications and Variations

- Use a split stance or change the bar type to an EZ-curl bar.
- Lean against a wall.
- Use a cable machine or dumbbells.

Figure 7.13 Barbell biceps curl: (a) beginning position; (b) curl.

Coaching Tips

- Do not swing the body to move the bar.
- Pause at the top and bottom of the exercise to prevent the use of momentum.
- Do not allow the elbows to leave the side of the body when the bar is returning to the body from the front of the shoulders.
- Keep the core tight to prevent the low back from flexing or extending.

DUMBBELL BICEPS CURL

Primary Muscles Trained

Biceps brachii, brachialis, brachioradialis

Beginning Position

- Start in an athletic stance. Hold the dumbbells by the side of the body with a neutral grip (a).
- Stand up tall and keep the knees slightly flexed (more than what is shown in figure 7.14).

Movement Phases

1. Flex one of the elbows and move the wrist forward and toward the front of the shoulder.
2. Gradually rotate (supinate) the dumbbell to a palms-up position at the top half of the movement until the dumbbell is at shoulder level (b). Keep the other arm stationary.
3. Lower the dumbbell by moving the hand forward, down, and away from the shoulder to keep the elbow tight to the side of the body. The hand should also pronate gradually so that the dumbbell is in a neutral position when the elbow achieves full extension.
4. Repeat the movement with the other arm.

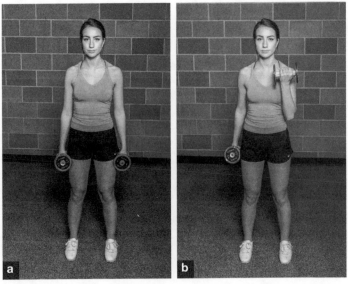

Figure 7.14 Dumbbell biceps curl: (a) beginning position; (b) curl.

Exercise Modifications and Variations

- Sit on a bench or ball.
- Curl with the hands in a hammer position (using a neutral grip) throughout the exercise.
- Use a cable machine with various grips.

Coaching Tips

- Minimize movement of the elbows forward or backward during the exercise.
- Keep the wrists stiff throughout the exercise.
- Do not swing the weights or arch the back to move the weights.

OVERHEAD DUMBBELL TRICEPS EXTENSION

Primary Muscle Trained

Triceps brachii

Beginning Position

- Sit on a bench with one dumbbell held in both hands behind the head and the feet flat on the floor.
- Position the upper arms next to the head and allow the elbows to flex to a relaxed position at approximately 90 degrees (a).

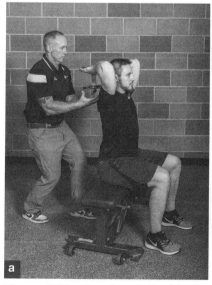
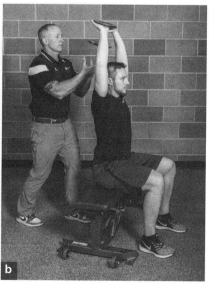

Figure 7.15 Overhead dumbbell triceps extension: (a) beginning position; (b) extend elbows.

Movement Phases

1. While keeping the upper arms fixed, extend the elbows to raise the dumbbell overhead until the elbows are fully extended (b).
2. Lower the dumbbell back to the beginning position.

Spotting Guidelines

The spotter stands behind the athlete to be sure that the athlete does not drop the dumbbell or to help the athlete get the dumbbell into the beginning position.

Exercise Modifications and Variations

- Use a cable machine or a barbell.
- Use two dumbbells.
- Perform the exercise with a single arm.

Coaching Tip

- Keep the upper torso still by squeezing the elbows toward the head to prevent back arching.

8

ANATOMICAL CORE EXERCISE TECHNIQUE

JOHN SHACKLETON

The **anatomical core**—as it pertains to the torso of the human body—refers to the musculature with attachments originating on the spine, rib cage, and skull. The spinal erectors, glutes, abdominals, and obliques all function together as support structures of the spine by providing stability as the athlete moves in all dimensions (1). Without a strong core, performance will be compromised and the athlete will be more susceptible to injuries (4). As a result, strengthening the core musculature is essential to the overall physical development of a basketball athlete.

The exercises selected in this chapter aim to improve the isometric and dynamic strength of the anatomical core musculature while considering the safety of the athlete. **Isometric exercise** is a form of exercise in which the muscles generate tension without a change in joint angle or fascicle length despite external forces acting on the body (3). An example of a basketball athlete demonstrating isometric anatomical core strength is a center trying to gain position in the low post as the defensive player tries to force the athlete out of position and off balance. To gain position, the offensive player must stay low and wide and keep the torso upright, which takes isometric anatomical core strength while absorbing contact from the defensive player. Dynamically, the anatomical core plays a pivotal role in transferring forces generated by the legs and hips to the upper body.

A basketball athlete's ability to accept body contact and maintain a stable torso on both offense and defense is a critical aspect of the game and must be addressed through anatomical core training. Therefore, exercises selected in this chapter challenge the deep stabilizers (transverse abdominis, erector spinae, multifidus, and quadratus lumborum) and the superficial muscles (rectus abdominis, internal and external obliques, and erector spinae) of the core in all dimensions to work together synergistically to provide core stability (2). The athlete's anatomical core will be challenged in a basketball-specific approach to improve performance and reduce the risk of injury.

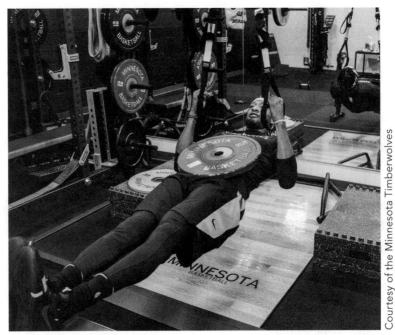

Courtesy of the Minnesota Timberwolves

The anatomical core is a bridge that transfers forces between the lower and upper body.

Exercise Finder

FRONT PLANK

Primary Muscles Trained
Transversus abdominis, rectus abdominis, multifidus, erector spinae

Beginning Position
- Lie face down on the floor.
- Position feet hip-width apart with toes pointed down.
- Fully extend legs and hips.
- Flex the elbows to 90 degrees and position them directly under the shoulders so that the forearms are in contact with the floor. Clench the hands to make fists with palms facing each other or place palms flat on the floor *(a)*.

Movement Phases
1. Begin by digging the toes into the floor and engage the muscles of the legs and hips.
2. While keeping the lower body engaged, drive the elbows into the floor and lift the hips off the floor to a neutral spine position *(b)*.
3. Hold this plank position for the prescribed amount of time.

Breathing Guidelines
Focus on controlled inhales matched with controlled exhales.

Exercise Modifications and Variations
This exercise can be regressed by having the athlete lift the feet off the floor and flex the knees to 90 degrees so that the lower body is supported at the knees.

Coaching Tip
When the athlete is in the plank position, make sure that the athlete maintains proper alignment with the ankle, knees, hips, torso, and head all in line.

Figure 8.1 Front plank: *(a)* beginning position; *(b)* static planked position.

V-UP

Primary Muscles Trained
Rectus abdominis, transverse abdominis, iliopsoas

Beginning Position
- Lie face up on the floor with the arms extended overhead.
- Position the legs closer together and point the toes up (a).

Movement Phases
1. Initiate movement with hip and spinal flexion by lifting the legs and arms simultaneously toward each other. Maintain full extension of the knees and elbows as the hips flex.
2. As the hands and feet travel toward each other, lift the shoulders and head off the floor, with the chin tucked, to allow the hands and feet to nearly meet over the hips (b). Hold this final position for approximately 1 second.
3. Return to the beginning position by demonstrating complete control of the arms and legs as the hips and spine extend back to the beginning position. Note that the elbows and knees remain extended through the full range of motion back to the beginning position.

Breathing Guidelines
At the beginning position, begin with a deep inhale. Exhale slowly with control as the feet and hands move toward each other. As the feet and hands meet, finish exhaling while pausing for 1 second. The next inhale should start as the arms and legs travel back toward the floor.

Exercise Modifications and Variations
If athletes have difficulty reaching their hands to their feet, have them focus on a point of contact with the hands somewhere on the lower leg between the knees and ankles.

Coaching Tip
As the athlete moves through the full range of motion, make sure that the knees and elbows remain fully extended.

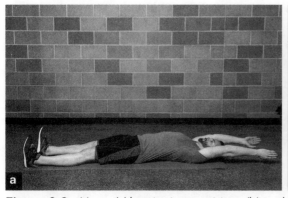

Figure 8.2 V-up: (a) beginning position; (b) end position.

SIDE ROTATIONAL V-UP

Primary Muscles Trained

Rectus abdominis, transverse abdominis, internal and external obliques, iliopsoas

Beginning Position

- Lie face up on the floor with the arms outstretched to the sides (in a "T"), legs and feet held together, and the torso and hips rotated to one side so half of the buttocks (one glute) and the outside (lateral) surface of the leg and foot (on that same side) is in contact with the floor.
- In this position, the contralateral arm, the back of the head, or both may or may not be touching the floor (it depends on the flexibility of the torso).

Movement Phases

1. Initiate movement with the anatomical core musculature to move into hip and spinal flexion and partial torso rotation by lifting the legs and the contralateral arm simultaneously toward each other.
2. Keel the other arm flat on the floor with the palm facing down to add stability to the exercise. Maintain full extension of the knees and elbow during the upward movement.
3. As the contralateral arm and feet travel toward each other, lift the shoulders and head off the floor to maximally "crunch" the torso. Hold the final position for approximately 1 second.
4. Return to the beginning position by lowering the arm and legs and gradually relaxing the torso back to the beginning position.
5. Repeat the movement but start with the torso and hips rotated to the other side and reach with the other arm.

Breathing Guidelines

In the beginning position, begin with a deep inhale. Exhale slowly and with control as the feet and hand move toward each other. Finish the exhale at the top while pausing for 1 second. The next inhale should start as the arm and legs travel back toward the floor.

Exercise Modifications and Variations

To progress the level of difficulty, hold a dumbbell or kettlebell in the hand of the contralateral arm.

Coaching Tip

Make sure that the athlete keeps the arms and legs extended through the full range of motion. The legs and arms should not touch the floor to ensure that the anatomical core musculature is engaged during the entire exercise.

DEADBUG

Primary Muscles Trained

Transverse abdominis, rectus abdominis, internal and external obliques

Beginning Position

- Lie face up on the floor with the knees and hips flexed at 90 degrees.
- Place the arms straight out in front of the body and hold a stability ball in place with the hands and knees (a).

Movement Phases

1. While keeping the entire back (neck to lower spine) in contact with the floor, apply light pressure with the knees and hands against the stability ball to engage the abdominal musculature.
2. Move contralateral limbs (e.g., the right leg and left arm) simultaneously in a controlled manner until both the leg and arm reach full extension a few inches (5-8 cm) off the floor. During the contralateral movement of the limbs, the other hand and knee should actively press into the ball to provide isometric anatomical core stability (b).
3. Hold the end position for a moment and return the contralateral hand and knee back to the ball in the beginning position (a).
4. Repeat the movement with the other contralateral limbs and continue to alternate for the prescribed repetitions.

Breathing Guidelines

During the initial set up, begin with a full exhalation and apply pressure into the ball with both the hand and knees. Inhale during the extension of the contralateral limbs. Exhale as the contralateral limbs return to the beginning position.

Exercise Modifications and Variations

If the athlete cannot maintain lower-back contact with the floor during contralateral limb movement, then regress and have the athlete hold the beginning position for a designated time.

Coaching Tip

Check to see if the lumbar spine is in contact with the floor during the initial setup. If there is a gap, slide a hand under the low back and cue the athlete to tilt the hips anteriorly (tuck the buttocks under) to get the lumbar spine in contact with the floor.

Figure 8.3 Deadbug: (a) beginning position; (b) contralateral movement.

SIDE PLANK

Primary Muscles Trained

Transverse abdominis, rectus abdominis, quadratus lumborum, multifidus, erector spinae, internal and external obliques

Beginning Position

- Lie on the floor on one side of the body.
- Stack the feet, knees, hips, and shoulders on top of each other and in line.
- Position the elbow of the bottom arm directly under the shoulder so that the upper arm is perpendicular to the floor (more than what is shown in figure 8.4a).

Movement Phases

1. Begin by driving the elbow and the side of the feet into the floor to lift the hips up until they are in neutral position and in line with the head, feet, and spine. At this point, the elbow and the bottom side foot become the only two points of contact with the floor (b).
2. Hold the side plank position for the prescribed time.
3. Change positions so that the plank is performed with the other side of the body in contact with the floor.

Breathing Guidelines

While in the side plank position, perform slow and controlled inhalation and exhalation.

Exercise Modifications and Variations

- To regress the exercise, flex the knees to 90 degrees to support the side plank position with the bottom knee.
- To progress the exercise, go from supporting the upper body with the elbow to extending the bottom elbow so that the hand is on the floor and supporting the weight of the upper body. This position requires strong shoulder stabilization ability.

Figure 8.4   Side plank: (a) beginning position; (b) static side planked position.

Suspension Side Plank

Lie on one side of the body with the elbow directly under the shoulder and forearm and wrist in contact with the floor. Stack the hips on top of each other and place the feet inside the loops of the suspension straps. The loops of the suspension straps should be in contact with the ankles. The shoulders, hips, and bottom knee and ankle should be in line. The top knee and ankle will be aligned slightly in front of the bottom knee and ankle. Simultaneously drive the forearm into the floor and bottom ankle into the suspension strap to lift the hips up into a neutral position. While in the side plank position, engage the musculature of the anatomical core, hips, and lower legs to maintain neutral alignment of the spine and hips for the prescribed amount of time.

Coaching Tips

- Cue the athlete to keep neck aligned with the rest of the spine.
- Cue the athlete to squeeze the buttocks and push the hips forward to keep aligned with the knees and shoulders. The nonsupport arm can also be extended and reaching up to help keep the shoulders stacked on top of each other.

BIRDDOG PLANK

Primary Muscles Trained

Transversus abdominis, rectus abdominis, multifidus, erector spinae, gluteus maximus

Beginning Position

- Lie face down on the floor.
- Position the feet hip-width apart with the toes pointed down into the floor.
- Fully extend the legs and hips.
- Flex the elbows to 90 degrees and position them directly under the shoulders. Place the forearms in contact with the floor. Make fists with the hands so that the palms are facing each other (a).

Movement Phases

1. Lift the contralateral arm and leg (i.e., right arm and left leg) simultaneously off the floor until the right arm is fully extended above the head and level with the shoulder (b). The left leg should remain fully extended as it lifts and the glute muscles contract. Hold the position for the prescribed time.
2. Return to the beginning position and repeat the exercise with the other arm and leg.

Breathing Guidelines

In the beginning position, exhale completely and engage the abdominal musculature. Inhale as the contralateral arm and leg lift. Once in the isometric hold, use deep and controlled inhalations and exhalations.

Figure 8.5 Birddog plank: *(a)* beginning position; *(b)* static planked position.

Exercise Modifications and Variations

- A quadruped beginning position (on the knees and hands) can be used as a modification to regress the level of difficulty.
- To progress the level of difficulty, the exercise can be made more dynamic. For example, lift the contralateral arm and leg, and hold the final position for about 2 seconds before switching to the other arm and leg. Continue performing the exercise while alternating arms and legs until the prescribed repetitions have been completed.

Coaching Tips

- As the athlete lifts the contralateral arm and leg, cue the athlete to keep the hips level with the floor. It is common to see the hips rotate down toward the floor as the leg is lifted.
- Check to make sure the athlete is not going into lumbar extension as the leg is lifted.

PALLOF PRESS

Primary Muscles Trained

Transverse abdominis, rectus abdominis, internal and external obliques

Beginning Position

- Grasp the handle with two hands from the cable column and kneel perpendicular to the cable column.
- Align the shoulders over the hips and the hips over the knees.
- Maintain an upright torso with the chest up and the shoulder blades pulled down and back.
- Tuck the elbows in next to the rib cage and hold the cable handle close to the chest *(a)*.

Movement Phases

1. Press the cable straight out from the chest with the hands until the elbows are fully extended and the cable handle is directly in line with the shoulders *(b)*.
2. After the arms are fully extended, the anatomical core will be challenged isometrically to the greatest degree.
3. Hold this position for the prescribed time while maintaining a neutral spine, holding the chest up, and keeping the shoulders down and back.

Figure 8.6 Pallof press: *(a)* beginning position; *(b)* static pressed out position.

Breathing Guidelines

While holding the cable handle straight out in front of the body, focus on controlled inhales matched with controlled exhales.

Exercise Modifications and Variations

The exercise can be progressed by performing the exercise in a standing position; assume an athletic stance by positioning the feet hip-width apart and slightly flexing the knees and hips.

Standing Pallof Press With Lateral Step

Grasp the handle with both hands and stand perpendicular to the cable column. Position the feet wider than the shoulders and assume an athletic, defensive stance by flexing at the hips and knees while keeping the torso upright with the chest up and shoulder blades back. Tuck the elbows in next to the rib cage and hold the cable handle close to the chest. Begin the exercise by pressing the cable straight out from the chest until the elbows are fully extended and the cable handle is directly in line with the shoulders. With the arms fully extended, the rotational force from the cable is at its greatest and the athlete's anatomical core musculature is challenged isometrically to resist any rotational movement. As the low and wide squat position is held with the cable pressed out, take one lateral step away from the cable column (pausing for a brief second) and then a lateral step toward the cable column (again pausing for a brief second). After that movement, either bring the cable back into the chest, pause, press back out, and complete another lateral step or hold the press and continue completing lateral steps.

Coaching Tips

- Make sure that the athlete maintains neutral alignment through the hips, torso, and shoulders. If any compensations occur, reduce the weight and have the athlete focus on maintaining proper alignment.
- To help keep the pelvis neutral, cue the athlete to contract the gluteal muscles.

STANDING PALLOF OVERHEAD PRESS

Primary Muscles Trained

Transverse abdominis, quadratus lumborum, internal and external obliques, rectus abdominis

Beginning Position

- Grasp the handle with both hands and stand perpendicular to the cable column.
- Assume an athletic stance by positioning the feet hip-width apart and slightly flexing the knees and hips.
- Keep the torso upright with the chest up.
- Tuck the elbows in next to the rib cage and hold the cable handle close to the chest *(a)*.

Movement Phases

1. Press the cable straight up overhead until the cable handle is above the head *(b)*.
2. With the cable handle above the head the anatomical core musculature will be challenged to contract isometrically and resist lateral flexion of the spine.
3. Hold this position for the prescribed time while maintaining a neutral spine and hips.

Breathing Guidelines

While holding the cable handle over the head, focus on controlled inhales matched with controlled exhales.

Figure 8.7 Standing Pallof overhead press: *(a)* beginning position; *(b)* static pressed up position.

Exercise Modifications and Variations

The exercise can be regressed by performing the exercise in a tall kneeling position with both knees on the floor or by flexing the elbows to 90 degrees. Doing this will lessen the degree of difficulty by reducing the rotational forces resisted by the anatomical core.

Standing Pallof Overhead Press With Lateral Step

Grasp the handle with both hands and stand perpendicular to the cable column. Position the feet wider than the shoulders and assume an athletic, defensive stance by flexing at the hips and knees while keeping the torso upright with the chest up and shoulder blades back. Tuck the elbows in next to the rib cage and hold the cable handle close to the chest. Begin the exercise by pressing the cable straight up overhead until the cable handle is above the head. With the cable handle above the head the anatomical core musculature will be challenged to contract isometrically and resist lateral flexion of the spine. Hold this position for a moment, take a lateral step back toward the cable column, pause for a moment, and either return the cable handle to the cable column or continue completing repetitions.

Coaching Tips

- Make sure that the athlete maintains neutral alignment through the hips, torso, and shoulders. If any compensations occur, reduce the weight and have the athlete focus on maintaining proper alignment.
- To help keep the pelvis neutral, cue the athlete to contract the gluteal muscles.

ELEVATED BRIDGE HOLD

Primary Muscles Trained

Gluteal muscles (maximus, medius, minimus), erector spinae, multifidus, transverse abdominis

Beginning Position

- Lie face up on the floor with the feet elevated on a bench.
- Flex the ankles so that the toes are pointed up.
- Flex the knees and hips to 90 degrees.
- Fully extend the arms at the sides of the body with palms facing down.
- The head should be in contact with the floor with the chin slightly tucked (a).

Movement Phases

1. Drive the heels into the bench to lift the hips up off the floor into a neutral spine position. The upper body is supported by the shoulders.
2. Actively drive through the heels to fully extend the hips (b); isometrically hold this position for the prescribed time.

Breathing Guidelines

Focus on controlled inhales matched with controlled exhales.

Figure 8.8 Elevated bridge hold: *(a)* beginning position; *(b)* lift hips.

Exercise Modifications and Variations

To regress this exercise, position the feet on the floor directly below the knees.

Elevated Bridge Hold With Alternating Leg Lift

Lie face up on the floor with the feet elevated on a bench. Flex the ankles so that the toes are pointed up and flex the knees and hips to 90 degrees. Fully extend the arms at the sides of the body with palms facing down. The head should be in contact with the floor with the chin slightly tucked. Drive the heels into the bench to lift the hips up off the floor into a neutral spine position with the upper body supported by the shoulders. Actively drive through the heels to fully extend the hips and isometrically hold this position for the prescribed time. Take one foot off the bench, fully extend the knee, and hold this position for 1 to 2 seconds before returning to the beginning position. Repeat the movement using the other leg. Continue until the prescribed repetitions have been completed.

Coaching Tips

- From a side view, the athlete's knees, hips, and shoulders should be in line.
- Cue the athlete to keep driving through the heels to keep the hips up and the gluteal muscles engaged to stabilize the hips.

REVERSE HIP EXTENSION HOLD

Primary Muscles Trained

Gluteal muscles (maximus, medius, minimus), erector spinae, multifidus

Beginning Position

- Lie face down on a high bench (or box) so that only the upper body is being supported. Hold on to the outer edges of the bench for support.
- Position the hips at the edge of the box and flex them to 90 degrees (or as far as the height of the bench or box will permit as shown in figure 8.9a).

Movement Phases

1. Keeping the knees extended and the toes pointed, pus he hips into the box (i.e., contract the glutes) while lifting the legs under control tc xtend the hips into a neutral position *(b)*.

2. After the legs reach the top and the hips are in neutral p. ion, hold this position for the prescribed amount of time.

Figure 8.9 Reverse hip extension hold: *(a)* beginning positio. b) raise legs.

Breathing Guidelines

Focus on controlled inhales matched with controlled exha when in the reverse hip extension hold position.

Exercise Modifications and Variations

This exercise can be regressed with the knees held in a 90-c ree flexed position.

Bosch Hip Extension Hold

Lie face up on the floor with one foot elevated on a bench an he other leg extended up toward the ceiling. With the ankle (of the foot that is on the nch) dorsiflexed, actively drive through the heel to fully extend the hips to lift them off tl loor. Hold this position for the prescribed time and then return back to the beginning pc on (or perform the movement for a prescribed number of repetitions). Repeat the mc ment using the other leg.

Coaching Tips

- Cue the athlete to contract the glutes when lifting the le into position.
- From a side view, the shoulders, hips, and knees are all i line at the top position.

WOOD CHOP

Primary Muscles Trained

Internal obliques, external obliques, transverse abdominis, rectus abdominis

Beginning Position

- Stand with the shoulders perpendicular to the cable column.
- Position the feet shoulder-width apart with the hips and knees slightly flexed.
- Keep the torso upright with the chest up and shoulders down and back.
- Reach up diagonally with both arms (outside arm comes across the body) and grip the cable above the inside shoulder *(a)*.

Movement Phases

1. With fully extended arms, pull the cable handle down in a diagonal pattern just below the outside hip by rotating the upper spine and shoulders *(b)*. The hips and lower back stay neutral throughout the entire movement.
2. Pause for 1 to 2 seconds at the final position of the rotation.
3. Reverse the movement by returning the cable handle back diagonally to the cable column under control, allowing the shoulders and upper spine to rotate back into the beginning position. Again, the hips and lower back stay neutral throughout the entire movement.

Breathing Guidelines

Exhale forcefully when rotating away from the cable column and inhale when returning the cable handle back to the column.

Figure 8.10   Wood chop: *(a)* beginning position; *(b)* diagonal movement.

Exercise Modifications and Variations

This exercise can be modified by changing the angle in which the chopping action occurs. For example, by adjusting the cable lower on the column (just below the hips) the movement would now start at the bottom and a low to high chopping pattern would be used. Two additional variations are to set the cable to standing shoulder height to perform a horizontal chopping pattern while standing or an angled chop while in a tall kneeling position. The exercise technique described earlier applies for each variation. The only differences is the beginning positions of the arms or body and the direction of the chop.

Coaching Tips

- When the athlete becomes comfortable with the movement pattern, have the athlete pull the cable more quickly when rotating away from the cable column.
- For safety, always have the athlete control the cable back to the beginning position.

PART III

PROGRAM DESIGN GUIDELINES AND SAMPLE PROGRAMS

9

POSTSEASON PROGRAMMING

JOSHUA BONHOTAL AND BRYCE DAUB

Following a long and demanding basketball season comes a critical point in the year when athletes begin to lay a foundation for the higher intensity training mesocycles soon to follow. The postseason begins soon after the competitive season and a brief transitional period. Athletes must be afforded the opportunity to recover from the accumulated stress of the season. A brief transitional period of detraining will occur, when athletes have the opportunity to rest and rejuvenate both physically and mentally, taking some much-needed time away from the court. After this period, the postseason phase serves as the starting point to a carefully planned out and progressive off-season resistance training program.

Depending on the length of the season, as determined by playoff success, the postseason training phase is short, lasting four to six weeks, and should be broken up into at least two microcycles: active recovery and general physical preparation (GPP). How long and how involved the resistance training program becomes is often determined by the outcome and length of the recently finished season. In a year when the athlete's team has been eliminated from play early, the opportunity will be greater to make positive training adaptations before the commencement of the off-season phase. Counter to this is the successful season in which a run to the championship is made. In this case, the postseason phase of training may be geared nearly in its entirety toward recovery. The first step when developing the postseason plan is to establish and consider the available timeline. The postseason plan must balance time away with moderate activity to promote recovery from the demands of the season while avoiding becoming completely deconditioned when resistance training is reintroduced.

Although encouraging some down time after the final game is important, taking too much time off can be detrimental. At the end of a season, basketball athletes, especially those playing high minutes, will likely be in good physiological condition. Totally disregarding their current physical state would be irresponsible. Detraining can occur in as little as two weeks in the absence of physical exercise. Rodriguez-Fernandez and colleagues (20) found that repeated maximal sprint ability (total time and best time) decreased after a two-week in-season break for both younger, high school (age 18.3 ± 0.8 years) and older, professional (age 24.0 ± 2.8 years) soccer athletes. Furthermore, faster athletes, regardless of age, showed larger decreases in repeated sprint ability. Intermittent endurance, as determined by the yo-yo intermittent recovery test, was not significantly affected, although distance covered did decrease slightly in both groups. In another study, Joo (9) found that two weeks of detraining impaired intermittent endurance. So, it appears that even as little as two weeks without exercise can result in detraining. On the other hand, because of the physical nature of basketball, a two-week break that includes physical exercise might have a positive effect on performance. For instance, Buchheit and colleagues (3) found that Australian football athletes who completed unsupervised, abbreviated resistance training programs over the course of a two-week Christmas break maintained or improved strength upon return. Therefore, athletes should be encouraged to begin physical activity in the form of exercise within two weeks after the end of a season.

This recommendation does not mean that athletes should get back onto the basketball court; rather, they should simply return to an active lifestyle. Often this activity will be some combination of soft-tissue work and light resistance training and participation in other non-basketball-related sports or cross-training activities like swimming, yoga, boxing, or biking. Before beginning the postseason phase, any underlying physical issues that may limit the athlete's participation in training must be diagnosed by the sports medicine staff. Initial assessment and the results of examination can be used to prescribe any necessary corrective or restorative training and rehabilitation measures. Because the athlete is less active during this time, a wise approach is to emphasize nutrition, lifestyle, and sleep to reduce and manage stress levels.

After a brief period of rest, the athlete will enter the first postseason microcycle focused on active recovery, typically lasting another two weeks. Note that depending on both biological and training age, as well as strength and power levels, detraining might still be occurring at this time. An athlete might go several weeks without reaching previous maximal strength and power thresholds. Highly trained athletes will have a tougher time maintaining strength and power during this time. Nevertheless, the purpose of this microcycle is to continue recovery and rehabilitation, to familiarize the athlete with the exercises and structure of a new program, and to improve the athlete's understanding of his or her overall strengths, weaknesses, and any restrictions that may not have been identified in the screening process.

Considering ways to change or vary the environment during this time is also important. Something as simple as training at a different location or training outdoors instead of indoors may be worth considering to help facilitate the postseason recovery process and break up the monotony that can exist with in-season training.

Another key element during the reintroduction of activity and training is to insert some level of fun, such as playing games like dodge ball, navigating obstacle courses, or taking on new challenges like hiking or ropes courses. These activities can be a great way to avoid monotony and overuse, both of which can lead to symptoms of overtraining. Ultimately, this active recovery period serves as a break for the athlete and offers critical time for the strength and conditioning professional to create a full off-season plan for the athlete.

In the active recovery microcycle the initial focus of the resistance training program is on restorative methods and tissue regeneration or retraining to optimize range of motion and movement patterns. This microcycle typically lasts two weeks and is designed to get the athlete reacclimated to resistance training. For high school, college, and professional athletes, the active recovery microcycle following competitive play can continue to serve as a time to evaluate the results of the season and set up a plan leading into the upcoming off-season mesocycles. The foundation of this plan will evolve from discussions between the strength and conditioning coach, basketball coaches, sports medicine staff, and, most important, the athlete. This microcycle can also serve useful as a time to assess the athlete's current state and developmental potential, which can be derived from movement analyses, athletic testing, body composition, and current training age. Moreover, the microcycle will be helpful in determining a comprehensive plan that will also address basketball-specific skill development needs that are structured around exploiting the athlete's physical strengths on the court and areas that need continued development. This critical part of the postseason phase ensures that the athlete is set up for future success both on the court and in the weight room.

GOALS AND OBJECTIVES

Coaches working with youth athletes need to know how sex and maturation might influence performance outcomes of a resistance program. **Peak height velocity** (PHV) refers to the period during which an adolescent experiences a maximum rate of growth. This developmental period is often also used to determine when resistance training can become more aggressive. Typically, girls experience PHV a couple of years before boys (12 years versus 14 years). Sex does not play a role in resistance training outcomes for pre- and post-PHV boys and girls (17). Both pre- and post-PHV boys and girls should expect strength gains with resistance training.

For direction in initial planning for youth resistance training programs, knowing what programs have been most effective is helpful. Slimani (23) concluded that programs lasting longer than eight weeks seem to work better than those lasting less than eight weeks. The overall focus of the post-season phase, targeting GPP, needs to carry over into the off-season, especially for youth athletes. According to Pietz and colleagues (17), two resistance training sessions per week performed using low to moderate loads at or below 60% of the 1RM for 2 to 4 sets of 6 to 12 repetitions per exercise with properly executed technique is advised for untrained youth (11). Because intensity measures based on the 1RM are difficult to attain with youth athletes, monitoring resistance training programs using velocity or the RPE scale might be best (23).

Again, the high school, college, or professional athlete has likely undergone a period of detraining by reducing the total workload in resistance training sessions toward the end of the competitive season and in the transitional rest and active recovery periods. As a result, total workload begins low and steadily increases. Exercise selection is relatively simple and prescribed under lower load and higher repetitions. Low-load, high-volume workloads induce neuromuscular adaptations that affect muscular endurance (24). Movement practice and tissue modeling and remodeling during the postseason is targeted using lighter loads, moderate to high repetitions per set, and longer time under tension through isometric holds and slow tempo repetitions (while staying away from failure) in which the concentric and eccentric phases are intentionally extended under low loads to facilitate recovery from the intense demands of the season (30).

At this time of year motor learning, or relearning, will be taking place. Athletes will be introduced to new exercises and will be exploring different movement patterns. For motor skill acquisition to occur, specific tasks must be practiced, and automation will be obtained through repetition (12). Repetitions train muscle memory and coordination to find the most efficient strategy to execute a given task. In fact, similar strength adaptations may be observed simply by performing 1RM tests versus performing a higher volume, moderate-load resistance training program that results in hypertrophy (14). Coaches should know that there are age-related differences in central versus peripheral fatigue as it relates to resistance training. For instance, when compared with adult men, prepubescent boys may maintain force output for longer while experiencing less peripheral fatigue but greater central fatigue when performing maximal isometric voluntary contractions (19). With higher resistance to fatigue, younger athletes, who are typically subject to lower resistance training loads anyway, can take on higher repetitions, which may support their need for motor skill and memory acquisition. At the same time, older basketball athletes or those who are not looking to put on muscle size can improve strength performance by practicing the specific action using loads close to a 1RM at a lower volume. In other words, if an athlete needs to improve unilateral lower body function, he or she needs to practice unilateral lower body exercises that stress the preferred function.

After the active recovery microcycle ends, a well-defined, clearly mapped-out plan should be communicated by the coach and understood by the athlete. The athlete should be aware of the upcoming training calendar, what is expected of her or him, as well as what she or he should expect from the strength and conditioning professional. The athlete should also be given the opportunity to openly discuss any pending concerns or questions. This open line of dialogue during the active recovery phase should be welcomed to encourage constant communication and active participation by the athlete in taking ownership of her or his individual development. Forming a partnership with the athlete is a critical yet often overlooked aspect that will largely determine the extent of the athlete's overall development.

Generally, athletes must develop four key components to enhance their overall performance (figure 9.1). These components can be shaped like a pyramid. General physical preparation (GPP) forms the base. GPP, which addresses work capacity, basic strength, and corrective strengthening exercises designed to improve postural and stability issues, is the developmental foundation on which further strength, power, and speed can be built. The primary goal of the entire postseason phase is to establish a sound structural foundation by increasing general strength and stability, while also removing limitations, deficiencies, and imbalances.

The goal of the postseason GPP microcycle is to build up the athlete's strength-endurance. Although a high anaerobic capacity is critical for basketball performance, aerobic mechanisms of energy production must not be overlooked. The aerobic system aids in recovery from anaerobic efforts in basketball (26). Aerobic capacity plays a role in maintaining high power output during repeated high-intensity bouts. This conclusion is supported by multiple sources that have reported an enhanced contribution from the aerobic energy system during high-intensity intermittent exercise (2, 7, 15, 22). **Concurrent training** refers to the simultaneous implementation of both resistance and aerobic endurance training (21). The basketball athlete requires a careful balance of strength, power, and aerobic endurance exercise. As a result, although athletes are participating in a lower load, high-repetition resistance training program at this time, a higher volume of aerobic endurance-related training should be taking place to maximize stamina and aerobic capacity and provide a base on which to train and develop anaerobic capacity.

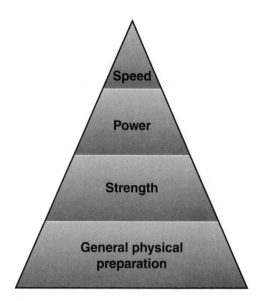

Figure 9.1 Four key components of athletic performance.

Adapted from NSCA, *Basics of Strength and Conditioning Manual.*

LENGTH, STRUCTURE, AND ORGANIZATION

GPP is relevant, even for the athlete with an advanced training background, and will carry over into the off-season mesocycle. The entire postseason phase typically lasts from four to six weeks and should be approached as a preparatory period for more intensive off-season training. Its length will ultimately determine how much time is needed to address GPP in the off-season phase. The initial intent of a GPP resistance training program is to increase work capacity to take on higher workloads in subsequent mesocycles. Although motor learning is achieved through repetitive practice, workloads will continue to progress by increasing training volume under submaximal loads with shorter rest periods. High-volume, moderate-load training elevates blood lactate and serum hormone concentrations and activates protein signaling pathways that may enhance resistance to fatigue (29).

Greater specificity will occur later in the off-season phase. In this postseason phase, however, individual programmatic differences largely depend on training age, preliminary assessment results, and current level of strength. These differences might also alter the types of equipment used or the way in which the load is applied. For instance, it might be determined that trained athletes use barbells, whereas less experienced athletes perform the same movements with dumbbells or only their body weight. Even with isometric training exercises, trained athletes may begin to perform these same basic holds while using external resistance or even performing maximal intensity isometrics against immovable loads.

The GPP and postseason phase should not be viewed simply as a low-intensity recovery period after in-season competition. Neither should it focus solely on aerobic and anaerobic conditioning in the form of running. Resistance training requires higher force production and activates a higher number of motor units than running does (27). Resistance training programs should be challenging and progressively tuned to increase total workload each week leading into the off-season phase.

For muscles to adapt, grow, and take on higher workloads, the postseason resistance training program should begin to address moderate loading and high volumes that push the athlete to volitional fatigue. Muscle remodeling activates satellite cells that stimulate an increase in muscle fiber size (5). Only eccentric and chronic concentric exercise leads to satellite cell activation. So, to achieve a proper training effect, postseason resistance training programs should prescribe exercises to be performed for a longer duration or time under tension.

To achieve a higher peripheral work capacity, **complex sets**, in which multiple exercises are performed consecutively with minimal rest time in between can be used with moderate loads (70-75% of the 1RM). In this season, alternating between agonist and antagonist muscles might serve useful. **Antagonist-paired sets** (APS) is a resistance training technique that alternates sets between antagonist and agonist muscle groups. Preactivating the antagonistic muscles facilitates greater performance of agonist muscles, resulting in increased repetition performance (27). In addition, allowing shorter rest intervals (30-60 seconds) between exercises has been shown to elicit improvements in repetition performance, which makes this technique especially appealing during the postseason phase when endurance is the goal (27).

Circuit resistance training has been shown to improve muscular endurance and aerobic capacity (7). Explosive circuit training, however, might be superior to traditional circuit training for the basketball athlete. High-intensity resistance circuit training has been demonstrated to be an effective mode of training to improve maximal strength and power, as well as shuttle run performance and lean muscle mass (1). Taipale and colleagues (27) showed that when combined with aerobic endurance training, explosive training mixed with maximal strength training was superior to body weight circuit training. More experienced athletes in good physiological condition may then find benefit in continuing to focus on strength-endurance targeting fast-twitch fibers during the GPP microcycle. Trained athletes can use explosive, Olympic movements with a barbell, and novice to intermediate athletes may perform similar explosive exercises with dumbbells. The postseason phase is also a prime time to focus on practicing explosive technique because repetitions are performed under lower loads.

Another reason that the postseason should not be viewed as an extension of the in-season is that preliminary assessments often reveal that muscle hypertrophy and improved body composition are major goals. As a result, the postseason should be used to begin that process and establish a foundation for more intensive and stressful bouts of training to follow in the off-season. Younger athletes and those with thin, underdeveloped frames will need many months to gain muscle. Overweight athletes may also need time to significant improvements in body composition. GPP will carry into the off-season phase (chapter 10), so it is important to begin to note the frequency, workload, and time needed to elicit improvements in work capacity through resistance training.

Other basketball athletes may also be looking to gain muscle mass but often find themselves taking on high-intensity conditioning workloads. Concurrent high-intensity interval training with resistance training might cause interference, however. Sabag and colleagues (21) concluded that the combination of HIIT and resistance training does not appear to influence resistance training-mediated hypertrophy or increases in upper body strength. HIIT, however, may interfere with resistance training-mediated improvements in lower body strength, especially if using cycling modalities. Another advanced technique that can be explored in GPP is a gradual increase in the frequency of resistance training sessions per week to work on multiple skills offsetting interference. Higher training frequencies equate to additional practice. If hypertrophy is the goal, this method might be used to increase total volume.

For highly trained athletes who are interested in improving resistance to fatigue, variable resistance training has been shown to be more effective than traditional resistance training performed using constant external resistance. For example, Walker and colleagues (29) demonstrated that in 10 weeks, subjects participating in both variable resistance training (in which the external resistance changes according to the force-angle relationship) and constant external resistance training improved the 1RM and muscle hypertrophy. In weeks 1 through 4 (which, in this case, could be a large portion of the postseason phase), 2 to 3 sets of 12 to 14 repetitions were completed at 60% to 70% of the 1RM. Weeks 5 through 7 used 2 to 3 sets of 10 to 12 repetitions at 70% to 80% of the 1RM, and weeks 8 through 10 required 3 to 4 sets of 8 to 10 repetitions at 75% to 85% of the 1RM. One minute of rest was given after each set for the duration of the 10-week program. During loading, variable resistance seems to result in a higher amount of total work completed, produce greater acute neuromuscular fatigue, and necessitate a greater hormonal response than constant resistance does (29). Variable resistance is discussed in more detail in chapter 11, which explains how this advanced technique can be used to improve rate of force production.

Overall, the postseason phase should focus on developing a progressive resistance training routine, mastering fundamental movement patterns, and establishing higher work capacity to take on heavier workloads at higher intensities in the upcoming off-season phase. This time offers an opportunity to address any underlying issues that may limit performance and trainability. Athletes need to develop each of the following motor patterns: bilateral, split stance, and unilateral squatting; lunging, jumping, and bounding; hip hinging; horizontal and vertical pulling and pushing; and reaching in multiple planes (i.e., overhead, below, side, and rotational behind). Each of these movements needs to be executed with sound mechanical qualities, both internally and externally.

High School

Because their in-season schedule is shorter and they play significantly fewer games, high school basketball athletes are typically afforded a longer postseason phase than college or professional athletes. A longer postseason is beneficial to young developing athletes because they likely lack significant experience in resistance training and exercise technique. In addition, because they typically possess a large window for development, they can make significant adaptations during this time. Multisport athletes and those athletes participating in spring and summer basketball leagues and tournaments are not likely to have much of a break. In these cases, a one-week active recovery period may take place, followed immediately by the continuation of an in-season resistance training program. In any case, considering that high school athletes generally lack resistance training experience, they have time to make significant neuromuscular improvements over the course of the postseason.

The initial one or two weeks of postseason training should ultimately be geared toward acclimation and establishing movement competency. Week-to-week exercise variation during this phase is not overly critical because positive adaptations will be made by increasing total volume and overall practice of specific tasks they need to learn in order to progress to more difficult tasks later. Extended practice leads to improved skill execution by reducing noise (25). In other words, significant emphasis is placed on high repetitions—while minimizing fatigue—to promote motor learning by repeatedly executing foundational movements with optimal technique. Young, healthy athletes do not need much time to learn basic movement patterns.

Note that fatigue may negatively affect exercise execution and motor learning, so repetitions and recovery times between sets should fit the task. Performing multiple sets of many repetitions within one session could lead to higher levels of fatigue, and thus specific attention is needed to maintain proper exercise technique and to terminate the exercise when technique is compromised (31). Fatigue could create poor technique and learning of bad habits. Given that most high school athletes possess limited training backgrounds, a wide array of exercises may facilitate variability and more well-rounded muscular development, but it should be programmed only after athletes have performed specific tasks that need to be practiced and learned. This mixed approach may create a more extensive base on which more intense and specialized resistance training can be built later in off-season and preseason phases.

College

The college basketball athlete's postseason training schedule is dictated nearly entirely by the success of the prior season. A long run in the tournament may significantly reduce any meaningful time that the strength and conditioning professional must work with athletes in preparation for the off-season phase. In such cases, when limited time is available to devote to a postseason resistance training phase beyond active recovery, it is wise to meet with the athlete, head coach, and sports medicine staff to outline a plan moving forward into the off-season. On the other hand, in the case of a less than successful season, more time can be devoted to training between the end of the basketball season and the close of the academic calendar. The postseason recovery phase may begin as early as one week following the last game.

The first week or two of the collegiate athlete's postseason phase are designed largely around recovery to minimize overall soreness and fatigue. This goal can often be accomplished with training modes used during the season. For instance, research has shown that higher frequency vibration training can effectively reduce perceived muscle soreness. Iodice and colleagues (8) found that high-frequency vibration restored posture and reduced perceived soreness in subjects experiencing delayed-onset muscle soreness after a bout of eccentric training. In this study, 15 minutes of local, continuous vibration at 120 Hz was applied 24 and 48 hours post exercise. Further, Magoffin and colleagues (13) concluded that whole-body vibration that is used as a *warm-up* can serve to diminish delayed-onset muscle soreness caused by eccentric exercise and Veqar and Imtiyaz (28) determined that whole-body vibration that is used *after exercise* has a similar positive effect to reduce muscle soreness.

Following the initial one- to two-week acclimation period, training volume can be increased quickly, especially for athletes approaching their third and fourth years. Exposing athletes to higher training volumes and developing their overall work capacity is critical in setting the stage for a successful off-season. But note as well that recovery between exercise sessions is important at this time when motor learning and repatterning are a major focus. Greater workloads will induce delayed-onset muscle soreness that may affect posture. For instance, hip kinematics can be altered after eccentric exercise targeting the quadriceps because of subsequent changes in center of mass of the head and pelvis (8). Eccentric exercise will be a primary mode of training in upcoming phases, but for the healthy athlete coming off a grueling season it might not be best suited for this time of year when attempting to retrain movement patterns.

Professional

For the professional athlete, resistance training during the postseason phase often focuses on recovery and may last two to four weeks. Depending on the duration of the season, which may include increased demands from additional playoff games, time for a traditional postseason phase may be limited. A successful season at the NBA level may result in more than 100 games played in an eight- to nine-month period. As such, recovery, both active and passive, should likely be prioritized when constructing the postseason resistance training plan. In fact, given that the postseason schedule for a professional athlete may be as short as two weeks, it may be composed entirely of recovery tactics. In such cases, the professional athlete is likely to have enough resistance training experience that little time is needed to learn proper exercise technique. Recovery and GPP can be interwoven to promote rejuvenation after the long season and develop a sound foundation to undergo more intensive resistance training in the off-season phase.

At this stage it is appropriate for the professional athlete to return to fundamental movement patterns to elicit neuromuscular adaptations and restore range of motion. More complex movement pattern combinations can simultaneously incorporate traditional lower body movements with traditional upper body movements. For example, holding a light dumbbell, an athlete can perform a lunge and move directly into a push press. This lunge to press helps to develop motor skills and functional coordination, postural control, and core stability while promoting adaptations to prepare the athlete to handle greater training loads and volumes in the quickly approaching off-season phase.

Techniques that use advanced technology can offer postseason variation to assist in both recovery and growth. **Blood flow restriction** (BFR) is thought to promote increases in strength, muscle mass, and muscular endurance. Over the years BFR has become a novel mode of training that uses pressure cuffs to the proximal portion of the lower or upper limbs. The appropriate amount of pressure applied maintains arterial inflow while restricting venous outflow to the distal ends of the limbs, resulting in metabolic acidosis, intracellular swelling, and an increase in protein synthesis and growth hormone release (18). When research has compared low-load resistance training with BFR with low-load resistance training without BFR, greater gains in strength and size are seen when training with BFR (10). BFR training with low loads ranging from 20% to 50% of the 1RM seem to be most beneficial. Often used in rehabilitation settings when heavy loads are not conducive or when it is preferred that an athlete not take on a high amount of mechanical stress, BFR seems to provide additional benefits. In the same way, loads are typically lower in the postseason phase, making BFR a useful tool to improve localized muscular endurance and hypertrophy.

BFR is a tool often used in rehabilitation protocols. For some athletes, a postseason phase might occur earlier than expected because of injury. BFR might serve as an appropriate method to maintain hypertrophy in both weight-bearing and non-weight-bearing instances. BFR may be applicable during the early phases of healing (4). In any case, BFR may not be suitable for every athlete; therefore, a strength and conditioning professional should consult with a BFR expert, and only a qualified clinician should recommend and apply this tool to an athlete.

Although BFR is a great tool to be used in the postseason phase, it should not be thought of as a replacement to heavy-load resistance training. A recent systematic review and meta-analysis concluded that heavy-load resistance training (>65% of the 1RM) was more effective than light-load resistance training with BFR in eliciting strength gains and comparable in terms of increasing muscle mass (10). As a result, as the athlete moves into the off-season phase, he or she should continue to address strength using traditional methods. When using BFR, the athlete should perform 2 to 4 sets at 30% to 50% of the 1RM to failure, resting 30 to 60 seconds between sets (18). Traditional bilateral and unilateral exercises like a squat or bench press can be used.

More traditional training protocols are used in the sample programming shown in this chapter. As mentioned previously, professional athletes are often more experienced and thus can initiate postseason training with more complex movements. Still, significant emphasis is placed on executing loaded bodyweight movements such as push-ups, inverted rows, and squats. In each example, the professional athlete can likely progress these movements by adding external load using a weighted vest. Again, resistance training takes on its simplest form during the postseason period. The emphasis should be centered simply on performing each movement with perfect technique through a full range of motion, with total load being of secondary importance. As such, much of the resistance training program during this short training block is performed between 8 and 12 repetitions per set using 60% to 70% of the 1RM. Set volume is kept relatively low at 3 sets per exercise. Although this prescription may be perceived as a light training block, it is crucial element in setting the foundation for a productive off-season training block.

CONCLUSION

Postseason resistance training is easy to overlook because it is often the shortest phase of the year. But this phase is an important planning and preparatory period. It should be used to evaluate the athlete's performance in the prior basketball season, his or her developmental status, and the athlete's current needs to create the most appropriate resistance training program in preparation for the off-season phase. Ultimately, the postseason phase may be the most critical of all in terms of developing the roadmap and effectively establishing the athlete's starting point. Resistance training programs consist primarily of the proper execution of fundamental movement patterns and focus on strength-endurance in preparation for the higher demands and specificity that will take place in the off-season phase.

Interpreting the Sample Program Tables

- DB = Dumbbell
- KB = Kettlebell
- RDL = Romanian deadlift
- PAP = Postactivation potentiation
- BW = Body weight
- RFD = Rate of force development
- BB = Barbell
- Order = Perform one set of each exercise (1a, 1b, 1c, and so on) in the group (1, 2, 3, and so on). Then go back to the first exercise in the group and do the second set of each exercise and so on. If certain exercises call for fewer sets than others in the group, perform those sets on the backend of the grouping. For instance, if exercise 1a and exercise 1b call for 4 sets and exercise 1c calls for 3 sets, perform exercise 1c during sets 2 through 4 of exercises 1a and 1b.
- Tempo = The time, in seconds, for each phase or portion of the exercise, written as "eccentric phase: top (or bottom) position: concentric phase" (King, I., How to write strength training programs. In *Speed of Movement*, 1998, p. 123). For example, a tempo of "1:5:1" for the back squat means 1 second to lower, 5 seconds held at the bottom position, and 1 second to stand back up. Note: An "X" means that the athlete should explode during that phase of the movement. A tempo of "X:X:X" is associated with power exercises because there is not a prescriptive time allotted to each portion of the movement.

Table 9.1 Guards: Postseason Microcycle 1, Active Recovery, Weeks 1-2

Total Body Focus (Day 1)

Order	Exercise	Set(s)	Reps or duration	Tempo	Rest
1a	Goblet squat (mobility focus)	3	12-15 reps	1:2:1	<30 s
1b	Inverted row*	3	12-15 reps	1:2:1	<30 s
1c	Reverse hip extension (mule kick)	3	8-10 reps	1:2:1	60 s
2a	DB step-up	2	12-15 reps	2:1:1	<30 s
2b	Push-up**	2	12-15 reps	2:2:1	<30 s
2c	Half-kneeling wood chop, high to low	2	12-15 reps	1:2:1	60 s

*Hold the end position of each repetition for 2 seconds. **Be slow and controlled on the descent and hold the bottom position for 2 seconds with the elbows and shoulders held at 90 degrees.

Total Body Focus (Day 2)

Order	Exercise	Set(s)	Reps or duration	Tempo	Rest
1a	One-arm cable chest press*	3	12-15 reps	1:2:1	<30 s
1b	Side lunge**	3	8-10 reps	1:2:1	<30 s
1c	Single-leg hip thrust	3	12-15 reps	1:2:1	60 s
2a	Straight-arm pulldown	2	12-15 reps	1:1:2	<30 s
2b	Single-leg RDL	2	12-15 reps	2:1:1	<30 s
2c	Side plank (stamina focus)	2	30- 60 s	Iso hold	60 s

*Substitute the one-arm incline bench press if a cable machine is not available. **Hold DB or KB in the front-racked or goblet position.

Table 9.2 Bigs: Postseason Microcycle 1, Active Recovery, Weeks 1-2

Total Body Focus (Day 1)

Order	Exercise	Set(s)	Reps or duration	Tempo	Rest
1a	Goblet squat (mobility focus)	3	12-15 reps	1:2:1	<30 s
1b	Inverted row*	3	12-15 reps	1:2:1	<30 s
1c	Half-kneeling DB or KB shoulder press**	3	8-10 reps	1:5:1	60 s
2a	DB step-up	2	12-15 reps	2:1:1	<30 s
2b	Push-up***	2	12-15 reps	2:2:1	<30 s
2c	Deadbug (with stability ball)	2	15-20 reps	1:3:1	60 s

*Hold the end position of each repetition for 2 seconds. **Perform a 5-second isometric hold in the bottom position with the elbows at 90 degrees. ***Be slow and controlled on the descent and hold the bottom position for 2 seconds with the elbows and shoulders held at 90 degrees.

Total Body Focus (Day 2)

Order	Exercise	Set(s)	Reps or duration	Tempo	Rest
1a	One-arm cable chest press*	3	12-15 reps	1:2:1	<30 s
1b	DB split squat	3	8-10 reps	1:2:1	<30 s
1c	Single-leg hip thrust	3	12-15 reps	1:2:1	60 s
2a	One-arm lat pulldown	2	12-15 reps	2:2:1	<30 s
2b	RDL	2	12-15 reps	2:1:1	<30 s
2c	Side plank (stamina focus)	2	30- 60 s	Iso hold	60 s

*Substitute the one-arm incline bench press if a cable machine is not available.

Table 9.3   Guards: Postseason Microcycle 2, GPP, Weeks 3-4

Total Body Focus (Day 1)

Order	Exercise	Set(s)	Load	Reps or duration	Tempo	Rest
1a	Front squat*	3	50%-65%	12-15 reps	1:3:1	<30 s
1b	Inverted row	3		12-15 reps	1:2:1	<30 s
1c	Prone Y's, T's, I's**	3	1-5 lb (0.5-2.3 kg)	5-6 reps	1:5:1	60 s
2a	DB reverse lunge	3		12-15 reps	2:1:1	<30 s
2b	Push-up	3		12-15 reps	2:1:2	<30 s
2c	Single-leg hip thrust**	3		8-10 reps	1:5:1	60 s
3a	Leg curl (on stability ball)	2		10-12 reps	2:1:1	<30 s
3b	Single-leg RDL	2		8-10 reps	3:1:1	<30 s
3c	One-arm cable row (with rotational reach)	2		10-12 reps	1:2:1	60 s

*Focus on holding the bottom position for 3 seconds. **Hold the end position of each repetition for 5 seconds.

Total Body Focus (Day 2)

Order	Exercise	Set(s)	Load	Reps or duration	Tempo	Rest
1a	Deadlift	3	50%-65%	6-8 reps	Concentric only	<30 s
1b	One-arm cable chest press*	3		12-15 reps	1:2:1	<30 s
1c	Cable D2 pattern—single-leg stance**	3		10-12 reps	1:5:1	60 s
2a	Side lunge***	3		12-15 reps	1:2:1	<30 s
2b	One-arm cable row (with split stance)****	3		12-15 reps	1:2:1	<30 s
2c	Barbell hip thrust**	3		8-10 reps	1:5:1	60 s
3a	Straight-arm pulldown (with hip extension)	2		10-12 reps	2:1:1	<30 s
3b	One-arm single-leg cable RDL (with a row)	2		8-10 reps	3:1:1	<30 s
3c	Plank hold—hand to chest taps	2		10-12 reps	1:1:1	60 s

*Substitute the one-arm incline bench press if a cable machine is not available. **Hold the end position of each repetition for 5 seconds. ***Hold DB in the front-racked position. ****Substitute the one-arm DB row if a cable machine is not available.

Table 9.4 Bigs: Postseason Microcycle 2, GPP, Weeks 3-4

Total Body Focus (Day 1)

Order	Exercise	Set(s)	Load	Reps or duration	Tempo	Rest
1a	Front squat*	3	50%-65%	12-15 reps	1:3:1	<30 s
1b	Inverted row	3		12-15 reps	1:2:1	<30 s
1c	Prone Y's, T's, I's**	3	1-5 lb (0.5-2.3 kg)	5-6 reps	1:5:1	60 s
2a	DB walking lunge	3		10-12 reps	2:1:1	<30 s
2b	Push-up	3		12-15 reps	2:1:2	<30 s
2c	Side plank***	3		8-10 reps	1:10:1	60 s
3a	Leg curl (on stability ball)	2		10-12 reps	2:1:1	<30 s
3b	Single-leg RDL	2		8-10 reps	3:1:1	<30 s
3c	Half-kneeling DB or KB shoulder press****	2		8-10 reps	1:5:1	60 s

*Focus on holding the bottom position for 3 seconds. **Hold the end position of each repetition for 5 seconds. ***Hold position for 10 seconds and then relax and repeat for recommended repetitions. ****Perform a 5-second isometric hold in the bottom position with the elbows at 90 degrees.

Total Body Focus (Day 2)

Order	Exercise	Set(s)	Load	Reps or duration	Tempo	Rest
1a	Deadlift	3	50%-65%	6-8 reps	Concentric only	<30 s
1b	One-arm cable chest press*	3		12-15 reps	1:2:1	<30 s
1c	Deadbug (with stability ball)**	3		15-20 reps	1:3:1	60 s
2a	DB single-leg squat (Bulgarian)***	3		6-8 reps	1:2:1	<30 s
2b	One-arm cable row (with split stance)****	3		12-15 reps	1:2:1	<30 s
2c	Barbell hip thrust	3		8-10 reps	1:5:1	60 s
3a	Straight-arm pulldown (with hip extension)	2		10-12 reps	2:1:1	<30 s
3b	One-arm single-leg cable RDL (with a row)	2		8-10 reps	3:1:1	<30 s
3c	Cable D2 pattern—single-leg stance*****	2		10-12 reps	1:5:1	60 s

*Substitute the one-arm incline bench press if a cable machine is not available. **Hold the extended position for 3 seconds before alternating. ***Hold DB in the front-racked position. ****Substitute the one-arm DB row if a cable machine is not available. *****Hold the end position of each repetition for 5 seconds.

10

OFF-SEASON PROGRAMMING

JOSHUA BONHOTAL AND BRYCE DAUB

The purpose of an off-season resistance training program is to prepare the basketball athlete to handle the intensity of future competition by reducing the likelihood of preventable injuries and optimizing athletic performance. Resistance training for basketball is unique in that it requires a careful balance of both muscular endurance and muscular strength adaptations. To design an effective off-season resistance training program, the demands of the game, style of play, position on the court, and training age all must be considered. Resistance training programs should specifically match the needs of the individual (12, 39, 47). Therefore, the off-season resistance training plan must address the physiological demands of the sport along with the physical strengths and weaknesses of each individual athlete. A well-planned off-season resistance training program will have a profound, positive effect on the basketball athlete's athletic development. If appropriate motor learning has occurred and the skills acquired can be performed repetitively without using compensatory strategies, an effective off-season resistance training program should adequately address external loading, as a stimulus, to maximize strength and power gains.

GOALS AND OBJECTIVES

Because of the complex physiological nature of the sport, off-season resistance training programs must address multiple training variables. Periodized plans containing programming variations within microcycles are likely more effective than nonperiodized plans (44). The primary goal of overall athletic development should be to create more efficient movement. Programs solely focused on movement, however, have limitations regarding the acquisition and application of sport-specific strength and power. If movement has been properly addressed in the postseason phase, athletes will have acquired greater work capacity to take on more difficult skill-oriented tasks, including intense strengthening and highly explosive, basketball-specific exercises with optimal movement strategies.

The primary goals of the off-season phase is to maximize strength and power. The basketball athlete is often subject to the concurrent implementation of both resistance and aerobic endurance training, however. Concurrent training is necessary for the basketball athlete. Unfortunately, time spent developing one quality may hinder the development of another. This interference is a critical element to consider when addressing off-season planning with each athlete. Larger improvements in lower body strength occur with resistance training alone than with a concurrent mix of high-intensity interval training and resistance training (36). Progressive conditioning protocols, which are out of the scope of this book and are not be discussed in detail here, should be implemented throughout the off-season, but coaches should be aware that intensive conditioning programs could limit strength and power gains.

The training components that will be addressed within the off-season phase are strength-endurance, high-load low-velocity strength, rate of force development, low-load high-velocity strength, and reactive strength. Each of these qualities provide slightly different benefits, but all contribute to the overall development of power and explosiveness. To meet sport-specific speeds, it is important to address and improve these components of strength within the resistance training program. Although there is typically an underlying trace of each of the various qualities present in the off-season resistance training program, some are more dependent on others so it is important to maintain focus on one or two qualities within each training cycle to maximize the athlete's development.

LENGTH, STRUCTURE, AND ORGANIZATION

A carefully planned and well-rounded resistance training program maintains a proper balance between the muscular strength and aerobic endurance components while maintaining a primary emphasis on the development of the most relevant strength quality for each athlete.

For the purpose of this chapter, the off-season resistance training programs have been designed to be carried out over a 12-week period. The length of the off-season phase depends on level of play. A typical high school off-season phase lasts anywhere from 12 to 16 weeks, whereas a typical off-season resistance training program for the collegiate or professional athlete lasts anywhere between 8 and 12 weeks.

The off-season resistance training phase can be divided into three microcycles: general physical preparation (GPP), strength, and power. The length of each microcycle depends on the training age of the athlete, his or her specific developmental considerations, and how the athlete adapts in response to training. Understanding how the different strength qualities interact and influence athletic performance outcomes on the court is vital to determining areas of emphasis and progressing properly throughout the off-season program. Every athlete possesses different physical characteristics, physical maturity, training experience, and responses to training stimuli, so different methods can be used to achieve developmental goals. Therefore, the off-season resistance training program must be individualized and progress according to the athlete's current level of development.

General Physical Preparation

The first microcycle of the off-season phase is a more advanced continuation of the postseason phase and continues to address endurance-strength. This period should be relatively short, but note that younger, less developed athletes may spend their entire off-season phase here. For the athlete with a more established training background who is afforded a complete postseason phase, devoting as little as two more weeks to the GPP may be sufficient before moving into the next microcycle. The GPP should continue to focus on improving neuromuscular adaptations with emphasis on fundamental movement patterns, optimization of mobility and core stability, and a concomitant increase in the overall workload. At least two resistance training sessions per week should be completed. Volume should remain high (3 sets × 8-12 repetitions at 70%-75% of the 1RM), and athletes should approach near-maximal effort for the given repetitions.

Load and intensity must be increased in an appropriate and relevant manner. Dynamic warm-up and mobility exercises help improve active flexibility. Core stabilization exercises should concentrate on improving muscular endurance and stability. A higher volume of isometric holds may be highly effective in improving any structural issues and increasing the muscular endurance of postural muscles to maintain appropriate positions during more stressful training (14, 40). Traditional strength and power exercises should focus on developing technical efficiency. Barbell exercises may be used to familiarize athletes with elements of the Olympic lifts and prepare them for later training microcycles provided they have no movement restrictions or other contraindications. When an appropriate strength level supports overall resistance to fatigue, the athlete can transition into the next microcycle, switching focus to developing maximal strength and power.

When programming resistance training programs, consider the frequency of resistance training sessions. Although growing evidence suggests that resistance training volume and intensity may be the primary drivers of adaptation to training, the frequency of training will influence the volumes, intensities, and selections of exercises programmed in each session (13b, 36b). Therefore, the time allowed between resistance training sessions should be carefully planned to allow sufficient recovery of muscles before again placing them under a high amount of stress.

During certain periods of training, the strength and conditioning professional may purposefully choose to increase volume, intensity, or frequency in a manner that challenges the athlete's ability to recover. This period, often referred to as an **overreaching** phase, may lead to greater performance enhancement if followed by a period of reduced training load, a phenomenon known as **supercompensation**. But if training loads are not carefully monitored and are excessive, and the necessary recovery is not allowed, performance can suffer. Over time, overtraining may be the result (12, 39).

Strength

The second microcycle places a major focus on improving maximal strength. The strength phase is initiated after the athlete has appropriately adapted to the objectives outlined in the GPP microcycle and built up enough work capacity. In this microcycle, the focus of resistance training is to improve maximal force production. During this time, training loads should gradually increase to induce the appropriate training effect.

As intensity goes up, total volume typically has to go down while rest times between sets and exercises increase. As a result, a coach should factor intensity into the volume equation when attempting to periodize a resistance training program. Mean **intensity relative volume** (IRV) formula is a simple formula (IRV = sets × reps × intensity) that can be used to calculate overall resistance training loads (30).

The strength microcycle should address the athlete's maximum capacity to generate force, irrespective of time. Ultimately, increasing maximum strength qualities allows improved adaptations during later, more advanced power and speed training, when time becomes a vital component of the force production equation. Loading depends on the athlete's resistance training experience and current state of fitness. Neuromuscular adaptations at the onset of resistance training can cause an increase in strength rather quickly for those just beginning a program with external load. For untrained athletes, loads can be fairly low. Loads at 45% to 50% of the 1RM can be effective in improving dynamic strength in untrained individuals (2), although they may not maximize strength adaptations (23b). For highly trained athletes, loads have to increase progressively. Greater strength gains are achieved working at above 80% of the 1RM at the athlete's 3 to 5RM compared with 9 to 11RM (2).

Resistance training focused on specific muscle contraction phases may be worth considering to help promote further strength gains. Time under tension during isometric exercise and its influence on strength development is often overlooked. Super slow repetitions are not beneficial for the basketball athlete. In fact, super slow repetitions (i.e., longer than a 10-second concentric action) are contraindicated at this time because intentional slow velocities require load reduction (2). Further, super slow repetitions do not necessarily help improve muscle growth (37).

Isometric resistance training has been demonstrated to be an effective method to improve dynamic strength and muscular performance. In the postseason, isometric exercises were introduced, primarily in the form of core stability exercises, executed with high time under tension under little to no external resistance. According to Lee and McGill (27), isometric exercise targeting the core effectively enhances core stiffness and, ultimately, axial load-bearing ability. In the off-season phase, isometric holds also aim to improve lower and upper body strength qualities using lower time under tension under heavier loads to reach maximal, or near-maximal, muscular activation. Ground-based bilateral exercises, like the isometric mid-thigh pull, and unilateral exercises, like the single-leg squat with an isometric hold, can be performed for longer time under tension using heavier loads when held in a static position.

To calculate workload and achieve a favorable response for isometric resistance training, both volume and total time under tension must be considered. Under low volume, maximal isometric exercise may have a potentiating effect. Xenofondos and colleagues (45) found that both three- and six-second maximal isometric contractions (4 sets × 6 repetitions) improved peak twitch torque and rate of twitch torque. In this case, six-second holds had a higher potentiating effect, whereas three-second holds had a longer lasting potentiating effect. In another study using the bench press, Bartolomei and colleagues (8) found that isometric preloading for 1 repetition at 100% of the 1RM resulted in significantly higher power output in subsequent bench presses at 20%, 30%, 40%, and 50% of the 1RM (three-minute recovery period) when compared with a lower load isometric contraction (70% of the 1RM) and a typical concentric contraction. As discussed in earlier chapters, muscle twitch force increases after a brief maximal voluntary contraction (45).

For general improvements in maximal force output, isometric resistance training can be incorporated by adding shorter, three- to six-second holds at or near the end range of either the concentric or eccentric portion of a movement. Holds near concentric end range occur when the athlete is most likely strongest and capable of resisting the heaviest loads. Holds near the eccentric end range occur when the athlete is most likely weakest and most vulnerable to heavy loads, which may also result in quicker onset of fatigue. For the isometric mid-thigh pull, Dos'Santos and colleagues (15) recommend a pull with a 145-degree hip angle. When compared with 175 degrees and 125 degrees (9), the hip angled at 145 degrees allows more rapid force production. Note that isometric exercise at various angles have been shown to have a positive transfer to acute, dynamic muscle strength. Examining the isometric squat, Tsoukos and colleagues (42) concluded that the knee positioned at 140 degrees produced larger increases in subsequent vertical jump performance 6, 9, and 12 minutes after the isometric bout.

The strength microcycle is an opportune time for the athlete to focus on eccentric loading. Eccentric actions involve the lengthening of a muscle, which occurs when the contractile forces generated by the muscle are less than the resistive force. Typically, resistance exercise loads are prescribed based on 1RM strength, which are typically limited by concentric, not eccentric, strength and may therefore fail to address eccentric force capacity appropriately (16). Up until this point in the off-season, load has primarily been dictated by concentric performance and the athlete's ability to overcome inertia. Accentuated eccentric training, however, may enhance adaptations to resistance training (43b), perhaps by promoting central nervous system adaptations related to enhanced cortical drive or through ultrastructural adaptations (28). These adaptations are particularly important when attempting to prevent injury or to rehabilitate an injured muscle or joint.

Eccentric training is the great stimulus for those seeking to maximize strength and is necessary for the basketball athlete. Douglas and colleagues (16) may have summarized it best:

> *Eccentric training is a potent stimulus for enhancements in muscle mechanical function, and muscle-tendon unit (MTU) morphological and architectural adaptations. The inclusion of eccentric loads not constrained by concentric strength appears to be superior to traditional resistance training in improving variables associated with strength, power and speed performance.*

Eccentric exercise offers numerous benefits to the basketball athlete. Eccentric exercise increases muscle cross-sectional area (potentially targeting type II muscle fibers), positively augments tendon properties, and enhances stretch-shortening cycle function (16, 28). Many athletes have neuromuscular control deficits that might place them at a higher risk for injury. For instance, poor neuromuscular control can lead to lateral trunk displacement and abnormal knee mechanics in loading (i.e., landing and planting), increasing the risk of ACL injuries (28). Eccentric strength enhances body control and, in a game that involves frequent, abrupt, and rapid decelerations, can decrease the likelihood of other knee and ankle injuries.

Eccentric strength can be improved using heavy load resistance training (>80% of the 1RM). Depending on strength level and experience, loads can range from 80% to 120% of the 1RM. Because of the heavy loading and nature of the action (e.g., active lengthening), eccentric exercise causes more muscle damage than concentrically based exercise (34). Mike and colleagues (31) conducted a four-week study in which subjects trained twice per week, performing 4 sets of 6 repetitions at 80% to 85% of the 1RM. Three eccentric groups performed the same exercise (Smith machine barbell squat) for an eccentric repetition duration of either two, four, or six seconds. All groups significantly improved their strength and power, but peak velocity during the squat jump decreased significantly in the six-second group, whereas soreness tended to be greatest in the two-second group.

Because eccentric exercise places the highest amount of stress on the joints and muscles and causes a larger amount of tissue damage, it is best used when appropriate postworkout recovery time is available. For example, the novice athlete should not perform a high-volume, heavy-load bout of eccentric exercise the day before a basketball game. Eccentrically induced muscle damage might put the athlete at higher risk for injury, so appropriate volume should be prescribed when juggling different activities around the resistance training program. Under heavy loads (>80% of the 1RM), longer eccentric repetition durations (greater than six seconds) might negatively affect explosive movement, whereas shorter eccentric repetition durations (less than two seconds) might cause increased soreness (31). Delayed onset muscle soreness and performance decrements need to be considered when designing off-season loading patterns.

Behm and colleagues (10) recommend that resistance training should precede power training (e.g., plyometrics) to build a proper foundation of strength. Especially for youth or untrained athletes, the lack of strength can be detrimental to performance. To improve sprinting and jumping ability, youth athletes benefit more from resistance training than power training. Maturity and inadequate eccentric strength affect unilateral propulsion and landing (10). As a result, youth athletes may remain in this strength microcycle for longer periods, perhaps the entire off-season, while still exhibiting great improvements in change of direction and speed.

For more trained athletes, supramaximal loads (above 100% of the 1RM) can be performed with proper supervision. Working at supramaximal loads induces greater force outputs with less time under tension. Eccentric hooks (and other advanced electronic methods) provide a novel way to apply additional load to the eccentric portion of an exercise. In a traditional strength exercise using a barbell, like a squat or bench press, additional weight is added onto two hooks which are then hung onto both sides of the barbell that also carries a specific load, typically based on a percentage of the athlete's 1RM. The weight placed on the barbell is typically less than 85% of the 1RM so that the athlete can effectively manage acceleration in the concentric phase. The additional weight on the hooks, which should be determined with discretion and used only for more trained athletes, can raise the total resistance applied during the eccentric phase to over 100% of the 1RM. As the athlete performs the eccentric phase of the exercise, the hooks contact the floor and at the lowest point release off the barbell, decreasing the load for the concentric phase. The height of eccentric hooks can be adjusted to meet appropriate joint angles. For this mode of eccentric overload, working at 120% of 1RM has been shown to improve concentric power and velocity (32). Note that training with suspended hooks, although effective, is also extremely challenging and potentially more dangerous than other training techniques, so proper prescription and supervision is warranted.

During the strength microcycle, older, more trained high school, collegiate, and professional athletes should begin to incorporate some explosive resistance techniques when appropriate to help develop rate of force development. Although not the major focus, Olympic lifts teach athletes how to apply force into the ground as well as how to absorb force. In fact, Jensen and Jensen (24) have further suggested that including Olympic lifts within the resistance training program may help prepare athletes for the forces of competition. Additionally, given the demand of improving jumping ability with basketball athletes, performing Olympic lifts may be especially valuable because of the similarities in vertical ground reaction forces (19). The volume of plyometrics should also start to increase with a subsequent increase in the intensity of drills as training begins to shift toward power and speed development. In this off-season phase, high volumes of conditioning can have a negative effect on strength improvements and increased force development. As a result, total volume of conditioning should be reduced.

Ultimately, the goal when training a basketball athlete is to build transferrable strength and power and apply it in timely fashion to run faster, jump higher, and change direction quicker. Working under heavy loads results in unintentional slow velocities. Excessive time spent training with heavy loads (>80% of the 1RM) can lead to a decrease in power (20, 21). Working at higher velocities is more effective when attempting to improve power and rate of force development (2). Therefore, when maximal strength appears to be sufficient and does not seem to be a limiting factor to higher performance, total time under tension and volume can be reduced and the program can turn its focus to power.

Power

The final off-season microcycle focuses on power development with an emphasis on movement velocity. The focus during the power phase shifts toward the development of explosive strength qualities. While moving up the developmental pyramid, it is important not to get completely away from maintaining qualities developed in the prior phases of training. As such, higher training loads and fewer repetitions continue to be used to maintain maximal force production. At the same time, greater emphasis is now placed on resistance training using power exercises. Olympic lifts and their derivatives are recommended. These exercises require rapid force production and have been shown to be effective in increasing power output (2). Although traditional resistance training exercises should continue to be performed with loads above 80%, power exercises are executed at lighter loads with careful attention to maximizing movement velocity.

Muscle contraction speed plays a large role in a basketball athlete's explosive strength. Rate of force development (RFD) is the measure of how fast a muscle or group of muscles generates force, derived from the slope of the force-time curve. Resistance training programs that appropriately address rapid force production improve power. Enhancing RFD characteristics is of importance to the basketball athlete, because most dynamic athletic movements called for on the court generate force in minimal time (less than 200-250 milliseconds) (3). As might be expected, increases in contractile RFD are often attributed to improved neural functions (rapid muscle activation, fiber size and architecture, musculotendinous stiffness, and reflexive properties) that occur in response to explosive-type training (29). Additionally, training with heavy loads has also shown to improve RFD, likely as a result of a rise in peak force capacity (26, 29). Aagaard and colleagues (1) suggest that the *intent* to move an assigned load as fast as possible may be more important than the actual speed of movement for inducing gains in contractile RFD. In other words, the first few hundredths of a second take precedence over peak velocity. Tillin and Folland (41) found that explosive contractions were more effective than maximal isometric contractions at improving early phase explosive strength. As a result, although training with heavy loads continues within this microcycle, it is now important to emphasize RFD when training with heavy loads to avoid any detrimental effects to power development.

The major difference between the power and strength microcycles is in the program structure and exercise selection. At this time, heavily loaded exercises must be accompanied by explosive exercises. Loading for traditional resistance training exercises remains high, but movements are quantified with respect to velocity rather than total load. Furthermore, an additional emphasis should be placed on explosive strength by programming Olympic lifts and other power exercises requiring rapid force production, while traditional resistance training exercises such as the back squat and bench press are performed with the intent to move the load quickly. Additional assistance exercises follow these primary exercises to add volume and stamina to the well-balanced program.

Isometric exercises introduced in earlier microcycles, like the mid-thigh pull, can also be used with a focus on rate of force production, or in other words, reaching peak force in the shortest amount of time. In these cases, athletes should be instructed to apply force as fast and as hard as possible to reach maximal or near-maximal contraction in less than 1 second, rest 5 to 10 seconds, and then repeat for the prescribed number of repetitions.

When training with resistance to improve power, both time under tension and volume should be lower than in previous cycles, and both eccentric and concentric RFD should be significantly higher. If not able to monitor RFD, movement tempo should remain under a one second-to-one second eccentric-to-concentric ratio. These faster tempos are more effective in improving power and rate of force development (2). Boffey and colleagues (11) researched different loading patterns for the bench throw on a Smith machine and concluded that performing 3 sets of 10 repetitions at moderate loads elicits fatigue and decreases peak power output after a few repetitions and the fatigue caused a reduction in power at 5 to 7 repetitions at 30% of the 1RM, at 3 to 4 repetitions at 45% of the 1RM, and at 2 to 3 repetitions at 60% of the 1RM (11). Furthermore, 45% of the 1RM seemed to be the optimal load to reach peak power. Athletes with lower levels of relative strength should train for power at a lower percentage (11). In general, when training for upper body power, 3 sets of no more than 4 to 5 repetitions should be used working between 30% and 60% of the 1RM depending on relative strength levels.

Leading into the preseason phase, the off-season resistance training program begins its transition into an emphasis on high-velocity strength, which provides the rationale for decreasing the load. Using light loads in explosive resistance training results in nervous system adaptations that positively affect RFD capabilities (26). Speed-strength can be incorporated into the off-season training program by using exercises that require the athlete to minimize contraction time and maximize RFD and power output.

At some point, especially for more trained athletes, traditional resistance training exercises become limited by concentric strength. Reactive strength is a particularly important characteristic in determining an athlete's success (6). **Reactive strength** can be defined as the ability to tolerate a relatively high stretch load and rapid transition from eccentric contraction to concentric contraction (33). In the eccentric portion of a movement, relatively low loads, executed slowly, deliver lower force output, but when the movement is executed quickly, internal loads can increase significantly. Increasing the rate of eccentric force production with resistance training exercises uses the stretch-shortening cycle better and ultimately leads to better sport-specific transfer.

Ballistic contractions are often performed using plyometric exercises, but resistance training techniques can also improve reactive strength. For instance, **accentuated eccentric loading** (AEL) offers a higher eccentric load over concentric load. When executed in similar fashion to a plyometric exercise, the increased rate of eccentric loading might potentiate concentric performance (43). AEL can be performed using jump squats holding bands in the hands (pulling downward vertically as with the Vertimax) and drop (depth) jumps holding dumbbells. In both instances the resistance is released at the end of the eccentric phase right before the athlete begins the concentric phase.

Although not the focus of this book, traditional plyometric exercises are often included in off-season programming. The volume of plyometric-based strengthening exercises is highly dependent on the athlete's strength, training experience, and conditioning level, so some insight into the appropriate protocols is warranted. For instance, for youth basketball athletes, plyometric exercises (117-183 jumps) performed in conjunction with basketball practice resulted in improved agility and speed, and lower body strength and power, compared with no improvements for athletes participating in practice only (5). For a potentiating effect, 1 set of three bounce drop jumps with 15 seconds of rest after each jump improved 5-, 10-, and 20-meter sprint performance executed at various times after the jump protocol (15 seconds to 12 minutes) (13).

One major goal of resistance training for basketball athletes should be to improve change-of-direction ability. According to Asadi and colleagues (4), basketball athletes seem to respond to plyometric training better than athletes in other sports. Furthermore, the incorporation of combinations of various jumps (countermovement jump, drop jump, and broad jump) has a greater influence on change-of-direction ability than a single type of jump (4). In this meta-analysis (4), the best recommendation regarding frequency and volume was 800 to 1,200 jumps distributed over two or three training sessions per week for six to eight weeks, with a mix of moderate to high training intensities and 60 to 120 seconds of rest between sets. In the absence of basketball practice during the off-season phase, this volume, with mixed intensities, might be suitable for a basketball athlete who performs many rapid accelerations or decelerations over the course of a game and needs to maintain explosive performance over many repetitions.

In terms of jumping, sprinting, and reactive strength, performance can be improved with lower volumes. For instance, Jeffreys and colleagues (23) concluded that a low-volume plyometric program (480 total contacts) was just as effective as a high-volume program (1,920 total contacts) in improving reactive strength within a six-week program. In this case, a mixture of 40 jumps performed twice per week for six weeks might be enough. For trained athletes using

AEL, this volume should be reduced. For children (and perhaps untrained individuals) who will most likely not take part in resisted plyometrics, Johnson and colleagues (25) recommend no more than 50 to 60 bodyweight jumps per session.

High School

Much of the discussion of this chapter to this point has centered on understanding the concept of periodized development without mention of a long-term athletic development model. When working with a young, maturing athlete, like a high school basketball athlete, the entire off-season might need to be devoted to the base of the developmental pyramid, the GPP, and improving strength. Resistance training programs for youth and high school athletes should not mimic those of older athletes with more experience. A young athlete who exhibits exceptional athletic ability on the court will not necessarily demonstrate excellent skill in the weight room. Creating a foundation with enough core stability, sound technique, and strength gains will lead to improvements in power and speed. Repeated exposures to basic movement patterns with a high degree of frequency will have a profound effect on development (18). The adaptations made at this time will stem from repeated exposure to fundamental resistance training exercises and an emphasis on technical mastery. To accommodate the high school basketball athlete, and even older athletes with little resistance training experience, success can be built by using general exercise progressions under higher volume and lower intensities. Positive adaptations to resistance training are built over time, sometimes over years, and as a result, having a long-term developmental plan in mind is critical when writing resistance training programs, establishing exercise progressions, and determining appropriate loads and volume.

The GPP microcycle is an extension of a shorter postseason program that continues to establish a strong foundation and familiarity with resistance training movements and lasts four weeks. For high school athletes, the emphasis may still be on bodyweight to low-load movements and, more important, a purposeful refrain from introducing external loads when technique is lacking. Even bodyweight exercises can be modified to account for the athlete's current strength level. For example, an athlete who is unable to execute a proper push-up from the floor must first be instructed to perform this exercise from an elevated position with the hands on a bench or box or even by pressing against the wall. This approach provides the necessary mechanical advantage for the athlete to establish and maintain proper positioning throughout the movement without any compensation.

Continual progression by adding external load to previously practiced movements begins in week 5. As total load is increased, repetitions per set decrease and total sets increase, depending on the overall strength level of the athlete. By this point, noting the difference between warm-up sets and working sets is important. To achieve a proper training effect (hypertrophy, strength, power, and so on), total volume might, or might not, include warm-up sets. In an example progression, 4 sets of 5 repetitions might be performed at 50%, 65%, 75%, and 85% of the athlete's 1RM. In this case, sets 1 through 3 might be considered warm-up sets, whereas set 4 is a working set. This arrangement is much different from the same progression that prescribes 3 working sets. Three working sets at 85% of the 1RM may have a much different training effect than 1 working set at 85% of the 1RM. Furthermore, for programs for teams, each athlete's strength level affects her or his warm-up progressions. The athlete using 3 working sets will ultimately perform 6 sets including warm-up sets in the progression described earlier. Therefore, prescribing a strict 4-set progression might negatively affect the stronger athlete who might need more sets to progress appropriately to working loads.

The final four weeks of the off-season phase focus on improving power. When movement competency in foundational movement patterns is well established, a shift toward more intensive loading schemes aimed at the development of maximal strength and RFD is necessary. Under heavier resistance training loads, movements now emphasize movement velocity. At the same time, exercise progressions and variations might be used to elicit a more powerful training effect. For instance, with the long-term developmental model in mind, a high school athlete might move from a dumbbell goblet squat (microcycle 1) to a barbell front squat (microcycle 2) to a barbell back squat (microcycle 3), thereby creating a neuromuscular learning curve and transitioning the athlete to take on greater loads in a more challenging environment. Over a few years (macrocycles), training age will increase, and less time will be needed to address the GPP.

College

For more experienced athletes, the GPP turns into warm-ups, and more complex protocols can begin sooner. Highly trained, third- and fourth-year collegiate athletes likely have a longer off-season time to focus on the development of maximal strength and power than less-trained teammates. As the trained collegiate athlete nears the end of the power microcycle, the goal is to have the athlete lifting the heaviest loads at high speeds.

A properly designed off-season resistance training program complements and enhances explosive, plyometric programs. In the preseason phase, external loads in many primary exercises decrease because these movements turn their focus to velocity. The off-season phase should be thought of as a preparatory period for the preseason phase when the athlete takes on an increased volume of plyometrics to maximize the stretch-shortening cycle. Maximizing strength and power are vital to performance outcomes in the preseason phase.

Professional

The status of a professional-level athlete does not necessarily equate with a higher training age, the assumption that he or she is already a strong athlete, or the need to treat these athletes' resistance training programs with more complexity. A young athlete, perhaps still a teenager, is markedly different from an experienced, older veteran in terms of physical maturity and preparedness. A rookie, therefore, cannot be expected to train the same way that a veteran athlete does, and vice versa. Furthermore, two athletes of the same age might have had vastly different resistance training experiences. This crucial factor must be considered when designing the appropriate off-season resistance training program for the professional athlete. Off-season resistance training goals for a young athlete entering professional basketball may require a sharper focus on the GPP and center primarily on getting the athlete acclimated to technique and external loading. On the other hand, for older, more experienced athletes, resistance training might be much more advanced and specific.

Assuming that the professional athlete has acquired a sufficient resistance training background throughout high school and college, he or she likely needs to spend the first one to two weeks of the off-season dedicated to GPP training before diving into more specific training. Those with a more advanced resistance training background can begin the off-season program by targeting more specific, underdeveloped strength qualities they need to compete at the highest level of basketball. As with a young athlete, movement competency and overall joint stability are important for the aging professional but for different reasons that might include, but are not limited to, past injuries and strength deficits. Although load and volume might be vastly different in programming for an 18-year-old rookie compared with a 34-year-old veteran, movements should not become so complex that advancements in strength and power are sacrificed.

CONCLUSION

The off-season phase for the basketball athlete should be dedicated to physical development and inducing positive, holistic changes in strength and power. Regardless of age or level of play, the off-season resistance training program must meet the specific needs of the individual athlete. Exercise selection, frequency, load, intensity, volume, speed, and recovery time are all factors to consider when designing an off-season resistance training program. An effective, 12-week off-season resistance training program optimizes the various qualities addressed in this chapter in a progressive manner so that basketball-specific movements, introduced in later preseason and in-season phases, can be executed in a more efficient and explosive fashion.

Interpreting the Sample Program Tables

- DB = Dumbbell
- KB = Kettlebell
- RDL = Romanian deadlift
- PAP = Postactivation potentiation
- BW = Body weight
- RFD = Rate of force development
- BB = Barbell
- Order = Perform one set of each exercise (1a, 1b, 1c, and so on) in the group (1, 2, 3, and so on). Then go back to the first exercise in the group and do the second set of each exercise and so on. If certain exercises call for fewer sets than others in the group, perform those sets on the backend of the grouping. For instance, if exercise 1a and exercise 1b call for 4 sets and exercise 1c calls for 3 sets, perform exercise 1c during sets 2 through 4 of exercises 1a and 1b.
- Tempo = The time, in seconds, for each phase or portion of the exercise, written as "eccentric phase: top (or bottom) position: concentric phase" (King, I., How to write strength training programs. In *Speed of Movement*, 1998, p. 123). For example, a tempo of "1:5:1" for the back squat means 1 second to lower, 5 seconds held at the bottom position, and 1 second to stand back up. Note: An "X" means that the athlete should explode during that phase of the movement. A tempo of "X:X:X" is associated with power exercises because there is not a prescriptive time allotted to each portion of the movement.

Table 10.1 Guards: Off-Season Microcycle 1, GPP, Weeks 1-2

Total Body With Lower Body Focus (Day 1)

Order	Exercise	Set(s)	Load	Reps or duration	Tempo	Rest
1a	Front squat (eccentric focus)	1	53%	8-10 reps	3:1:1	<30 s
		2	67%	8-10 reps	3:1:1	<30 s
		3	70%-76%	8-10 reps	3:1:1	<30 s
		4	70%-76%	8-10 reps	3:1:1	<30 s
1b	One-arm cable row (with split stance)*	4		8-10 reps	1:3:1	<30 s
1c	Barbell hip thrust hold**	4		8-10 reps	1:5:1	60 s
2a	Isometric pull (in a rack with split stance)***	3		5-6 reps	1:5:1	<30 s
2b	One-arm cable chest press (with step back)	3		10-12 reps	1:2:1	<30 s
2c	Plank hold (with alternating leg lift)	3		15-20 reps	1:2:1	60 s
3a	Leg curl (on stability ball)	3		10-12 reps	3:1:1	<30 s
3b	RDL (with DB)	3		8-10 reps	3:1:1	<30 s
3c	One-arm cable shoulder press (with single-leg stance)****	3		10-12 reps	1:2:1	60 s

*Substitute the one-arm DB row if a cable machine is not available. **Hold the end position of each repetition for 5 seconds. ***Rapidly and forcefully pull bar and then isometrically hold for 5 seconds then relax; repeat for recommended repetitions. ****Face the cable machine and press one handle overhead while standing on one leg.

Total Body With Upper Body Focus (Day 2)

Order	Exercise	Set(s)	Load	Reps or duration	Tempo	Rest
1a	Bench press*	1	53%	8-10 reps	1:3:1	<30 s
		2	67%	8-10 reps	1:3:1	<30 s
		3	70%-76%	8-10 reps	1:3:1	<30 s
		4	70%-76%	8-10 reps	1:3:1	<30 s
1b	DB split squat**	4		8-10 reps	1:3:1	<30 s
1c	Prone Y's, T's, I's***	4	1-5 lb (0.5-2.3 kg)	8-10 reps	1:3:1	60 s
2a	Lat pulldown	3		10-12 reps	3:1:1	<30 s
2b	Single-leg cable hip abduction***	3		10-12 reps	1:3:1	<30 s
2c	Side rotational V-up	3		10-12 reps	1:1:1	60 s
3a	Pallof press (with isometric hold)****	2		5-6 reps	1:5:1	<30 s
3b	Single-leg squat on box	2		8-10 reps	3:1:1	<30 s
3c	Shoulder external rotation	2		10-12 reps	1:2:1	60 s

*Perform a 3-second isometric hold in the bottom position with the elbows at 90 degrees. **Perform a 3-second isometric hold in the bottom position. ***Hold the end position of each repetition for 3 seconds. ****Perform a 5-second isometric hold in the end position.

Total Body Velocity-Based (Day 3)

Order	Exercise	Set(s)	Load	Reps or duration	Tempo	Rest
1a	Deadlift	1	53%	6-8 reps	Concentric only	<30 s
		2	67%	6-8 reps	Concentric only	<30 s
		3	76%-85%	4-6 reps	Concentric only	<30 s
		4	76%-85%	4-6 reps	Concentric only	<30 s
1b	Push press (or jerk)	4		6-8 reps	2:X:X	<30 s*
1c	Bosch hip extension hold	4		8-10 reps	1:5:1	60 s
2a	Step-up	3		5-6 reps	2:1:1	<30 s
2b	One-arm DB row	3		10-12 reps	1:2:1	<30 s
2c	Side plank**	3		15-20 reps	1:5:1	60 s
3a	Hamstring slide	2		10-12 reps	1:1:1	<30 s
3b	Straight-arm pulldown (with hip extension)	2		10-12 reps	1:1:1	<30 s
3c	Single-leg squat to reach	2		10-12 reps	1:1:1	60 s

*The rest period is short because the athlete moves from a functional performance-based exercise (push press) to a more isolated injury prevention exercise (Bosch hip extension hold). **Hold position for 5 seconds and then relax and repeat for recommended repetitions.

Table 10.2 Bigs: Off-Season Microcycle 1, GPP, Weeks 1-2

Total Body With Lower Body Focus (Day 1)

Order	Exercise	Set(s)	Load	Reps or duration	Tempo	Rest
1a	Front squat (sit down to box; eccentric focus)	1	53%	8-10 reps	3:1:1	<30 s
		2	67%	8-10 reps	3:1:1	<30 s
		3	70%-76%	8-10 reps	3:1:1	<30 s
		4	70%-76%	8-10 reps	3:1:1	<30 s
1b	Half-kneeling one-arm cable row*	4		8-10 reps	1:3:1	<30 s
1c	Barbell hip thrust hold**	4		8-10 reps	1:5:1	60 s
2a	DB walking lunge	3		5-6 reps	1:3:1	<30 s
2b	One-arm cable chest press (with step back)	3		10-12 reps	1:2:1	<30 s
2c	Plank hold (with alternating arm forward reach)	3		15-20 reps	1:2:1	60 s
3a	Leg curl (on stability ball)	3		10-12 reps	3:1:1	<30 s
3b	RDL (with DB)	3		8-10 reps	3:1:1	<30 s
3c	One-arm cable shoulder press (with single-leg stance)***	3		10-12 reps	1:2:1	60 s

*Hold the end position of each repetition for 3 seconds. **Hold the end position of each repetition for 5 seconds. ***Face the cable machine and press one handle overhead while standing on one leg.

Total Body With Upper Body Focus (Day 2)

Order	Exercise	Set(s)	Load	Reps or duration	Tempo	Rest
1a	Bench press*	1	53%	8-10 reps	1:3:1	<30 s
		2	67%	8-10 reps	1:3:1	<30 s
		3	70%-76%	8-10 reps	1:3:1	<30 s
		4	70%-76%	8-10 reps	1:3:1	<30 s
1b	Single-leg squat (Bulgarian)**	4		8-10 reps	1:3:1	<30 s
1c	Prone Y's, T's, I's**	4	1-5 lb (0.5-2.3 kg)	8-10 reps	1:3:1	<30 s
2a	Lat pulldown	3		10-12 reps	3:1:1	<30 s
2b	Single-leg cable hip abduction**	3		10-12 reps	1:3:1	<30 s
2c	Side rotational V-up	3		10-12 reps	1:1:1	60 s
3a	Drop step wood chop, low to high***	2		5-6 reps	1:5:1	<30 s
3b	Single-leg squat on box	2		8-10 reps	3:1:1	<30 s
3c	Shoulder external rotation	2		10-12 reps	1:2:1	60 s

*Hold the bottom position for 3 seconds with the elbows at 90 degrees. **Hold the end position of each repetition for 3 seconds. ***Hold the end position of each repetition for 5 seconds.

Total Body Velocity-Based (Day 3)

Order	Exercise	Set(s)	Load	Reps or duration	Tempo	Rest
1a	Deadlift	1	53%	6-8 reps	Concentric only	<30 s
		2	67%	6-8 reps	Concentric only	<30 s
		3	76%-85%	4-6 reps	Concentric only	<30 s
		4	76%-85%	4-6 reps	Concentric only	<30 s
1b	Push press (or jerk)	4		6-8 reps	2:X:X	<30 s*
1c	Bosch hip extension hold	4		8-10 reps	1:5:1	60 s
2a	Step-up	3		5-6 reps	2:1:1	<30 s
2b	One-arm DB row	3		10-12 reps	1:2:1	<30 s
2c	Side plank**	3		15-20 reps	1:5:1	60 s
3a	Hamstring slide	2		10-12 reps	1:1:1	<30 s
3b	Straight-arm pulldown (with hip extension)	2		10-12 reps	1:1:1	<30 s
3c	Single-leg squat to reach	2		10-12 reps	1:1:1	60 s

*The rest period is short because the athlete moves from a functional performance-based exercise (push press) to a more isolated injury prevention exercise (Bosch hip extension hold). **Hold position for 5 seconds and then relax and repeat for recommended repetitions.

Table 10.3   Guards: Off-Season Microcycle 2, Strength, Weeks 3-10

Lower Body Focus (Day 1)

Order	Exercise	Set(s)	Load	Reps or duration	Tempo	Rest
1	Back squat	1	53%-67%	5 reps	3:3:1	1 min
		2	67%-76%	5 reps	3:1:1	2 min
		3	76%-85%	5 reps	3:1:1	3 min
		4	85%-92%	3-5 reps	3:1:1	3 min
		5	>92%	1 rep*	Eccentric only	3 min
2a	Power (or hang) clean (peak velocity of 1.3-1.4 m/s)	1	25%-45%	4-5 reps	X:X:X	<30 s
		2	45%-65%	4-5 reps	X:X:X	<30 s
		3	45%-65%	4-5 reps	X:X:X	<30 s
		4	45%-65%	4-5 reps	X:X:X	<30 s
2b	Barbell hip thrust hold**	4		5-6 reps	1:5:1	2 min
3a	Reverse lunge	3		6-8 reps	2:1:1	<30 s
3b	One-arm split snatch	3		4-5 reps	X:X:X	<30 s
3c	Nordic hamstring curl	3		5-6 reps	1:5:1	<30 s
3d	Birddog hold (opposite arm and opposite leg)***	3		5 reps	1:10:1	2 min
Additional advanced complex—college or pro athlete						
4a	Single-leg RDL	2		6-8 reps	2:1:1	<30 s
4b	Reverse hip extension hold***	2		5-6 reps	1:10:1	60 s

*Perform 5 to 6 total repetitions but take a 20-second intraset rest between repetitions. **Hold the end position of each repetition for 5 seconds. ***Hold position for 10 seconds and then relax and repeat for recommended repetitions.

Upper Body Focus (Day 2)

Order	Exercise	Set(s)	Load	Reps or duration	Tempo	Rest
1	Bench press (eccentric focus)	1	53%-67%	5 reps	3:3:1	1 min
		2	67%-76%	5 reps	3:1:1	2 min
		3	76%-85%	5 reps	3:1:1	3 min
		4	85%-92%	3-5 reps	3:1:1	3 min
		5	>92%	1 rep*	Eccentric only	3 min
2a	Lat pulldown	4		8-10 reps	2:1:1	<30 s
2b	Turkish get-up	4		2-4 reps	Slow, steady	2 min
3a	One-arm cable row**	3		8-10 reps	1:3:1	<30 s
3b	One-arm shoulder press (with split stance)	3		8-10 reps	1:1:1	<30 s
3c	Prone Y's, T's, I's***	3	2-8 lb (0.9-3.6 kg)	8-10 reps	1:2:1	<30 s
3d	Side rotational V-up	3		10-15 reps	1:1:1	2 min
Additional advanced complex—college or pro athlete						
4a	One-arm cable chest press (with step back)	2		8-10 reps	1:2:1	<30 s
4b	Single-leg V-up	2		10-15 reps	1:1:1	60 s

*Perform 5 to 6 total repetitions but take a 20-second intraset rest between repetitions. **Substitute the one-arm DB row if a cable machine is not available. ***Hold the end position of each repetition for 2 seconds.

Lower Body Focus, Velocity-Based (Day 3)

Order	Exercise	Set(s)	Load	Reps or duration	Tempo	Rest
1	Deadlift (average velocity of 0.75-1.0 m/s)	1	53%-67%	5 reps	Concentric only	1 min
		2	67%-76%	5 reps	Concentric only	2 min
		3	76%-85%	5 reps	Concentric only	3 min
		4	85%-92%	2-4 reps	Concentric only	3 min
		5	85%-92%	2-4 reps	Concentric only	3 min
2a	Split squat	4		5-6 reps	5:1:1	<30 s
2b	Side plank (with hip abduction hold)*	4		5-6 reps	1:10:1	2 min
3a	Single-leg squat on box	3		6-8 reps	3:1:1	<30 s
3b	Hamstring slide**	3		6-8 reps	2:1:X	<30 s
3c	RDL	3		6-8 reps	3:1:1	<30 s
3d	Pallof press (with isometric hold)***	3		5-6 reps	1:5:1	2 min
Additional advanced complex—college or pro athlete						
4a	DB walking lunge	2		6-8 reps	1:1:1	<30 s
4b	Single-leg squat to reach (stamina focus)	2		10-15 reps	1:3:1	60 s

*Hold position for 10 seconds and then relax and repeat for recommended repetitions. **Slow and controlled eccentric phase, explosive concentric phase. ***Perform a 5-second isometric hold in the end position.

Upper Body Focus, Velocity-Based (Day 4)

Order	Exercise	Set(s)	Reps or duration	Tempo	Rest
1	One-arm cable row (split stance, with rotation)	5	6-8 reps	1:1:X	3 min
2a	One-arm push press	4	6-8 reps	1:1:X	<30 s*
2b	Wood chop, low to high	4	6-8 reps	2:2:1	2 min
3a	One-arm bench press	3	6-8 reps	2:1:X	<30 s
3b	Cable row into rear deltoid raise (with hip rotation)	3	6-8 reps	3:1:1	<30 s
3c	Single-leg V-up	3	10-15 reps	1:1:1	<30 s
3d	Shoulder external rotation (stamina focus)	2	10-15 reps	3:2:1	2 min
Additional advanced complex—college or pro athlete					
4a	D2 pattern, single-leg stance	2	10-15 reps	2:1:1	<30 s
4b	Birddog plank (opposite arm and opposite leg raise) (stamina focus)	2	10-15 reps	1:2:1	<30 s

*The rest period is short because the athlete moves from a functional performance-based exercise (push press) to a more isolated injury prevention exercise (wood chop).

Table 10.4 Bigs: Off-Season Microcycle 2, Strength, Weeks 3-10

Lower Body Focus (Day 1)

Order	Exercise	Set(s)	Load	Reps or duration	Tempo	Rest
1	Back squat (eccentric focus)	1	53%-67%	5 reps	3:3:1	1 min
		2	67%-76%	5 reps	3:1:1	2 min
		3	76%-85%	5 reps	3:1:1	3 min
		4	85%-92%	3-5 reps	3:1:1	3 min
		5	>92%	1 rep*	Eccentric only	3 min
2a	Power (or hang) clean (peak velocity of 1.3-1.4 m/s)	1	25%-45%	4-5 reps	X:X:X	<30 s
		2	45%-65%	4-5 reps	X:X:X	<30 s
		3	45%-65%	4-5 reps	X:X:X	<30 s
		4	45%-65%	4-5 reps	X:X:X	<30 s
2b	Barbell hip thrust hold**	4		5-6 reps	1:5:1	2 min
3a	Side lunge	3		6-8 reps	2:1:1	<30 s
3b	Lateral DB clean	3		4-5 reps	X:X:X	<30 s
3c	Leg curl (on stability ball)	3		5-6 reps	2:1:1	<30 s
3d	Birddog hold (opposite arm and opposite leg)****	3		5 reps	1:10:1	2 min
Additional advanced complex—college or pro athlete						
4a	Single-leg RDL***	2		6-8 reps	2:1:X	<30 s
4b	Reverse hip extension hold****	2		5-6 reps	1:10:1	60 s

*Perform 5 to 6 total repetitions but take a 20-second intraset rest between repetitions. **Hold the end position of each repetition for 5 seconds. ***Slow and controlled eccentric phase, explosive concentric phase. ****Hold position for 10 seconds and then relax and repeat for recommended repetitions.

Upper Body Focus (Day 2)

Order	Exercise	Set(s)	Load	Reps or duration	Tempo	Rest
1	Bench press (eccentric focus)	1	53%-67%	5 reps	3:3:1	1 min
		2	67%-76%	5 reps	3:1:1	2 min
		3	76%-85%	5 reps	3:1:1	3 min
		4	85%-92%	3-5 reps	3:1:1	3 min
		5	>92%	1 rep*	Eccentric only	3 min
2a	Lat pulldown	4		8-10 reps	2:1:1	<30 s
2b	Turkish get-up	4		2-4 reps	Slow, steady	2 min
3a	One-arm cable row**	3		8-10 reps	1:3:1	<30 s
3b	One-arm shoulder press (with split stance)	3		8-10 reps	1:1:1	<30 s
3c	Prone Y's, T's, I's***	3	2-8 lb (0.9-3.6 kg)	8-10 reps	1:2:1	<30 s
3d	Side rotational V-up	3		10-15 reps	1:1:1	2 min
Additional advanced complex—college or pro athlete						
4a	One-arm cable chest press (with step back)	2		8-10 reps	1:2:1	<30 s
4b	Single-leg V-up	2		10-15 reps	1:1:1	60 s

*Perform 5 to 6 total repetitions but take a 20-second intraset rest between repetitions. **Substitute the one-arm DB row if a cable machine is not available. ***Hold the end position of each repetition for 2 seconds.

Lower Body Focus, Velocity-Based (Day 3)

Order	Exercise	Set(s)	Load	Reps or duration	Tempo	Rest
1	Deadlift (off blocks if needed) (average velocity of 0.75-1.0 m/s)	1	53%-67%	5 reps	Concentric only	1 min
		2	67%-76%	5 reps	Concentric only	2 min
		3	76%-85%	5 reps	Concentric only	3 min
		4	85%-92%	2-4 reps	Concentric only	3 min
		5	85%-92%	2-4 reps	Concentric only	3 min
2a	Single-leg squat (Bulgarian) (eccentric focus)	4		5-6 reps	5:1:1	<30 s
2b	Side plank (with hip abduction hold)*	4		5-6 reps	1:10:1	2 min
3a	Single-leg squat on box	3		6-8 reps	3:1:1	<30 s
3b	Hamstring slide**	3		6-8 reps	2:1:X	<30 s
3c	RDL	3		6-8 reps	3:1:1	<30 s
3d	Cable rotational drop step pull overhead***	3		5-6 reps	1:3:1	2 min
Additional advanced complex—college or pro athlete						
4a	DB walking lunge	2		6-8 reps	1:1:1	<30 s
4b	Single-leg squat to reach (stamina focus)	2		10-15 reps	1:3:1	60 s

*Hold position for 10 seconds and then relax and repeat for recommended repetitions. **Slow and controlled eccentric phase, explosive concentric phase. ***Hold the end position of each repetition for 3 seconds.

Upper Body Focus, Velocity-Based (Day 4)

Order	Exercise	Set(s)	Reps or duration	Tempo	Rest
1	One-arm cable row (split stance, with rotation)	1	6-8 reps	1:1:X	1 min
		2	6-8 reps	1:1:X	2 min
		3	6-8 reps	1:1:X	3 min
		4	6-8 reps	1:1:X	3 min
		5	6-8 reps	1:1:X	3 min
2a	One-arm push press	4	6-8 reps	1:1:X	<30 s*
2b	Wood chop, low to high	4	6-8 reps	2:2:1	2 min
3a	One-arm bench press	3	6-8 reps	2:1:X	<30 s
3b	Cable row into rear deltoid raise (with hip rotation)	3	6-8 reps	3:1:1	<30 s
3c	Single-leg V-up	3	10-15 reps	1:1:1	<30 s
3d	Shoulder external rotation (stamina focus)	3	10-15 reps	3:2:1	2 min
Additional advanced complex—college or pro athlete					
4a	D2 pattern, single-leg stance	2	10-15 reps	2:1:1	<30 s
4b	Birddog plank (opposite arm and opposite leg raise) (stamina focus)	2	10-15 reps	1:2:1	<30 s

*The rest period is short because the athlete moves from a functional performance-based exercise (push press) to a more isolated injury prevention exercise (wood chop).

Table 10.5 Guards: Off-Season Microcycle 3, Power, Weeks 11-14

Lower Body Focus (Day 1)

Order	Exercise	Set(s)	Load	Reps or duration	Tempo	Rest
1a	Back squat (average velocity of 0.5-0.75 m/s)	1	53%	10-12 reps	2:1:X	1 min
		2	67%	8-10 reps	2:1:X	1 min
		3	76%	5-6 reps	2:1:X	2 min
		4	76%-85%	4-5 reps	2:1:X	2 min
		5	40%-50%	2 reps*	1:1:X	2 min
1b	Barbell jump squat (PAP effect)	1	BW	4-5 reps	X:X:X	1 min
		2	BW	4-5 reps	X:X:X	2 min
		3	BW	4-5 reps	X:X:X	3 min
	Accentuated eccentric load	4	20%-40%	4-5 reps	X:X:X	3 min
	Accentuated eccentric load	5	20%-40%	4-5 reps	X:X:X	3 min
2a	Power (or hang) clean (peak velocity of 1.3-1.4 m/s)	1	25%-45%	5-6 reps	X:X:X	<30 s
		2	50%-65%	2-4 reps	X:X:X	<30 s
		3	50%-65%	2-4 reps	X:X:X	<30 s
		4	50%-65%	2-4 reps	X:X:X	<30 s
2b	Barbell hip thrust hold**	4		5-6 reps	1:5:1	2 min
3a	Single-leg squat (Bulgarian)	4		5-6 reps	5:1:1	<30 s
3b	Split squat jump	4		4-5 reps	X:X:X	<30 s
3c	Birddog hold (opposite arm and opposite leg)****	4		5 reps	1:10:1	2 min
Additional advanced complex—college or pro athlete						
4a	Nordic hamstring curl	3		5-6 reps	5:1:1	<30 s
4b	Single-leg RDL***	3		5-6 reps	2:1:X	<30 s
4c	Reverse hip extension hold****	3		5-6 reps	1:10:1	60 s

*Perform 3 to 4 sets of 2 repetitions but take a 20-second intraset rest between sets. **Hold the end position of each repetition for 5 seconds. ***Slow and controlled eccentric phase, explosive concentric phase. ****Hold position for 10 seconds and then relax and repeat for recommended repetitions.

Upper Body Focus (Day 2)

Order	Exercise	Set(s)	Load	Reps or duration	Tempo	Rest
1a	Bench press (average velocity of 0.5-0.75 m/s)	1	53%	10-12 reps	2:1:X	1 min
		2	67%	8-10 reps	2:1:X	1 min
		3	76%	5-6 reps	2:1:X	2 min
		4	76%-85%	4-5 reps	2:1:X	2 min
		5	40%-50%	2 reps*	2:1:X	2 min
1b	Explosive push-up (hands leave ground; PAP effect)	1	BW	5-6 reps	X:X:X	1 min
		2	BW	5-6 reps	X:X:X	2 min
		3	BW	5-6 reps	X:X:X	3 min
		4	BW	5-6 reps	X:X:X	3 min
		5	BW	5-6 reps	X:X:X	3 min

(continued)

Upper Body Focus (Day 2) *(continued)*

Order	Exercise	Set(s)	Load	Reps or duration	Tempo	Rest
2a	Lat pulldown	4		6-8 reps	2:1:X	<30 s
2b	Turkish get-up	4		1-2 reps	Slow, steady	2 min
3a	One-arm DB row	4		6-8 reps	1:2:1	<30 s
3b	One-arm shoulder press (with split stance)	4		8-10 reps	1:1:1	<30 s
3c	Side rotational V-up	4		10-15 reps	1:1:1	2 min
Additional advanced complex—college or pro athlete						
4a	One-arm cable chest press (with step back)	3		10-12 reps	1:2:1	<30 s
4b	Bent-over lateral raise	3		10-12 reps	1:2:1	<30 s
4c	Single-leg V-up	3		10-15 reps	1:1:1	60 s

*Perform 3 to 4 sets of 2 repetitions but take a 20-second intraset rest between sets.

Lower Body Focus, Velocity-Based (Day 3)

Order	Exercise	Set(s)	Load	Reps or duration	Tempo	Rest
1a	Deadlift (average velocity of 0.75-1.0 m/s)	1	53%-67%	5 reps	Concentric only	1 min
		2	67%-76%	5 reps	Concentric only	1 min
		3	76%-85%	5 reps	Concentric only	2 min
		4	85%-92%	3-5 reps	Concentric only	2 min
		5	>92%	1-2 reps	Concentric only	2 min
1b	Box jump	5		4-5 reps	X:X:X	3 min
2a	Side lunge	4		6-8 reps	2:1:X	<30 s
2b	Side plank (with hip abduction hold)*	4		5-6 reps	1:10:1	2 min
3a	Single-leg squat on box	4		6-8 reps	3:1:1	<30 s
3b	One-arm split snatch	4		4-5 reps	X:X:X	<30 s
3c	Pallof press (with isometric hold)**	4		5-6 reps	1:5:1	2 min
Additional advanced complex—college or pro athlete						
4a	Hamstring slide***	3		6-8 reps	2:1:X	<30 s
4b	RDL**	3		6-8 reps	1:2:1	<30 s
4c	Single-leg squat to reach (stamina focus)	3		10-15 reps	1:2:1	60 s

*Hold position for 10 seconds and then relax and repeat for recommended repetitions. **Perform a 5-second isometric hold in the end position. ***Slow and controlled eccentric phase, explosive concentric phase.

Upper Body Focus, Velocity-Based (Day 4)

Order	Exercise	Set(s)	Load	Reps or duration	Tempo	Rest
1a	Seated row (or bent-over row)	1		5-6 reps	1:1:X	1 min
		2		5-6 reps	1:1:X	1 min
		3		5-6 reps	1:1:X	2 min
		4		5-6 reps	1:1:X	2 min
		5		5-6 reps	1:1:X	2 min
1b	Med ball slam	1		5-6 reps	X:X:X	1 min
		2		5-6 reps	X:X:X	2 min
		3		5-6 reps	X:X:X	3 min
		4		5-6 reps	X:X:X	3 min
		5		5-6 reps	X:X:X	3 min
2a	Alternating DB bench press	4		5-6 reps	1:1:X	<30 s
2b	Wood chop, low to high	4		6-8 reps	2:2:1	2 min
3a	Standing one-arm shoulder press (split stance)	4		8-10 reps	1:1:1	<30 s
3b	Prone Y's, T's, I's*	4	2-8 lb (0.9-3.6 kg)	8-10 reps	1:2:1	<30 s
3c	One-arm cable row (with rotation)	4		8-10 reps	1:1:1	2 min
Additional advanced complex—college or pro athlete						
4a	D2 pattern, single-leg stance	3		10-15 reps	2:1:1	<30 s
4b	Birddog plank (opposite arm and opposite leg raise)	3		10-15 reps	1:2:1	<30 s
4c	Shoulder external rotation (stamina focus)	3		10-15 reps	3:2:1	60 s

*Hold the end position of each repetition for 2 seconds.

Table 10.6 Bigs: Off-Season Microcycle 3, Power, Weeks 11-14

Lower Body Focus (Day 1)

Order	Exercise	Set(s)	Load	Reps or duration	Tempo	Rest
1a	Back squat (average velocity of 0.5-0.75 m/s)	1	53%	10-12 reps	2:1:X	1 min
		2	67%	8-10 reps	2:1:X	1 min
		3	76%	5-6 reps	2:1:X	2 min
		4	76%-85%	4-5 reps	2:1:X	2 min
		5	40%-50%	2 reps*	1:1:X	2 min
1b	Barbell jump squat (PAP effect)	1	BW	4-5 reps	X:X:X	1 min
		2	BW	4-5 reps	X:X:X	2 min
		3	BW	4-5 reps	X:X:X	3 min
	Accentuated eccentric load	4	20%-40%	4-5 reps	X:X:X	3 min
	Accentuated eccentric load	5	20%-40%	4-5 reps	X:X:X	3 min
2a	Power (or hang) clean (peak velocity of 1.0-1.2 m/s)	1	25%-45%	5-6 reps	X:X:X	<30 s
		2	50%-65%	2-4 reps	X:X:X	<30 s
		3	50%-65%	2-4 reps	X:X:X	<30 s
		4	50%-65%	2-4 reps	X:X:X	<30 s
2b	Barbell hip thrust hold**	4		5-6 reps	1:5:1	2 min
3a	Single-leg squat (Bulgarian)	4		5-6 reps	5:1:1	<30 s
3b	Split squat jump	4		4-5 reps	X:X:X	<30 s
3c	Birddog hold (opposite arm and opposite leg)****	4		5 reps	1:10:1	2 min
Additional advanced complex—college or pro athlete						
4a	Leg curl (on stability ball)	3		5-6 reps	5:1:1	<30 s
4b	Single-leg RDL***	3		5-6 reps	2:1:X	<30 s
4c	Reverse hip extension hold****	3		5-6 reps	1:10:1	60 s

*Perform 3 to 4 sets of 2 repetitions but take a 20-second intraset rest between sets. **Hold the end position of each repetition for 5 seconds. ***Slow and controlled eccentric phase, explosive concentric phase. ****Hold position for 10 seconds and then relax and repeat for recommended repetitions.

Table 10.6 Bigs: Off-Season Microcycle 3, Power, Weeks 11-14 *(continued)*

Upper Body Focus (Day 2)

Order	Exercise	Set(s)	Load	Reps or duration	Tempo	Rest
1a	Bench press (average velocity of 0.5-0.75 m/s)	1	53%	10-12 reps	2:1:X	1 min
		2	67%	8-10 reps	2:1:X	1 min
		3	76%	5-6 reps	2:1:X	2 min
		4	76%-85%	4-5 reps	2:1:X	2 min
		5	40%-50%	2 reps*	2:1:X	2 min
1b	Med ball overhead wall throw (bilateral stance; PAP effect)	5	15-30 lb (6.8-13.6 kg)	5-6 reps	X:X:X	3 min
2a	Lat pulldown	4		6-8 reps	2:1:X	<30 s
2b	Turkish get-up	4		1-2 reps	Slow, steady	2 min
3a	One-arm DB row	4		6-8 reps	1:2:1	<30 s
3b	One-arm shoulder press (with split stance)	4		8-10 reps	1:1:1	<30 s
3c	Side rotational V-up	4		10-15 reps	1:1:1	2 min
Additional advanced complex—college or pro athlete						
4a	One-arm cable chest press (with step back)	3		10-12 reps	1:2:1	<30 s
4b	Standing one-arm cable rear raise	3		10-12 reps	1:2:1	<30 s
4c	Single-leg V-up	3		10-15 reps	1:1:1	60 s

*Perform 3 to 4 sets of 2 repetitions but take a 20-second intraset rest between sets.

Lower Body Focus, Velocity-Based (Day 3)

Order	Exercise	Set(s)	Load	Reps or duration	Tempo	Rest
1a	Isometric mid-thigh pull	1	75% effort	4- 5 reps	Concentric only	1 min
		2	85% effort	4-5 reps	Concentric only	1 min
	Max RFD; pull hard and fast	3	100% effort	4-5 reps	Concentric only	2 min
	Max RFD; pull hard and fast	4	100% effort	3-5 reps	Concentric only	2 min
	Max RFD; pull hard and fast	5	100% effort	1-2 reps	Concentric only	2 min
1b	Box jump	1		4-5 reps	X:X:X	1 min
		2		4-5 reps	X:X:X	2 min
		3		4-5 reps	X:X:X	3 min
		4		4-5 reps	X:X:X	3 min
		5		4-5 reps	X:X:X	3 min
2a	DB side lunge	4		6-8 reps	2:1:X	<30 s
2b	Side plank (with hip abduction hold)*	4		5-6 reps	1:10:1	2 min
3a	Single-leg squat on box	4		6-8 reps	3:1:1	<30 s
3b	One-arm split snatch	4		4-5 reps	X:X:X	<30 s
3c	Cable rotational drop step pull overhead**	4		5-6 reps	1:3:1	2 min
Additional advanced complex—college or pro athlete						
4a	Hamstring slide***	3		6-8 reps	2:1:X	<30 s
4b	RDL***	3		6-8 reps	1:2:1	<30 s
4c	Single-leg squat to reach (stamina focus)	3		10-15 reps	1:2:1	60 s

*Hold position for 10 seconds and then relax and repeat for recommended repetitions. **Hold the end position of each repetition for 3 seconds. ***Slow and controlled eccentric phase, explosive concentric phase.

Table 10.6 Bigs: Off-Season Microcycle 3, Power, Weeks 11-14 *(continued)*

Upper Body Focus, Velocity-Based (Day 4)

Order	Exercise	Set(s)	Load	Reps or duration	Tempo	Rest
1a	Bent-over row (or seated row)	1		5-6 reps	1:1:X	1 min
		2		5-6 reps	1:1:X	1 min
		3		5-6 reps	1:1:X	2 min
		4		5-6 reps	1:1:X	2 min
		5		5-6 reps	1:1:X	2 min
1b	Med ball slam	1		5-6 reps	X:X:X	1 min
		2		5-6 reps	X:X:X	2 min
		3		5-6 reps	X:X:X	3 min
		4		5-6 reps	X:X:X	3 min
		5		5-6 reps	X:X:X	3 min
2a	Alternating DB bench press	4		5-6 reps	1:1:X	<30 s
2b	Wood chop, high to low	4		6-8 reps	2:2:1	2 min
3a	Standing one-arm shoulder press (bilateral neutral stance)	4		8-10 reps	1:1:1	<30 s
3b	Prone Y's, T's, I's*	4	2-8 lb (0.9-3.6 kg)	8-10 reps	1:2:1	<30 s
3c	One-arm cable row (with rotation)	4		8-10 reps	1:1:1	2 min
Additional advanced complex—college or pro athlete						
4a	D2 pattern, single-leg stance	3		10-15 reps	2:1:1	<30 s
4b	Birddog plank (opposite arm and opposite leg raise)	3		10-15 reps	1:2:1	<30 s
4c	Shoulder external rotation (stamina focus)	3		10-15 reps	3:2:1	60 s

*Hold the end position of each repetition for 2 seconds.

11

PRESEASON PROGRAMMING

NIC HIGGINS AND SCOTT THOM

As athletes begin to approach their basketball season, their preseason resistance training should reflect the sport- and position-specific demands so that they can attain the highest transfer of training from the weight room to the court. The preseason mesocycle bridges basketball performance with physical qualities developed in previous mesocycles to elicit the highest performance on the court. This chapter discusses more advanced methods of resistance training to apply throughout the preseason phase, as well as provides programming recommendations for basketball athletes competing at the high school, college, and professional levels.

GOALS AND OBJECTIVES

The complex nature of the game of basketball requires the improvement of strength, power, and aerobic endurance. As basketball athletes begin to increase workload on the court—by the addition of practice, scrimmages, or conditioning—during the preseason, concurrent training in the weight room develops strength and power to prepare them for the physical demands of jumping, cutting, and sprinting. A study by Balabinis and colleagues (1) examined basketball athletes in the preseason phase and determined that concurrent training can significantly increase strength, power, and aerobic endurance during the preseason if the program is properly structured.

For the basketball athlete, although aerobic endurance is extremely important, preseason strengthening programs can still be effective using a concurrent training model. Note that in the previously mentioned study (1), athletes performed aerobic endurance training in the morning and did resistance training seven hours later. It is important to provide appropriate rest between resistance training sessions and basketball activities for both recovery and performance. If strength and power gains are a primary goal, resistance training sessions should take place before conditioning events, but separating skill sessions and conditioning sessions might be most beneficial to allow more complete recovery and limit interference.

During the preseason, resistance training programs increase in intensity and address the development of strength across the entire force-velocity curve while maintaining a balance between power development and basketball-specific conditioning. As a result, the preseason phase should remain relatively short, lasting only four to six weeks regardless of level of play. The off-season should be a longer period that is focused on physical development, where earlier phases of a macrocycle should not have to account for a detrimentally high volume of basketball demands. Unlike other resistance training phases, the preseason introduces a higher volume of basketball-related activities. Therefore, most basketball athletes preparing for the basketball season are taking on high workloads, in both sporting activities and resistance training activities. Athletes are required to complete both resistance training sessions and all basketball activities, causing the preseason mesocycle to align and complement sport-specific skill development.

With appropriate progression, athletes should have completed previous mesocycles focusing on aerobic endurance, hypertrophy, maximal strength, and power. After athletes have completed an off-season resistance training program that has addressed these components, the preseason resistance training program should focus on the athlete's ability to use the stretch-shortening cycle, boosting the athlete's ability to produce high amounts of force in very short periods. As a result, the primary focus is placed on movement velocity to convert the strength and power they have developed in previous mesocycles into more sport-specific reactive strength and explosiveness. A thorough knowledge of basketball requirements is central to the proper selection of programming methods, including frequency, exercise selection, intensity, volume, and other strength and conditioning parameters for preseason training.

LENGTH, STRUCTURE, AND ORGANIZATION

Resistance training sessions during the preseason phase should consist of a minimum of one to two total body resistance training sessions per week. Although determining the optimal frequency of resistance training sessions is difficult because of variables such as exercise selection, volume, intensity, training status, and so on with the increase in basketball-related activities and workload during the preseason phase, reducing the resistance training volume from previous off-season cycles allows the athlete to acclimate to the increase in total workload. Untrained athletes will benefit from two to three resistance training sessions per week (15). More trained athletes who need to continue to build strength and size should work out more often using total body sessions or resistance training sessions focused on the upper and lower body split over four days per week. In any case, these recommendations on frequency are only for resistance training sessions aimed to improve strength and power and do not include the additional conditioning, agility, change-of-direction, plyometrics, and speed drills that also need to be written into the overall strength and conditioning program. Therefore, in general, one or two resistance training sessions focused solely on strength and power will suffice to improve performance for younger, untrained athletes. Intermediate and trained athletes can perform power training three to four times per week, while retaining strength with one to two sessions per week (15).

With increased basketball workloads during this phase, resistance training should not only improve basketball performance but also build on a foundation to support durability and the ability to handle the demands of an entire season. As a result, resistance training programs are altered by manipulating the exercise order, intensity, and volume to elicit improvements in power and proper transfer onto the court. Workouts should be structured to include one to three primary exercises and two to four assistance exercises to provide power and strength development, as well as structural balance. In general, preseason resistance training programs should include robust, multijoint exercises that recruit muscles in a coordinated manner, similar to movement patterns associated with basketball. Foundational movements such as squatting and deadlifting, as well as unilateral lower body exercises and upper body exercises in the sagittal, frontal, and transverse planes, remain appropriate in the preseason phase. This approach allows the athlete to continue to build on previously developed stability, strength, and power. In addition, with the preseason emphasis on improving basketball-specific explosiveness, routines now emphasize Olympic movements and their derivatives, loaded jumps, and other velocity-based exercises that athletes can complete with high technical efficiency.

Assistance exercises selected in the preseason resistance training program should focus on areas that assist in basketball performance and, more important, support overall muscle function and strength to prepare the body to endure an entire season. Programs need to maintain a careful balance between sport-specific explosiveness and general strength that includes a selection of assistance exercises.

Methods of structuring a preseason program can include clusters, complex, and contrast set and repetition schemes. The **cluster method**, which involves short rest intervals between smaller groupings of repetitions has shown to be beneficial to programs that aim to maximize power and velocity (5, 6). Brief rest periods usually lasting 15 to 45 seconds between sets of 1 to 3 repetitions increase power output in subsequent sets. Phosphocreatine and ATP stores are at least partially restored during these recovery periods. Traditional resistance training sets and repetition schemes may be configured such as 3×10, 4×6, or 5×5. Athletes perform the repetitions within each set consecutively, without any rest between repetitions. As athletes perform the sets, however, fatigue accumulates and leads to a reduction in power and velocity (5, 6). The cluster method splits sets into multiple intrasets. For example, instead of performing 1 set of 10 repetitions, the athlete performs 5 intrasets of 2 repetitions while taking a brief, 15-second rest after each intraset. After completing the 5 intrasets (e.g., a cluster set), the athlete takes a long 3- to 4-minute break to recover fully before completing another cluster set. This method allows athletes to complete repetitions with greater velocities and power output, as well as better technique, because the rest provides the athletes the ability to recover, reset, and complete quality movements.

Cluster training can be broken down into three variations in terms of intensity prescribed during the set: standard, undulating, and ascending (8). In the standard method, athletes complete the entire set using the same load throughout. The undulating method is completed in pyramid fashion in which the load is manipulated to increase and then decrease, which theoretically may take advantage of postactivation potentiation. Lastly, in the ascending method the load is increased throughout the intraset. Note that these methods should be applied to athletes who have a foundation of resistance training experience and appropriate strength levels (8).

Postactivation potentiation (PAP) is the enhancement of neuromuscular performance that occurs in response to a near-maximal load stimulus (12, 19). In other words, to elicit the PAP response, the athlete performs an exercise requiring a maximal or near-maximal muscle contraction before typically performing a more explosive, bodyweight exercise. The acute neuromuscular alterations caused by the first, near-maximal or maximal exercise elicit a potentiating effect by phosphorylating myosin regulatory light chains, increasing calcium release from the sarcoplasmic reticulum, and perhaps by enhancing the recruitment of type II motor units, thus improving muscular performance (2, 10). For example, a near-maximal load squat may improve subsequent countermovement jump performance.

Complex and contrast sets use PAP by pairing a heavy resistance training exercise with a plyometric exercise. These methods can be beneficial during the preseason phase when the goal is to maximize sport-specific explosiveness. Combining heavy resistance training with plyometric training can improve stretch-shortening capabilities and ultimately increase power (8). **Complex training** involves the completion of all the heavy sets first followed by lighter power and plyometric exercises (3b). **Contrast training** alternates between heavy and light exercises each set; the athlete performs a heavy resistance training exercise (i.e., a back squat) and then a biomechanically similar plyometric exercise (i.e., a countermovement vertical jump) (3b). Both types of training seem to take advantage of the PAP response. Older, more skilled athletes seem to benefit more from complex training (9). Less-skilled athletes may not be using heavy enough loads to elicit a PAP response. Moreover, having these athletes complete exercises under heavy loads may not be safe if they cannot execute them properly. In addition, weaker athletes may experience greater fatigue and be unable to recover before the subsequent plyometric exercises (11).

The **French contrast method** combines four exercises and alternates between heavy and light loads. According to Hernandez-Preciado (9), the French contrast method combines a near-maximal resistance exercise, a plyometric exercise, a velocity-based resistance exercise, and a reactive (short ground contact time) plyometric exercise. For example, a basketball athlete might perform a heavy back squat paired with a box jump and then move into a barbell jump squat paired with a band-assisted repetitive countermovement vertical jump. Hernandez-Preciado and colleagues (9) examined the acute effects of the French contrast method on vertical jump performance using an isometric partial squat (85% of the 1RM for a three-second hold), three drop jumps, three dynamic squats at 50% of the 1RM, and three hurdle jumps (50 cm [20 in.] high), resting 20 seconds after each exercise. Posttesting revealed significant improvements in countermovement jump height.

Note that these set schematics used to induce a PAP response are reserved for athletes with advanced training experience, greater fast-twitch fiber distribution, greater strength capabilities, and lower power-to-strength ratios (7). Again, recovery time between exercises can have either a positive or negative effect. If not instituted properly, both complex and contrast sets can often turn into metabolic conditioning circuits and result in a completely different training effect. Recovery intervals of five to seven minutes and single-set maximal training is more effective at inducing a PAP response in stronger athletes, but weaker athletes respond better to longer recovery intervals (over 8 min) and multiple sets of submaximal training (17).

Because the PAP response may be highly dependent on the individual, Gołaś (4) recommends experimenting with rest times between 2 and 12 minutes. Regardless, care must be taken that the manner in which an exercise is performed does not create a fatiguing effect. According to Seitz and Haff (17), when using a squat to evoke the PAP response, shallower depth has a greater effect regardless of the athlete's strength level. They mention that isometrics also cause a negative effect. The study conducted by Hernandez-Preciado and colleagues (9) used only 1 repetition for the initial isometric squat exercise at a partial, self-selected depth.

When using these methods, the first movement should be properly loaded with intensities greater than 80% of the 1RM to provide sufficient load to potentiate the following exercises. Depending on the method used, the second exercise may be completed as a ballistic bodyweight plyometric or loaded exercise like a barbell jump squat in the power ranges of 30% to 50% of the 1RM. Other contrast pairings that can be implemented during the preseason phase are barbell lunges with bodyweight split squats, barbell bench press with medicine ball chest passes, and RDLs with resisted horizontal broad jumps. Remember that the movements should be similar in muscles recruited and ranges and planes of movement.

Young or inexperienced athletes may not have the strength required to complete advanced methods such as complex or contrast methods, so training focused on traditional strength and power development may be more appropriate. If this is the case, explosive and ballistic exercises should be programmed first within the workout before the athlete completes the heavier, primary strength exercises; assistance exercises should be performed near the end of the program, so that fatigue does not compromise power and strength development.

In many instances, coaches might find that multiple skills need to be addressed but total training time per session is limited. When under time constrictions, younger athletes and, especially, less-skilled athletes in large team settings still can benefit from purposeful supersets. While in these settings, strength gains remain a major priority. Motor learning and functional movement patterns still need to be addressed, and when under time constraints, complex and contrast set schematics can be an efficient programming strategy. When programming these methods for movement-based protocols for younger or less-experienced athletes, resistance training exercises can be coupled with plyometric exercises with an emphasis on optimal technique, mobility, and stability. Providing enough recovery between sets is still essential, but active rests can address movement competency with additional mobility or stability exercises. To prevent fatigue, keep volume of intense activities low. An example of an adjusted contrast set in this scenario would be to move from a primary lower body exercise (i.e., front squat) to an explosive plyometric (i.e., box jump) followed by a hip mobility exercise (i.e., hip flexor or quad stretch) tied in as an active rest. Athletes with a higher training age and greater fitness may be able to complete the subsequent exercises with shorter rest because they may recover quicker (11).

Volume

The volume of basketball-specific activity during the preseason may influence the timing, frequency, volume, and intensity of resistance training sessions. For a resistance training session before practice, a coach might keep the intensity high but reduce the volume, ensuring that the primary exercises are completed. Alternatively, for a session after a demanding practice, resistance training may take on a higher volume at a lower intensity and focus more on assistance exercises. The coach must make informed choices and appropriate adjustments to the training session depending on the basketball schedule and demands.

Preseason resistance training is always challenging because of the scheduling and workloads of basketball or other sports, but the fact is that this phase remains the most important time to prepare the basketball athlete to meet the physical demands of the upcoming season.

Intensity

While training during the preseason phases, intensities should be assigned based on training goals and adaptations such as increasing force, developing strength, and training for power and velocity. As previously discussed, during this phase a training session may include training sets across the force-velocity curve or use methods to elicit power development by combining exercises with different intensity loading. During this phase the athlete may be able to complete more repetitions than prescribed for primary exercises. Previous phases focused on aerobic endurance, hypertrophy, and in later stages, absolute strength, all of which featured higher volumes and slower movement velocities, eliciting fatigue. Thus, the adaptations result in a resistance to fatigue. The major focus of preseason resistance training is acceleration and speed-strength. Therefore, although the quality of training remains intact, reducing total volume during this phase becomes important. Each repetition should focus on explosiveness with the intent to move as fast as possible.

Assistance work in the preseason is included for the maintenance of hypertrophy and muscular endurance. For assistance exercises, athletes should complete 1 to 3 sets of 8 to 12 repetitions.

Velocity-Based Training

Velocity-based training is an advanced resistance training method that allows the coach to designate target speeds to elicit a desired training effect and regulates load based on the athlete's ability to accelerate the resistance. Whether the goal of the preseason program remains absolute strength or switches focus to power and explosiveness, velocity-based resistance training serves as a preferred preseason training method for the explosive basketball athlete. Training to improve rate of force development and power output with the assistance of external feedback provides insight into the athlete's current state of training and the appropriateness of the load being applied. The feedback helps to autoregulate intensity and, in a team environment, it can become an important motivational tactic.

When implementing velocity-based resistance training, using different training zones allows coaches to select velocity targets to help train the desired training adaptation (figure 11.1). During earlier phases, coaches focus on movements under higher loads while still paying attention to the lower velocity output. For example, rather than prescribing a percentage of the athlete's 1RM, a coach who wants to focus on accelerative strength can select a target velocity range between 0.45

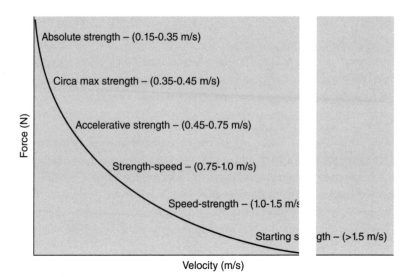

Figure 11.1 Velocity-based training curve.

Reprinted by permission from NSCA, Advanced Power Technic~~s, D.N. French, in~~ *Developing Power*, edited by M. McGuigan (Champaign, IL: H~~u~~~~n Kinetics, 2017),~~ 191.

and 0.75 m/s. Traditional sets of 4 to 6 sets of 3 to 5 repetitions m   ht still be instituted, but the load depends on the athlete's ability to move the most amount of   istance at that speed. As the athlete progresses into the preseason phase, loads and volume can b   nanipulated according to the athlete's current state. Target zones shift toward lower loads execu   at higher velocities, moving from maximal and accelerative strength to strength-speed and sp   l-strength.

When completing the Olympic lifts and their derivatives, peak   locity during the concentric portion of the movement (table 11.1) should be recorded rather   n average velocity, which is traditionally used for the bench press, squat, and deadlift (or their   ations) (13). With this infor- mation and an understanding of the demands of the Olympic li   training with lower volume loads for 2 to 5 sets is recommended to generate maximum peak   ocity. These movements are intended to be explosive and should not be trained in or to failur

The experienced athlete preparing for high-level competition   displays sufficient strength and power might require more advanced methods of training tha   n be introduced during the preseason phase. For instance, accentuated eccentric loading in   p jumps has been shown to improve performance. Bridgeman and colleagues (2) observed that   et of five drop jumps holding a load of 20% body mass was more effective for improving count   ovement jump performance than performing the drop jumps unloaded. To perform a drop ju   with accentuated eccentric load, the athlete holds, for instance, dumbbells in each hand and d   s down to the ground. After landing, the athlete lets the dumbbells go and performs an unloa   vertical jump. The external resistance produces an eccentric overload that is thought to enha   e neuromuscular activation. Moreover, habitual accentuated eccentric loading has been showr   elicit greater improvements in strength, power, reactive strength, and sprinting performance

Variable Resistance Training

Another advanced method that can be implemented in the presea   phase is variable resistance. Variable resistance, frequently implemented in free-weight exerc   with steel chains or elastic bands, delivers more dynamic loading throughout the range of n   ion of a movement. Chains, for example, carry a higher load when hanging off the floor, t   cally when a muscle is in a

Table 11.1 Peak Velocities for the Olympic Lifts and Their Derivatives

Exercise	Peak velocity
Snatch from floor	1.52-1.67 m/s
Snatch power pull	1.81 m/s
Snatch power shrug	1.45 m/s
Hang snatch	1.96 m/s
Power clean	1.2-1.32 m/s
Hang clean	1.3-1.4 m/s
Power shrug	1.15 m/s

Reprinted by permission from J. B. Mann, "Power and Bar Velocity Measuring Devices and Their Use for Autoregulation," *NSCA's Hot Topic Series*, 2011.

stronger position to deliver a higher force output. Using a squat to 90 degrees as an example, as the athlete descends and the lower body muscles lengthen, the chains fall onto the ground and the load decreases. In the bottom position, when the lower body muscles are in a lengthened and weakened position, the load reaches its lowest point, making it more manageable for the athlete to change direction and begin the ascent. As the athlete ascends, the chains are gradually lifted off the floor and the load increases. As a result, the athlete encounters his or her highest loads in a more extended position, coincidentally when the lower body muscles are able to deliver more force.

Variable resistance training offers a greater training stimulus than traditional resistance training, having the ability to induce greater improvements in strength, velocity, and power (16). Rivière and colleagues (16) offer the following possible reasons for this training effect: (a) Higher initial loads may increase muscle activation and the recruitment of larger motor units, and (b) variable resistance may result in greater elastic energy storage during the eccentric phase that results in greater release of energy when transitioning to the concentric phase.

Variable resistance has been shown to induce greater constant acceleration throughout the concentric portion of the exercise by reducing the deceleration that typically occurs toward the end of the concentric phase and increasing muscle tension. Furthermore, at the lowest point of an exercise the muscles are lengthened and the joints are at a mechanical disadvantage. At this point, a loss of velocity is observed (18). When placed under heavy loads the muscles must work much harder. Variable resistance may also serve as a useful in-season method when trying to limit muscle damage and soreness, because mechanical stress is lower in the most weakened position.

High School

High school athletes most likely have low to moderate experience and low technical skills in resistance training. Furthermore, they typically take on a daily schedule that includes academics, extracurricular events, and basketball-specific activities while in this resistance training phase. As a result, exercise selection, load, intensity, and volume should be programmed appropriately while considering the athlete's training age and experience in the weight room. Properly designed resistance programs often follow linear or undulated progressions with a major focus on technique. This approach allows the athlete to establish movement patterns, gain confidence, and build a foundation of fitness and strength before engaging in more advanced methods of training. Finding opportunities to schedule the resistance training program before school, during physical education class, or after basketball practice is a challenge that can be met with appropriate communication.

High school basketball athletes' preseason resistance training phase ranges between four to six weeks and between one and two total body training sessions per week, typically lasting 30 to

45 minutes per session. Because the volume of basketball-specific activities continue to increase with the inclusion of practices and live scrimmages, resistance training sessions should be complementary to basketball skill development. Varying the training load of the sessions between heavy, medium, and light allows athletes to recover between sessions and balance their total training workload both on the court and in resistance training sessions. This undulating periodization approach is covered in chapter 4.

At the high school level, special considerations should be given to athletes who participate in multiple sports. As outlined in previous chapters, when athletes complete a mesocycle they often transition into the next mesocycle by focusing on restoration and active recovery. This brief period allows the athlete to recover from previous training loads, practice, and competition before beginning the next phase. For basketball athletes who participate in fall sports, transition from the competitive season of the fall sport into the basketball season disregards the traditional periodization model. As a result, the strength and conditioning professional needs to recognize that this athlete's strength levels and physical capabilities will be different from those who are able to complete a full off-season mesocycle. Making appropriate adjustments in volume and intensity is vital for long-term success. For example, fall sport athletes may be coming off a program that focused on either maintenance or peaking and tapering goals, so a preseason phase for them may require a more gradual reintroduction to resistance training. Additional recovery for these athletes may be encouraged by modifying frequency, load, intensity, or volume of resistance training sessions.

College

Collegiate basketball athletes may have been introduced to resistance training programs in high school but understanding the difference between their biological age and their training age is important. An athlete may be the biological age of 21 but have a lower training age, referring to her or his experience in resistance training and ability to perform movement patterns with high technical efficiency. Previous mesocycles should have allowed time to evaluate, educate, and address movement and technical deficiency that prepare the athlete to take on a more advanced preseason resistance training program appropriate for that individual. In a team setting, coaches may find it useful to divide athletes into groups based on their training age, training goals, or proficiency in resistance training movements. Whichever systemic structure is used, exercises, volume, intensity, and resistance training methods should fit the individual in a group setting so that each athlete reaps the full rewards of the program.

The preseason phase for collegiate basketball athletes occurs over four to six weeks. A typical strength and conditioning schedule should include a minimum of one or two total body resistance training sessions per week, with each session typically lasting 30 to 45 minutes. As with the high school athlete, the volume of basketball-specific activities will continue to increase with the inclusion of practices and live scrimmages, so resistance training sessions need to complement basketball skill development. The academic calendar and student-athlete demands on the college athlete are different from those of the high school athlete, and coaches need to consider these aspects when scheduling and programming resistance training sessions. High school basketball athletes typically have a set classroom study time such as 8:30 a.m. to 3:30 p.m., Monday through Friday. A college basketball athlete's academic class time varies throughout the day or week and often carries into the evening hours. The strength and conditioning professional should work closely with the academic advisor, coaching staff, and the athlete to help coordinate the resistance training session schedule.

Collegiate athletes and their coaches also need to adhere to NCAA rules and regulations. At specific times of the year, the NCAA has rules and regulations regarding how many hours a student-athlete can be required to practice or train. The duration of each resistance training session and frequency (per week) need to be coordinated to remain compliant with the NCAA rules. Therefore, resistance training sessions need to be timely and efficient, while still yielding a positive return. Again, communication with the coaching staff is important for planning and programming preseason resistance training sessions. Coaches need to remain flexible and make quick adjustments in instances when resistance training sessions must be modified because of time restrictions or changes in the overall schedule. Knowing which programming methods and exercises within the program are the most important is essential to creating a successful preseason training program.

Professional

When programming preseason resistance training programs for the professional basketball athlete, the strength and conditioning professional must take age into consideration. Biological age will vary from late teens to early 40s; in the NBA the average age is about 28. The coach must consider each athlete's biological age as well as training age when developing preseason resistance training programs. Programming for a teenage athlete who is coming into her or his first year will differ from that of an older athlete. Furthermore, two athletes of the same age may come from different training backgrounds. Younger athletes need to be educated about the importance of strength and resistance training and its influence on basketball performance, durability, and career longevity. Completing movement and performance evaluations regularly is important to the design of an appropriate resistance training program. Although an elite athlete may demonstrate great basketball skills, those talents do not necessarily carry over into the weight room and resistance training movements. Professional athletes with a low training age require greater attention to sound technique and movement pattern instruction before they can use advanced exercises and training methods geared to maximizing strength and power.

Preseason programming for the professional athlete is always a challenge for the coach because often the athlete is not required to live and train in the same city as the team plays. Professional basketball athletes need to arrive at preseason training camp prepared, so follow-up is necessary to ensure that they are adhering to resistance training programs that prepare them for the demands of their sport. Rookies and young developing athletes may be asked to stay and train at the team's facility, allowing more control over their physiological readiness entering preseason camp. Veteran athletes who have accumulated high volumes of basketball throughout their careers come from different off-season programs, so coaches need to assess their current state of readiness when they return to preseason camp and make proper modifications to the volume and intensity of the resistance training program based on those assessments. The environment influences the preseason mesocycle, but as a general approach with an athlete who sufficiently adheres to an intense off-season regimen, the preseason resistance training phase should be designed and tailored to continue on return to the team's facility for training camp and preseason exhibition games and continue until the first regular season game.

A professional basketball athlete's preseason resistance training programs should range from four to six weeks with two to four training sessions per week, with each session lasting 30 to 45 minutes. Again, this time should include preseason training camp and exhibition games. For the most part, these resistance training programs should remain global in nature and address total body strength in each session. As explained for the high school and collegiate athlete, the volume of basketball-specific activity in the preseason will continue to increase with the inclusion of practices and live scrimmages, so resistance training sessions should complement basketball skill development. Fatigue could decrease basketball performance and possibly lead to overuse injuries, so explaining the purpose and overall goals of this mesocycle will provide better direction for the athletes and an understanding of how to prepare sufficiently before arrival to training camp.

As preseason exhibition games are played, constraints due to time, practice and game schedule, and travel will have an effect on the resistance training program. When traveling, contacting other team's coaches and hotels in advance is helpful in coordinating access to local facilities and equipment. Proper planning and being able to make quick adjustments based on what is offered in different places will promote an effective program delivery with consistent follow-through.

Regardless of level, the schedule of resistance training sessions should be discussed with the coaching staff, medical staff, and the athlete to determine the most appropriate days and times. In the high school or collegiate setting, a schedule may be in place for the team to complete resistance training sessions as an entire group. In the professional setting, a full commitment to basketball is afforded to the athletes, so programming becomes more flexible, often taking place in individual or small-group sessions at various times throughout the day. Organizations and coaching staffs have their own rules, standards, and structure to basketball practice and resistance training sessions, so strength and conditioning professionals should tailor a program that is optimal for their environment.

CONCLUSION

Preseason resistance training is the final approach before in-season training commences at the start of a grueling season. Therefore, the selection of training methods, intensities, volumes, exercise, and other strength development parameters is crucial to establishing a successful in-season resistance training program. By manipulating methods and schemes such as those listed earlier, the strength and conditioning professional can develop resistance training sessions that will assist in overall physical performance and transfer to sport-specific skills. Understanding the needs, goals, and other programming considerations when dealing with individual athletes will help the coach establish and deliver the most effective preseason resistance training program.

Interpreting the Sample Program Tables

- DB = Dumbbell
- KB = Kettlebell
- RDL = Romanian deadlift
- PAP = Postactivation potentiation
- BW = Body weight
- RFD = Rate of force development
- BB = Barbell
- Order = Perform one set of each exercise (1a, 1b, 1c, and so on) in the group (1, 2, 3, and so on). Then go back to the first exercise in the group and do the second set of each exercise, and so on. If certain exercises call for fewer sets than others in the group, perform those sets on the backend of the grouping. For instance, if exercise 1a and exercise 1b call for 4 sets and exercise 1c calls for 3 sets, perform exercise 1c during sets 2 through 4 of exercises 1a and 1b.
- Tempo = The time, in seconds, for each phase or portion of the exercise, written as "eccentric phase: top (or bottom) position: concentric phase" (King, I., How to write strength training programs. In *Speed of Movement*, 1998, p. 123). For example, a tempo of "1:5:1" for the back squat means 1 second to lower, 5 seconds held at the bottom position, and 1 second to stand back up. Note: An "X" means that the athlete should explode during that phase of the movement. A tempo of "X:X:X" is associated with power exercises because there is not a prescriptive time allotted to each portion of the movement.

Table 11.2 Guards: Preseason Microcycle 1, Reactive Strength and Velocity, Weeks 1-6

Lower Body Pushing Focus (Day 1)

Order	Exercise	Set(s)	Load	Reps or duration	Tempo	Rest
1a	Back squat (average velocity of 0.8-1.0 m/s)	1	53%	10 reps	3:1:1	1 min
		2	67%	8 reps	3:1:1	1 min
		3	76%	5 reps	3:1:1	2 min
	Variable resistance	4	76%-85%	5 reps	1:X:X	2 min
	Variable resistance	5	76%-85%	5 reps	1:X:X	2 min
1b	Box depth jump (PAP effect)	1		3-5 reps	X:X:X	1 min
		2		3-5 reps	X:X:X	2 min
		3		3-5 reps	X:X:X	3 min
		4		3-5 reps	X:X:X	3 min
		5		3-5 reps	X:X:X	3 min
2a	Single-leg squat on box	4		4-6 reps	2:1:X	<30 s
2b	Single-leg curl (on stability ball)	4		6-8 reps	3:1:1	<30 s
2c	RDL	4		4-6 reps	3:1:1	2 min
Additional advanced complex—college or pro athlete						
3a	Single-leg squat - Reactive stiffness hop*	2		3-5 reps	1:X:1	<30 s
3b	Standing stability ball groin squeeze**	2		10-15 reps	1:3:1	60 s

*Cal Dietz version: quick explosive hops in lowered position. **Squeeze and hold for 3 seconds, release tension, and then repeat for recommended repetitions.

Upper Body Pushing Focus (Day 2)

Order	Exercise	Set(s)	Load	Reps or duration	Tempo	Rest
1a	Bench press (average velocity of 0.8-1.0 m/s)	1	53%	10 reps	3:1:1	1 min
		2	67%	8 reps	3:1:1	1 min
		3	76%-85%	5 reps	3:1:1	2 min
		4	76%-85%	5 reps	1:X:X	2 min
		5	76%-85%*	5 reps	1:X:X	2 min
1b	Med ball reactive chest pass (wall throws; PAP effect)	1		3-5 reps	X:X:X	1 min
		2		3-5 reps	X:X:X	2 min
		3		3-5 reps	X:X:X	3 min
		4		3-5 reps	X:X:X	3 min
		5		3-5 reps	X:X:X	3 min
2a	One-arm DB shoulder press**	4	40-50%	4-6 reps	2:1:X	<30 s
2b	One-arm cable row (with split stance)***	4		4-6 reps	3:1:1	<30 s
2c	Side rotational V-up	4	5 lb (2.3 kg)	8-12 reps	3:1:1	2 min
Additional advanced complex—college or pro athlete						
3a	Prone Y's, T's, I's****	2		5-8 reps	1:3:1	<30 s
3b	Birddog plank (opposite arm and opposite leg raise)	2		10-12 reps	1:2:1	60 s

*Intensity may be closer to 60% to 70%. **Slow and controlled eccentric phase, explosive concentric phase. ***Substitute the one-arm DB row if a cable machine is not available. ****Hold the end position of each repetition for 3 seconds.

Lower Body Pulling Focus (Day 3)

Order	Exercise	Set(s)	Load	Reps or duration	Tempo	Rest
1a	Power (or hang) split snatch (peak velocity of 1.2-1.4 m/s)	1	25%-45%	4-5 reps	X:X:X	1 min
		2	25%-45%	4-5 reps	X:X:X	1 min
	Peak velocity >1.9 m/s	3	25%-45%	4-5 reps	X:X:X	2 min
	Peak velocity >1.9 m/s	4	25%-45%	4-5 reps	X:X:X	2 min
	Peak velocity >1.9 m/s	5	25%-45%	4-5 reps	X:X:X	2 min
1b	Lateral skater to box jump	1		3-5 reps	X:X:X	1 min
		2		3-5 reps	X:X:X	2 min
		3		3-5 reps	X:X:X	3 min
		4		3-5 reps	X:X:X	3 min
2a	Walking lunge	4		4-6 reps	1:1:1	<30 s
2b	Standing Pallof press (with side lunge)*	4		4-6 reps	2:1:1	<30 s
2c	Single-leg RDL (isometric focus)	4		4-6 reps	2:1:1	2 min
Additional advanced complex—college or pro athlete						
3a	Bosch single-leg hip extension hold	2		5-6 reps	1:3:1	<30 s
3b	Single-leg squat to reach (stamina focus)	2		10-15 reps	1:3:1	60 s

*Side lunge toward the cable machine while holding the arms extended.

Upper Body Pulling Focus (Day 4)

Order	Exercise	Set(s)	Reps or duration	Tempo	Rest
1a	Lat pulldown (or pull-up*)	1	5-6 reps	1:1:X	1 min
		2	5-6 reps	1:1:X	1 min
		3	5-6 reps	1:1:X	2 min
		4	5-6 reps	1:1:X	2 min
		5	5-6 reps	1:1:X	2 min
1b	Reactive med ball overhead throwdown (bouncing ball)	1	3-5 reps	X:X:X	1 min
		2	3-5 reps	X:X:X	2 min
		3	3-5 reps	X:X:X	3 min
		4	3-5 reps	X:X:X	3 min
2a	One-arm DB row	4	4-6 reps	2:1:X	<30 s
2b	One-arm cable chest press (with split stance)**	4	4-6 reps	2:1:X	<30 s
2c	Two-legged V-up***	4	10-15 reps	1:2:1	2 min
Additional advanced complex—college or pro athlete					
3a	D2 pattern, single-leg stance****	2	10-15 reps	1:3:1	<30 s
3b	Side plank (with hip abduction hold) (stamina focus)	2	10-15 reps	1:3:1	60 s

*Add a weight vest to advance the load. **Slow and controlled eccentric phase, explosive concentric phase. ***Pause for 2 seconds before moving into concentric phase. ****Pause with arm extended overhead for 3 seconds.

Table 11.3 Bigs: Pre-Season Microcycle 1, Reactive Strength and Velocity, Weeks 1-6

Lower Body Pushing Focus (Day 1)

Order	Exercise	Set(s)	Load	Reps or duration	Tempo	Rest
1a	Back squat (average velocity of 0.8-1.0 m/s)	1	53%	10 reps	3:1:1	1 min
		2	67%	8 reps	3:1:1	1 min
		3	76%	5 reps	3:1:1	2 min
	Variable resistance	4	76%-85%	5 reps	1:X:X	2 min
	Variable resistance	5	76%-85%	5 reps	1:X:X	2 min
1b	Box depth jump (PAP effect)	1		3-5 reps	X:X:X	1 min
		2		3-5 reps	X:X:X	2 min
		3		3-5 reps	X:X:X	3 min
		4		3-5 reps	X:X:X	3 min
		5		3-5 reps	X:X:X	3 min
2a	Single-leg squat on box	4		4-6 reps	2:1:X	<30 s
2b	Single-leg curl (on stability ball)	4		6-8 reps	3:1:1	<30 s
2c	RDL	4		4-6 reps	3:1:1	2 min
Additional advanced complex—college or pro athlete						
3a	Single-leg squat - Reactive stiffness hop*	2		3-5 reps	1:X:1	<30 s
3b	Standing stability ball groin squeeze**	2		10-15 reps	1:3:1	60 s

*Cal Dietz version: quick explosive hops in lowered position. **Squeeze and hold for 3 seconds, release tension, and then repeat for recommended repetitions.

Upper Body Pushing Focus (Day 2)

Order	Exercise	Set(s)	Load	Reps or duration	Tempo	Rest
1a	Bench press (average velocity of 0.8-1.0 m/s)	1	53%	10 reps	3:1:1	1 min
		2	67%	8 reps	3:1:1	1 min
		3	76%-85%	5 reps	3:1:1	2 min
		4	76%-85%	5 reps	1:X:X	2 min
		5	76%-85%*	5 reps	1:X:X	2 min
1b	Overhead med ball wall throw (single-leg stance; PAP effect)	1		3-5 reps	X:X:X	1 min
		2		3-5 reps	X:X:X	2 min
		3		3-5 reps	X:X:X	3 min
		4		3-5 reps	X:X:X	3 min
		5		3-5 reps	X:X:X	3 min
2a	One-arm push press	4	40%-50%	4-6 reps	2:1:X	<30 s
2b	One-arm cable row (with split stance)**	4		4-6 reps	3:1:1	<30 s
2c	Side rotational V-up	4	5 lb (2.3 kg)	8-12 reps	3:1:1	2 min
Additional advanced complex—college or pro athlete						
3a	Prone Y's, T's, I's***	2		5-8 reps	1:3:1	<30 s
3b	Birddog plank opposite arm and opposite leg raise	2		10-12 reps	1:2:1	60 s

*Intensity may be closer to 60%-70%. **Substitute the one-arm DB row if a cable machine is not available. ***Hold the end position of each repetition for 3 seconds.

Lower Body Pulling Focus (Day 3)

Order	Exercise	Set(s)	Load	Reps or duration	Tempo	Rest
1a	Power (or hang) clean (peak velocity of 1.3 m/s or greater)	1	25%-45%	4-5 reps	X:X:X	1 min
		2	45%-65%	4-5 reps	X:X:X	1 min
		3	45%-65%	4-5 reps	X:X:X	2 min
		4	45%-65%	4-5 reps	X:X:X	2 min
		5	45%-65%	4-5 reps	X:X:X	2 min
1b	Lateral skater to box jump	1		3-5 reps	X:X:X	1 min
		2		3-5 reps	X:X:X	2 min
		3		3-5 reps	X:X:X	3 min
		4		3-5 reps	X:X:X	3 min
		5		3-5 reps	X:X:X	3 min
2a	Step-up	4		4-6 reps	1:1:1	<30 s
2b	Standing Pallof press (with lateral step)*	4		4-6 reps	2:1:1	<30 s
2c	Single-leg squat to reach	4		4-6 reps	2:1:1	2 min
Additional advanced complex—college or pro athlete						
3a	Landmine squat to rotational press	2		5-6 reps	1:3:1	<30 s
3b	Birddog hold (opposite arm and opposite leg)**	2		10-15 reps	1:3:1	60 s

*Extend the arms and keeping them extended, step away from the cable machine and then step back toward the cable machine. **Hold the end position of each repetition for 3 seconds.

Upper Body Pulling Focus (Day 4)

Order	Exercise	Set(s)	Reps or duration	Tempo	Rest
1a	Lat pulldown (or pull-up*)	1	5-6 reps	1:1:X	1 min
		2	5-6 reps	1:1:X	1 min
		3	5-6 reps	1:1:X	2 min
		4	5-6 reps	1:1:X	2 min
		5	5-6 reps	1:1:X	2 min
1b	Reactive med ball overhead throwdown (bouncing ball)	1	3-5 reps	X:X:X	1 min
		2	3-5 reps	X:X:X	2 min
		3	3-5 reps	X:X:X	3 min
		4	3-5 reps	X:X:X	3 min
		5	3-5 reps	X:X:X	3 min
2a	One-arm DB row	4	4-6 reps	2:1:X	<30 s
2b	One-arm cable chest press (with split stance)**	4	4-6 reps	2:1:X	<30 s
2c	Deadbug (with stability ball)***	4	10-15 reps	1:2:1	2 min
Additional advanced complex—college or pro athlete					
3a	D2 pattern, single-leg stance****	2	10-15 reps	1:3:1	<30 s
3b	Side plank (with hip abduction hold) (stamina focus)	2	10-15 reps	1:3:1	60 s

*Add a weight vest to advance the load. **Slow and controlled eccentric phase, explosive concentric phase. ***Hold extended position for 2 seconds and then repeat on other side. ****Pause with arm extended overhead for 3 seconds.

12

IN-SEASON PROGRAMMING

NIC HIGGINS AND SCOTT THOM

After an off-season when strength and power have been developed and a preseason that has prepared the athletes for the demands of basketball, in-season resistance training should continue to bridge the weight room and the court by continuing to develop the power qualities needed for basketball, as well as maintaining the strength qualities established during the off-season. Basketball athletes should continue to resistance train during the competitive season not only to continue building on physical attributes but also to gain experience and improve movement technique.

GOALS AND OBJECTIVES

Throughout the off-season, basketball athletes may be placed into programs with a different training emphasis based on their training age, specific goals, position, and overall team training focus. For example, training groups such as beginners, intermediate, and trained may be created and athletes can be categorized according to their resistance training status, experience, and proficiency. Beginner athletes who are untrained or have minimal training experience should follow a progression and sequences of exercises that are different from those used by trained athletes who have been performing resistance training for multiple years. For instance, beginner athletes in the developmental group may use exercise progressions with a central focus on fundamental movements executed with technical proficiency and less emphasis on increasing intensity or load during that time. During the in-season phase, resistance training groups and programs can also be differentiated by those who are starters, those who are receiving moderate game minutes, and those who are receiving low to no game minutes. Injured athletes, redshirt freshmen, and athletes consistently not dressing for games typically require a completely different program during this time from those who are competing. Again, categorizing basketball athletes into training groups can be effective for in-season resistance training when considering frequency, volume, and intensity.

LENGTH, STRUCTURE, AND ORGANIZATION

The in-season phase is a significant period that athletes need to take advantage of, and they should continue to develop general and specific aspects of strength while competing in-season. This period can last 16 to 20 weeks for high school, up to 24 weeks for college, and as long as 30 weeks for professional basketball athletes. As a result, this phase is likely be the longest mesocycle of the year, offering a significant opportunity to implement a resistance training program. Although these weeks are filled with practices, games, travel, and other obstacles, proper planning and programming of resistance training sessions will prevent regression and aid in the continual growth of a developing athlete. The emphasis of in-season resistance training should be to continue to develop overall athleticism and ultimately maximize athletic performance in playoff competition.

High School

High school basketball athletes should be expected to complete one to two resistance training sessions per week strategically scheduled around their classes, practices, game schedule, and extracurricular activities. Total body resistance training programs for the high school athlete should last 30 to 45 minutes and include a proper warm-up and cool-down. The frequency per week of resistance training sessions should be adjusted around the volume of basketball activities, providing not only adequate recovery periods between resistance training sessions but also appropriate recovery leading up to the next game.

College

The collegiate basketball athlete's in-season phase ranges between 20 and 24 weeks and should consist of a minimum of one to two total body resistance training sessions per week. Each session should last 30 to 45 minutes and include a proper warm-up and cool-down. In-season training frequency should be structured around game schedule, travel schedule, academic calendar, and extracurricular activities. Previous training cycles may have allowed consistent training schedules such as a four-day or five-day training split with no basketball requirements, but in-season resistance training programs require coordination with academics, practices, games, and NCAA regulations.

Professional

The professional season can last anywhere between 24 and 30 weeks including playoffs. The overall game distribution, the length of the season, and travel requirements present a unique challenge when attempting to maximize performance for the professional athlete. One of the challenges that a strength and conditioning professional faces because of the demands of longer travel stints is access to a weight room that fits the basketball athlete's training needs. In the professional setting three to four games can spread throughout the week, including games on back-to-back nights that are sometimes played on the road for one and at home for the other. But with the redesign of the NBA schedule, games typically take place every other day. This setting can make it challenging for the coach to balance workloads on practice days and determine when it is time either to push an athlete or to promote recovery. In general, a professional athlete should take part in a minimum of one to two total body resistance training sessions per week lasting 30 to 45 minutes.

RECOMMENDED EXERCISES

Because resistance training continues throughout the in-season phase, one aspect that must be considered when programming is exercise selection. The exercises that will be performed are crucial for athletes' continued physical development and their ability to play basketball at a high level.

When selecting exercises, it is important to refer to the needs analysis for basketball athletes at the high school, college, and professional level. Generally, exercises should be prioritized using ground-based, multijoint movements over single-joint movements. The primary exercises selected during the in-season phase should contribute to the athlete's performance on the court. Microcycles built into the in-season mesocycle allow for training variation, but for transfer to occur, exercises included within the program should be completed using movement patterns and speeds commonly executed in the game. In other words, most exercises selected within a hectic in-season schedule should reflect the sport and be specific to its demands. For example, in-season resistance training for basketball athletes may include barbell squat jumps emphasizing quick contraction times with high effort and intent, resulting in maximal power output. Other examples of primary exercises that can be programmed during the in-season phase at basketball-specific speeds and intensities are loaded unilateral and bilateral squat variations, traditional and hex bar deadlifts, and Olympic lifting variations.

Assistance exercises provide structural balance and focus on areas of high concern due to the demands of basketball and should be assigned and included for in-season resistance training for athletes of all ages. These exercises may contribute to basketball performance but more importantly, they are necessary because they can be prescribed more specifically to the individual and address areas that contribute to the overall health and durability of the athlete. Variations of exercises might be programmed based on the body part being used, the plane or planes of movement, or both. For example, horizontal pulling exercises can include dumbbell rows and inverted rows, and vertical pulling variations such as lat pulldowns, pull-ups, and chin-ups can be selected. Lower body posterior chain exercises that focus on the development of the hamstring, glutes, and erectors are essential to the basketball athlete and might include Romanian deadlifts (bilateral and unilateral) and good mornings, reverse hip or low back extensions, or posterior bridging variations. Although some of these movements may not mimic specific movements in sport, they still contribute to the athlete's performance, durability, and overall health. Because basketball is a complex, multiplanar sport, athletes should use exercises that place an external load in the sagittal, frontal, and transverse planes. For example, assistance exercises might include variations of a forward, side, and reverse lunge, and step-ups with dumbbell or barbell loading can be performed in all three planes. Upper body reaching tasks like shoulder pressing in various directions not only promote strength but also address varied loading patterns in multiple planes of motion that allow the athlete to develop and strengthen the muscle in positions and movements that occur in basketball.

Other assistance exercises necessary in the in-season resistance training program include those that focus on smaller muscles that provide support to the joints. For example, the shoulder joint and its supporting scapular stabilizers and rotator cuff muscles take on a high amount of stress in basketball, so its stability and strength are important to the overall health of the athlete. These exercises can be nonfatiguing to the primary or other assistance exercises and paired with the movements during rest periods, creating a training program that is focused on both performance and durability.

In summary, the exercises programmed within the in-season phase should include primary exercises that focus on improving performance and the continued physical development of the athlete. At the same time, the program should include assistance exercises that improve balance and function while providing support to combat the workload of the basketball season.

When resistance training sessions are programmed twice per week, one lower body assistance exercise included in the program may be a unilateral, sagittal plane exercise. For example, the exercise programmed in the first session might be a barbell step-up, and a dumbbell walking lunge may be programmed in the second session. Microcycles within the in-season phase help to maintain a progressive approach and provide structure and variation. The coach can implement these exercises within the first microcycle and manipulate tempo rather than exercise variation. As the athlete progresses to the second microcycle during the in-season phase, the coach can introduce new and perhaps more challenging exercises to make further improvements in strength or movement velocity. As another example, the coach may decide to program a dumbbell lateral step-up and progress to a barbell lateral step-up, both performed under heavy load as lower body lateral plane assistance exercises in the first microcycle. During the second microcycle the athlete may progress by performing the same exercises while focusing on executing the movement ballistically, at a higher velocity. These exercise variations and program progressions will continue to reinforce in-season strength development. During the in-season phase slight variations to exercises should be made by manipulating parameters such as range of motion, intensity, velocity, exercise pairings, and equipment, rather than by introducing completely new exercises. With the high workloads from basketball activities and other in-season stressors, familiarity may help limit soreness and fatigue.

Frequency

The frequency of in-season resistance training programs depends not only on the level of basketball but also on the individual athlete's playing time and schedule. Also, unlike previous mesocycles during the off-season, the in-season includes scheduling conflicts resulting from practices, games, and travel. In some cases, depending on the level of play, a team might not play a game for several days; as a result, athletes might be able to complete their resistance training sessions as planned. But during weeks where one or two games are played or when other conflicts exist, identifying the optimal time to participate in a resistance training session may be difficult. For example, a day that would typically serve as a great opportunity to schedule a resistance training session might turn out to be an off-school day for the high school student or a travel day for the collegiate or professional athlete. Furthermore, the NCAA and NBA regulate days off and travel; although a particular day might otherwise serve as a great opportunity for a resistance training session, the coach must be able to make adjustments. Therefore, although it may not be optimal, scheduling a session during the only available time may be necessary in some circumstances. In these cases, workloads and working intensities will have to be adjusted to ensure that athletes can recover properly before the next competition.

In some instances when resistance training sessions are completed after a game or the day after a game, coaches need to account for and manage programs because of fatigue and soreness. For example, in the NBA, where the game schedule structure results in games being played every other day, implementing resistance training programs after games can be useful for athletes who take on high game workloads. Because these athletes are already fatigued, sessions should focus on assistance exercises and address strength-endurance under a higher volume. Although exercises that focus on explosiveness, aimed to develop power and maximal strength, can continue to be implemented on nongame days, assistance exercises that emphasize hypertrophy and muscular endurance like lunging, RDLs, and hamstring curls can be instituted in a postgame resistance training program.

Intensity

When prescribing intensities for exercises and for overall sessions, coaches should consider the athletes' training age, basketball volume, the calendar, and their ability to handle the demands of the current in-season workload.

In general, lighter relative loads might present more sport-specific transfer than heavier loads. From a joint kinetics perspective, vertical jumping resistance training movements in the sagittal plane are not all the same, nor do athletes execute these movements with the same strategies. A push jerk is more like the internal kinetics (joint moments) of a countermovement jump in jumpers who show high knee dominance (3). For hip dominant jumpers, the push jerk becomes a general exercise rather than a sport-specific exercise. For another example, Cushion and colleagues (3) mention that the load applied on the back of the shoulders during jump squats alters trunk kinematics, such that higher intensities correspond less to countermovement jump performance than lower intensities. As previously mentioned, during the in-season phase, coaches should prioritize exercises within a program that focus on improving performance transferrable to the basketball court. As load increases, joint kinetics might change. In addition, absolute intensity increases with each repetition. Therefore, what began as a lighter load and more sport-specific exercise when performed for 1 or 2 repetitions may become more intense and less sport-specific when performed for many repetitions. Therefore, the number of repetitions prescribed is a critical factor to consider when programming exercises during the in-season phase.

Several tools for prescribing intensity can assist coaches in making informed decisions on load and intensity. Prilepin's chart, the relative intensity scale, and the rate of perceived exertion scale all assist the strength and conditioning professional in selecting the desired level of difficulty, intensity, and load for an exercise or session. These tools can serve as useful guides to making quick adjustments within a resistance training session and assigning an appropriate workload for primary and assistance exercises over the course of a season.

Prilepin's Chart

Prilepin's chart (table 12.1) offers general guidance for choosing loads and optimal repetition ranges specifically for power and explosive exercises (7).

Relative Intensity Scale

The relative intensity scale (table 12.2) considers absolute load but adjusts it according to volume, which is helpful in-season when soreness and fatigue are a concern. For example, a training session 48 hours postgame has a repetition scheme for the back squat of 5 × 2. For an athlete who played high minutes or experiences increased fatigue or soreness, a coach may believe it is best for him or her to complete the same volume of exercise but under a slightly lighter load compared with an athlete who has the same level of strength but played less than 15 minutes in the game. The high-minute athlete might complete the 5 sets of 2 repetitions at

Table 12.1 Prilepin's Chart

Percent (% of the 1RM)	Optimal number of reps per set per exercise	Optimal number of total reps* per exercise	Optimal range of total reps* per exercise
55-65	3-6	24**	18-30***
70-80	3-6	18	12-24
80-90	2-4	15	10-20
>90	1-2	4	4-10

*Total reps = sets × reps. **For example, 8 × 3, 4 × 6, or 6 × 4. ***For example, 3 × 6, 4 × 5, 5 × 4, and so on as long as 3 to 6 reps per set are performed.

Adapted from N.P. Laputin and V.G. Oleshko, *Managing the Training of Weightlifters* (Kiev: Zdorov'ya Publishers, 1982).

Table 12.2 Relative Intensity Scale

Relative intensity		Absolute intensity							
Difficulty level		1 rep/set	2 reps/set	3 reps/set	4 reps/set	5 reps/set	6 reps/set	8 reps/set	10 reps/set
Maximum	100%	100% 1RM	95% 1RM	92.5% 1RM	90% 1RM	87.5% 1RM	85% 1RM	80% 1RM	72.5% 1RM
Heavy +	97.5%	97.5	92.8	90.3	87.8	85.5	83	78	70.8
	95%	95	90.3	88	85.5	83.3	80.8	76	69
Heavy	92.5%	92.5	88	85.8	83.3	81	78.8	74	67.3
	90%	90	85.5	83.3	81	78.8	76.5	72	65.3
Moderate +	87.5%	87.5	83.3	81	78.8	76.8	74.5	70	63.5
	85%	85	80.8	78.8	76.5	74.5	72.3	68	61.8
Moderate	82.5%	82.5	78.5	76.5	74.3	72.3	70.3	66	60
	80%	80	76	74	72	70	68	64	58
Light +	77.5%	77.5	73.8	71.8	69.8	68	66	62	56.3
	75%	75	71.3	69.5	67.5	65.8	63.8	60	54.5
Light	72.5%	72.5	69	67.3	65.3	63.5	61.8	58	52.8
	70%	70	66.5	64.8	63	61.3	59.5	56	50.8
Too light	67.5%	67.5	64.3	62.5	60.8	59.3	57.5	54	49
	65%	65	61.8	60.3	58.5	57	55.3	52	47.3

Adapted by permission from D. Boucher, *Citadel Football S&C*, Presented at the NSCA Coaches Conference (Indianapolis, IN, 2004). Based on Jerry Martin, University of Connecticut.

an absolute load of 69% of the 1RM, whereas the low-minute athlete completes the 5 sets of 2 repetitions at an absolute load of 78.5% of the 1RM. In relative terms, the high-minute athlete would be working at a "light" difficulty level of 72.5%, whereas the low-minute athlete would be asked to take on a more demanding task, working at a "moderate" difficulty level of 82.5%. Furthermore, an athlete who played zero minutes in the previous game might be assigned an even higher level of difficulty. For example, the athlete can be prescribed an intensity of 85.5% for 5 sets of 2 repetitions, resulting in a "heavy" difficulty level of 90%.

Understanding the cumulative effect of volume and its correlation to fatigue and stress brought on by the competitive season helps the coach understand the importance of using guides like the relative intensity table to make more educated decisions in the programming of in-season intensities.

Rating of Perceived Exertion Scale

Another method that for many years has assisted coaches in prescribing appropriate working intensities is the **rating of perceived exertion (RPE) scale**, in which the athlete subjectively rates the level of difficulty of an exercise set, the overall resistance training session, or both (table 12.3). In the later stages of the season it can be difficult to prescribe resistance training intensities from the previously determined 1RM, typically determined two to three months earlier. Using the RPE scale in the later microcycles may be a valuable way to determine appropriate load and intensities. Knowledgeable athletes can self-select weight and complete the desired volume based on their subjective rating of difficulty.

Autoregulation using the RPE scale appears to be a useful method in quantifying resistance training intensities (4, 14). This approach has limitations, and it might not be best for novice athletes. Research has shown that strength levels can fluctuate up to 18% day to day, and even

Table 12.3   Resistance Training–Specific Rating of Perceived Exertion

Rating	Description of perceived exertion
10	Maximum effort
9.5	No further repetitions but could increase the load
9	1 repetition remaining
8.5	1-2 repetitions remaining
8	2 repetitions remaining
7.5	2-3 repetitions remaining
7	3 repetitions remaining
5-6	4-6 repetitions remaining
3-4	Light effort
1-2	Little to no effort

Reprinted by permission from M.C. Zourdos et al., "Novel Resistance Training-Specific RPE Scale Measuring Repetitions in Reserve," *Journal of Strength Condition Research.* 30 (2016): 267-275.

the most experienced athlete can misinterpret perceived versus actual intensities (6). Athletes must have a strong understanding of their current physical state, previous strength levels, and the language being used for the RPE scale. According to Day and colleagues (4), the level of perceived difficulty is higher when performing the least number of repetitions at the highest absolute intensity. The authors found that subjects reported less difficulty when performing 15 repetitions at lighter resistances (50% of the 1RM) than when they performed 5 (90% of the 1RM) or 10 (70% of the 1RM) repetitions at higher resistances, when in fact they are doing more total work when performing 15 repetitions at 50% of the 1RM. Therefore, the RPE scale may be most accurate when using heavier loads (greater than 70% of the 1RM). This method of prescribing intensities may also be more appropriate for experienced athletes who have a good understanding of their strength levels, effort required for specific intensities, and overall repetition schemes based on load (6).

To institute the RPE scale most accurately, a rating of 10 should be equivalent or close to 100% on the relative intensity table (see table 12.2). For example, an accurate implementation of this method would show that an athlete who attributed a 10 to an exercise performed for 8 to 10 repetitions would most likely have been working at somewhere between 72.5 and 80% of his or her absolute intensity level and thus performed the exercise to the point of failure. A high school athlete who is inexperienced and has a low training age may not truly understand the language and association to the scale compared with a more experienced collegiate or professional basketball athlete and may over- or underrate the level of difficulty. An inaccurate assessment of difficulty is a limiting factor to successful implementation of this method. Athletes can produce a helpful learning tool by keeping a record of their workouts, the resistance they used, and the RPE associated with those workouts.

COMPETITIVE TRAINING PHASES

Because physical performance rises and drops over the course of a season, coaches need to construct in-season microcycles to allow athletes to reach optimal performance levels. Optimistically, the later in-season microcycles performed during the regular season will be a preparation period for the playoff push and be used to reach maximal performance during championship play. Within each in-season microcycle, training goals for the team and each individual need to be determined, and resistance training routines should be organized to address the most appropriate strength qualities for that period. In general, the in-season mesocycle can be broken down into two smaller microcycles, competitive phase I and competitive phase II.

Competitive Phase I

In competitive phase I, greater emphasis is placed on the maintenance or continued development of maximal strength, and athletes complete exercises at a higher intensity and lower volume. A lower volume of work should be performed earlier in the season because the athlete might still be getting accustomed to higher basketball-specific workloads and in-game intensity. Research suggests that maximal strength during the competitive season can be maintained with volumes of 1 to 6 sets of 1 to 6 repetitions at 85% to 100%, whereas the development of strength and power can be maintained by prescribing working sets at 70% to 88% of the 1RM for 3 to 6 sets of 4 to 10 repetitions in periodized fashion (10). Thus, if an appropriate preseason phase was completed, primary exercises within this microcycle can be performed at a lower volume (1-2 repetitions) at intensities between 80% and 90% of the 1RM focused on maintaining maximal strength, and further development of power can be achieved using velocity-based methods. Emphasizing this portion of the force-velocity curve allows the athlete to maintain or continue to develop absolute strength and strength-speed qualities. Primary exercises are performed between 0.3 m/s and 0.6 m/s (8). Although intensities will have been carefully selected to continue to develop and retain strength during the competitive season, the correct volume must be applied to provide adequate exposure to higher intensities while providing a dosage that allows the athlete to recover and perform at a high level.

In a traditional routine, exercise order begins with more explosive movements, is followed by heavier loaded structural exercises, and ends with relatively higher volume assistance exercises. When time is limited, performing primary resistance training exercises under heavy loads before explosive movements may improve performance in both vertical and horizontal tasks (11, 12). With basketball movements needing to be executed at high velocities, pairing heavy resistance exercises with those that focus on higher velocities is time efficient and ensures that both ends of the force-velocity curve are being addressed.

During competitive phase I, assistance exercise volume is reduced when compared with off-season workloads. When programming assistance exercises during competitive phase I, the best approach is to start with low volume to offset the fatiguing effects of increased basketball activity. The intensities should remain moderate to high with volume prescribed in the hypertrophic ranges to assist in the maintenance of previously developed muscle mass. Instead of performing 4 or more sets of an exercise, athletes might perform 2 or 3 sets of 8 to 12 repetitions, because this prescription promotes muscular development and strength-endurance as discussed in previous chapters.

Within the basketball season, the athletes' current state of readiness to take on specific loads and intensities within a resistance training session depends on multiple factors including fatigue from basketball activities and other stressors such as travel, academic load, extracurricular involvement, and recovery status, which is influenced by nutrition, sleep, and hydration. As a result, the coach must recognize that all team members enter a resistance training session in a different state of readiness. Therefore, sessions may need to be adjusted depending on an athlete's training status. Rather than prescribing loads based on absolute load and the traditional percentages associated with it, the coach can use the velocity-based method, covered in detail in chapter 11, to assist in regulating load and volume based on the athlete's day-to-day performance. Proper execution of an exercise with each repetition can influence sport-specific transfer (3). Velocity-based resistance training permits fluctuation in resistance training loads while still providing useful feedback through target velocity zones, which are ideal for the explosive basketball athlete (9).

As described previously, velocity-based training zones can be applied for traditional exercises like the squat, deadlift, and bench press and for Olympic lifts such as the clean, snatch, jerk, and their derivatives. An advantage to incorporating velocity-based training during the competition season is the external feedback that provides instantaneous information to the athletes, serving as motivation as well as creating a competitive environment. The data collected is useful not only to the strength and conditioning professional but also to the athletes during workouts by serving as motivation for them to compete against themselves and their teammates (5).

Variable resistance, detailed in chapter 11, is also a useful advanced method that can be applied in-season when attempting to implement heavy loads. Under heavy loads (greater than 80% of the 1RM) movement velocity is compromised near the sticking point (13). As a result, variable resistance can be implemented when working with loads greater than 80% of the 1RM. When applying variable resistance, the load calculated must include the variable resistance being implemented. A coach must first decide what load is desired in the top position of the movement and then determine how much of this load will come from variable resistance. Typically, variable resistance load is calculated as a percentage. For example, if the desired initial load of a back squat is 200 pounds (91 kg), the coach might decide that 20% of this load comes from chains. In this case the coach would add 160 pounds (73 kg) of weight to the barbell and a total of 40 pounds (18 kg) of chains (20 pounds [9 kg] on each side of the bar). After the barbell has been loaded correctly, some chains should still be in contact with the floor when the athlete moves into the beginning position. If the chains are allowed to sway while the athlete is moving, the movement will be extremely challenging and place the athlete at increased risk.

When attempting to structure the in-season delivery method of strength and power exercises, a coach should value quality over quantity. Transitioning from the in-season competitive phase I to competitive phase II, a gradual reduction in total volume should occur. Detailed in chapter 11, the cluster method can also serve as an excellent way to manage in-season resistance training volume and maintain high-intensity work output at sport-specific velocities. In-season resistance training will continue to address intensity through either load or velocity, so clusters can be used to reduce the onset of fatigue and promote high-quality movement (9). Because of basketball demands and concurrent maintenance of strength qualities, total volume should be reduced during the in-season phase when compared with preseason volume. For example, if during the preseason phase, 5 intrasets of 2 repetitions (10 total repetitions) were completed in cluster fashion with a 20-second rest after each intraset, during the in-season phase, 3 intrasets of 2 repetitions (6 total repetitions) can be used.

Competitive Phase II

As the season progresses, quality remains high, but the emphasis shifts to higher velocity movement. In competitive phase II, greater emphasis is placed on accelerative strength or speed-strength through high-velocity and explosive, transferrable movement patterns. The overall volume and workload of sessions is lower compared with competitive phase I, and total session duration also deceases. Basketball athletes should continue to train a minimum of once or twice a week with total body training sessions strategically planned around basketball activities. The goals of resistance training may also become more specific for each athlete. As discussed earlier, in situations when athletes are redshirting, not dressing, playing limited minutes, or returning from injury, a coach may decide to continue to focus on foundational strength. The coach needs to assess each athlete's current state and determine what specific aspects of strength will best serve the athlete as the regular season ends and the playoffs approach.

Competitive phase II can serve multiple purposes depending on the success of the team. For the athlete on a team that will not be participating in playoff competition, the final microcycle can serve as a preparatory period to the off-season, ensuring that each athlete enters the off-season healthy with a greater foundation of strength. In other cases, a team might be preparing for playoff or tournament competition. As a result, competitive phase II should use an approach somewhat similar to that taken in the preseason phase, with the goal being to maximize athleticism and reach peak performance levels.

For younger athletes such as high school basketball athletes or athletes with a low training age, maintaining strength-speed may be advantageous because they can train at a higher intensity and continue to build on their foundation. Even though a season might be ending, the coach needs to keep the long-term development goals of these athletes in mind. Consistent exposure to resistance training movements will help speed future growth.

During competitive phase II, velocity-based training may also be used, and the focus should continue to progress to speed-strength with load dictated by velocity and proper execution. In earlier resistance training phases, volume might gradually increase to maintain progress. During this microcycle, however, volume can remain the same or decrease, but target velocity gradually increases over sessions. Thus, late into the season the quality of training remains high by attempting to achieve higher power and velocity outputs.

To address both sides of the force-velocity curve in more novel ways during the in-season and perhaps make quicker improvements in power and explosiveness heading into playoff competition, coaches may decide to take advantage of complex sets. Defined in chapter 11, postactivation potentiation (PAP) complexes might be useful for trained athletes and perhaps, in competitive phase II, more fitting for college and pro athletes making a playoff push. Both accentuated eccentric load drop jumps and heavy loaded squats have been shown to improve countermovement jump performance and linear acceleration when performed in succession (2, 11), especially in stronger athletes (11). When recovery is a major concern during the later stages of the season, nonfatiguing power- and velocity-based workouts might be best before a game. Turki and colleagues (15) hypothesized that dynamic warm-ups improve performance through enhanced motor unit excitability, recruitment, and synchronization. Performing these workouts before a game may possibly also serve to enhance in-game performance if performed at appropriate intensities and volumes. As mentioned and covered in detail in chapter 11, although complex sets can certainly be time efficient, rest times will affect the PAP response.

In competitive phase II, many athletes may still need to continue to implement assistance exercises in hypertrophic repetition ranges to maintain their muscle mass. At this stage, total volume should again be reduced when compared with previous mesocycles during the off-season and competitive phase I. The assistance exercises selected should continue to address multiple planes of movement, incorporate both bilateral and unilateral movements, and challenge stability, posture, and range of motion, while focusing on the overall health of the athlete. Special attention should be given to including both total body and lower body movements in multiple planes, while also ensuring the inclusion of posterior chain exercise and a careful balance of upper body push and pull exercises.

CONCLUSION

From the start of the season to the final championship game, peaks and valleys will occur in the performance state of each individual. The strength and conditioning professional's job is to outline a plan and make necessary adjustments to allow the athlete to perform at her or his peak in time for the playoffs. If implemented strategically, the various methods discussed in this chapter can help to deliver a highly effective in-season resistance training program that maintains or increases strength and power, rather than causes strength or power losses. To achieve this goal, in-season resistance training programs need to be scheduled properly in two or more microcycles. Various methods can be implemented to complement basketball development and performance and address individual needs.

Regardless of level of play, following an in-season resistance training program that is developed based on sound, research-based principles and implemented on a consistent basis allows the athlete to continue to build on previous gains in strength and power. Applying various resistance training methods, selecting exercises that have high transfer to the sport, and applying the correct intensities and loads at the appropriate times of the season are all important in addressing the demands of the basketball season while ensuring maintenance or progression. Both basketball performance and physical development can improve throughout the season with the support and inclusion of an in-season resistance training program.

Interpreting the Sample Program Tables

- DB = Dumbbell
- KB = Kettlebell
- RDL = Romanian deadlift
- PAP = Postactivation potentiation
- BW = Body weight
- RFD = Rate of force development
- BB = Barbell
- Order = Perform one set of each exercise (1a, 1b, 1c, and so on) in the group (1, 2, 3, and so on). Then go back to the first exercise in the group and do the second set of each exercise, and so on. If certain exercises call for fewer sets than others in the group, perform those sets on the backend of the grouping. For instance, if exercise 1a and exercise 1b call for 4 sets and exercise 1c calls for 3 sets, perform exercise 1c during sets 2 through 4 of exercises 1a and 1b.
- Tempo = The time, in seconds, for each phase or portion of the exercise, written as "eccentric phase: top (or bottom) position: concentric phase" (King, I., How to write strength training programs. In *Speed of Movement*, 1998, p. 123). For example, a tempo of "1:5:1" for the back squat means 1 second to lower, 5 seconds held at the bottom position, and 1 second to stand back up. Note: An "X" means that the athlete should explode during that phase of the movement. A tempo of "X:X:X" is associated with power exercises because there is not a prescriptive time allotted to each portion of the movement.

Table 12.4 Guards: In-Season Microcycle 1, Competitive Phase I

Total Body Strength Focus (Day 1)

Order	Exercise	Set(s)	Load	Reps or duration	Tempo	Rest
1a	Back squat (average velocity of 0.6-0.8 m/s)	1	53%	10 reps	3:1:1	1 min
		2	67%	8 reps	3:1:1	2 min
		3	76%	5-6 reps	3:1:1	3 min
		4	76%-85%	5-6 reps	3:1:1	3 min
1b	Barbell jump squat (PAP effect)	4	BW	3-5 reps	X:X:X	<30 s
1c	One-arm cable row (with split stance, high to low)	4		6-8 reps	3:1:1	2 min
2a	Push press	3		5-8 reps	X:X:X	<30 s
2b	Walking lunge (or reverse lunge)	3		5-8 reps	2:1:1	<30 s
2c	Leg curl (on stability ball)	3		8-10 reps	2:1:1	<30 s
2d	Single-leg RDL	3		8-10 reps	2:1:1	2 min
Additional advanced complex—college or pro athlete						
3a	Reverse hip extension hold*	2		5 reps	1:10:1	<30 s
3b	Single or double leg V-up	2		10-15 reps	2:1:1	60 s

*Hold position for 10 seconds and then relax and repeat for recommended repetitions.

Total Body Strength Focus (Day 2)

Order	Exercise	Set(s)	Load	Reps or duration	Tempo	Rest
1	Power (or hang) clean (peak velocity of 1.2-1.4 m/s)	1	25%-45%	3-5 reps	X:X:X	<30 s
		2	45%-65%	3-5 reps	X:X:X	<30 s
		3	45%-65%	3-5 reps	X:X:X	<30 s
		4	45%-65%	3-5 reps	X:X:X	<30 s
2a	Bench press	1	53%	10 reps	3:1:1	1 min
		2	67%	8 reps	3:1:1	2 min
		3	76%	5-6 reps	3:1:1	3 min
		4	76%-85%	5-6 reps	3:1:1	3 min
2b	Barbell hip thrust hold*	4		3-5 reps	1:3:1	2 min
3a	Single-leg squat on box	3		6-8 reps	3:1:X	<30 s
3b	Seated row	3		8-10 reps	1:3:1	<30 s
3c	Prone Y's, T's, I's**	3		5-6 reps	1:5:1	<30 s
3d	Standing Pallof press (with hip rotation)	3		5-6 reps	1:5:1	2 min
Additional advanced complex—college or pro athlete						
4a	Turkish get-up	2		2-4 reps	Slow, steady	<30 s
4b	Birddog hold (opposite arm and opposite leg)***	2		5 reps	1:10:1	60 s

*Hold the end position of each repetition for 3 seconds. **Hold the end position of each repetition for 5 seconds. ***Hold position for 10 seconds and then relax and repeat for recommended repetitions.

Table 12.5 Bigs: In-Season Microcycle 1, Competitive Phase I

Total Body Strength Focus (Day 1)

Order	Exercise	Set(s)	Load	Reps or duration	Tempo	Rest
1a	Back squat (average velocity of 0.6-0.8 m/s)	1	53%	10 reps	3:1:1	1 min
		2	67%	8 reps	3:1:1	2 min
		3	76%	5-6 reps	3:1:1	3 min
		4	76%-85%	5-6 reps	3:1:1	3 min
1b	Barbell jump squat (PAP effect)	4	BW	3-5 reps	X:X:X	<30 s
1c	One-arm cable row (with split stance, high to low)	4		6-8 reps	3:1:1	2 min
2a	Split jerk	3		5-8 reps	X:X:X	<30 s
2b	Walking lunge (or reverse lunge)	3		5-8 reps	2:1:1	<30s
2c	Leg curl (on stability ball)	3		8-10 reps	2:1:1	<30 s
2d	Single-leg RDL	3		8-10 reps	2:1:1	2 min
Additional advanced complex—college or pro athlete						
3a	Reverse hip extension hold*	2		5 reps	1:10:1	<30 s
3b	Single or double leg V-up	2		10-15 reps	2:1:1	60 s

*Hold position for 10 seconds and then relax and repeat for recommended repetitions.

Total Body Strength Focus (Day 2)

Order	Exercise	Set(s)	Load	Reps or duration	Tempo	Rest
1	Power (or hang) clean (peak velocity of 1.2-1.4 m/s)	1	25%-45%	3-5 reps	X:X:X	<30 s
		2	45%-65%	3-5 reps	X:X:X	<30 s
		3	45%-65%	3-5 reps	X:X:X	<30 s
		4	45%-65%	3-5 reps	X:X:X	<30 s
2a	Bench press	1	53%	10 reps	3:1:1	1 min
		2	67%	8 reps	3:1:1	2 min
		3	76%	5-6 reps	3:1:1	3 min
		4	76%-85%	5-6 reps	3:1:1	3 min
2b	Barbell hip thrust hold*	4		3-5 reps	1:3:1	2 min
3a	Single-leg squat on box	3		6-8 reps	3:1:X	<30 s
3b	Seated row	3		8-10 reps	1:3:1	<30 s
3c	Prone Y's, T's, I's**	3		5-6 reps	1:5:1	<30 s
3d	Standing Pallof press (with hip rotation)	3		5-6 reps	1:5:1	2 min
Additional advanced complex—college or pro athlete						
4a	Turkish get-up	2		2-4 reps	Slow, steady	<30 s
4b	Birddog hold (opposite arm and opposite leg)***	2		5 reps	1:10:1	60 s

*Hold the end position of each repetition for 3 seconds. **Hold the end position of each repetition for 5 seconds. ***Hold position for 10 seconds and then relax and repeat for recommended repetitions.

Table 12.6 Guards: In-Season Microcycle 2, Competitive Phase II

Total Body Strength Push and Pull Focus (Day 1)

Order	Exercise	Set(s)	Load	Reps or duration	Tempo	Rest
1a	Back squat (average velocity of 0.8-1.0 m/s)	1	53%	10 reps	2:1:1	1 min
		2	67%	8 reps	2:1:1	2 min
		3	76%	4-5 reps	1:X:X	3 min
		4	85%	4-5 reps	1:X:X	3 min
1b	Box depth jump	4		4-5 reps	X:X:X	<30 s
2a	BB or DB split snatch	3		5-6 reps	X:X:X	<30 s
2b	Lat pulldown (or pull-up)*	3		6-8 reps	2:1:X	<30 s
3a	Turkish get-up	3		1-2 reps	Slow, steady	<30 s
3b	Cable pressout hold (with lateral step)	3		4-5 reps	1:1:1	2 min
Additional advanced complex—playoff prep						
4a	DB walking lunge	2		5-6 reps	2:1:1	<30 s
4b	Single-leg squat to reach (stamina focus)	2		10-15 reps	1:2:1	60 s

*Slow, controlled eccentric phase, explosive concentric phase.

Total Body Strength Push and Pull Focus (Day 2)

Order	Exercise	Set(s)	Load	Reps or duration	Tempo	Rest
1a	Power (or hang) clean (peak velocity of 1.2-1.4 m/s)	1	25%-45%	3-5 reps	X:X:X	<30 s
		2	45%-65%	3-5 reps	X:X:X	<30 s
		3	45%-65%	3-5 reps	X:X:X	<30 s
		4	45%-65%	3-5 reps	X:X:X	<30 s
1b	DB bench press*	1	53%	10 reps	2:1:1	1 min
		2	67%	8 reps	2:1:1	2 min
		3	76%	4-5 reps	1:X:X	3 min
		4	76%-85%	4-5 reps	1:X:X	3 min
2a	Step-up	4		4-5 reps	1:1:1	<30 s
2b	Seated row**	3		6-8 reps	2:1:X	<30 s
3a	RDL	3		6-8 reps	2:1:X	<30 s
3b	Birddog plank (opposite arm and opposite leg raise) (sagittal plane)	3		10-12 reps	1:1:1	2 min
Additional advanced complex—playoff prep						
4a	D2 pattern, single-leg stance***	2		10-15 reps	1:2:1	<30 s
4b	Side plank hold (stamina focus)	2		45-60 s	Iso hold	<30 s

*Slower, controlled eccentric phase with quick transition and explosive concentric phase. **Longer eccentric phase with explosive concentric phase. ***Pause with arm extended overhead for 2 seconds.

Table 12.7 Bigs: In-Season Microcycle 2, Competitive Phase II

Total Body Strength Push and Pull Focus (Day 1)

Order	Exercise	Set(s)	Load	Reps or duration	Tempo	Rest
1a	Back squat (average velocity of 0.8-1.0 m/s	1	53%	10 reps	2:1:1	1 min
		2	67%	8 reps	2:1:1	2 min
		3	76%	4-5 reps	1:X:X	3 min
		4	85%	4-5 reps	1:X:X	3 min
1b	Box depth jump	4		4-5 reps	X:X:X	<30 s
2a	Single-leg squat on box	3		5-6 reps	2:1:1	<30 s
2b	Lat pulldown (or pull-up)*	3		6-8 reps	2:1:X	<30 s
3a	Turkish get-up	3		1-2 reps	Slow, steady	<30 s
3b	Cable pressout hold (with lateral step)	3		4-5 reps	1:1:1	2 min
Additional advanced complex—playoff prep						
4a	DB walking lunge	2		5-6 reps	2:1:1	<30 s
4b	Single-leg squat to reach (stamina focus)	2		10-15 reps	1:2:1	60 s

*Slow, controlled eccentric phase, explosive concentric phase.

Total Body Strength Push and Pull Focus (Day 2)

Order	Exercise	Set(s)	Load	Reps or duration	Tempo	Rest
1a	Step-up	4		4-5 reps	1:1:1	<30 s
1b	DB bench press*	1	53%	10 reps	2:1:1	1 min
		2	67%	8 reps	2:1:1	2 min
		3	76%	4-5 reps	1:X:X	3 min
		4	76%-85%	4-5 reps	1:X:X	3 min
2a	One-arm push press	3		5-6 reps	X:X:X	<30 s
2b	Landmine squat to rotational press**	3		4-5 reps	2:1:X	<30 s
3a	RDL	3		6-8 reps	2:1:1	<30 s
3b	Birddog plank (opposite arm and opposite leg raise) (sagittal plane)	3		10-12 reps	1:1:1	2 min
Additional advanced complex—playoff prep						
4a	D2 pattern, single-leg stance***	2		10-15 reps	1:2:1	<30 s
4b	Side plank hold (stamina focus)	2		45-60 s	Iso hold	<30 s

*Slower, controlled eccentric phase with quick transition and explosive concentric phase. **Slow, controlled eccentric phase with explosive concentric phase. ***Pause with arm extended overhead for 2 seconds.

REFERENCES

Chapter 1

1. Atkins, S, Bentley, I, Hurst, H, Sinclair, J, and Hesketh, C. The presence of bilateral imbalance of the lower limbs in elite youth soccer players of different ages. *J Strength Cond Res* 30(4):1007-1013, 2016.

2. Allerton, TD, Earnest, CP, and Johannsen, NM. Metabolic and mechanical effects of laddermill graded exercise testing. *J Strength Cond Res* 32(1):195-200, 2018.

3. Baptista, F, Mil-Homens, P, Carita, A, Janz, K, and Sardinha, L. Peak vertical jump power as a marker of bone health in children. *Int J Sports Med* 37(8):653-658, 2016.

4. Barker, LA, Harry, JR, and Mercer, JA. Relationships between countermovement jump ground reaction forces and jump height, reactive strength index, and jump time. *J Strength Cond Res* 32(1):248-254, 2018.

5. Beck, BR, Daly, RM, Singh, MA, and Taaffe, DR. Exercise and Sports Science Australia (ESSA) position statement on exercise prescription for the prevention and management of osteoporosis. *J Sci Med Sport* 20(5):438-445, 2017.

6. Bolotin, A, and Bakayev, V. Efficacy of using isometric exercises to prevent basketball injuries. *Journal of Physical Education and Sport* 16(4):1177, 2016.

7. Bridgeman, LA, McGuigan, MR, Gill, ND, and Dulson, DK. Relationships between concentric and eccentric strength and countermovement jump performance in resistance trained men. *J Strength Cond Res* 32(1):255-260, 2018.

8. Brigatto, FA, Braz, TV, Cristina da Costa Zanini, T, Germano, MD, Aoki, MS, Schoenfeld, BJ, Marchetti, PH, and Lopes, CR. Effect of resistance training frequency on neuromuscular performance and muscle morphology after eight weeks in trained men. *J Strength Cond Res*. Post acceptance, March 6, 2018.

9. Caia, J, Weiss, LW, Chiu, LZF, Schilling, BK, Paquette, MR, and Relyea, GE. Do lower-body dimensions and body composition explain vertical jump ability? *J Strength Cond Res* 30(11): 3073-3083, 2016.

10. Campbell, BI, Bove, D, Ward, P, Vargas, A, Dolan, J. Quantification of training load and training response for improving athletic performance. *Strength and Conditioning Journal* 39(5):3-13, 2017.

11. Cholewa, JM, Rossi, FE, MacDonald, C, Hewins, A, Gallo, S, Micenski, A, Norton, L, and Campbell, BI. The effects of moderate- versus high-load resistance training on muscle growth, body composition, and performance in collegiate women. *J Strength Cond Res* 32(6):1511-1524, 2018.

12. Colquhoun, RJ., Gai, CM, and Aguilar, D. Training volume, not frequency, indicative of maximal strength adaptations to resistance training. *J Strength Cond Res* 32(5):1207-1213, 2018.

13. Contreras, B, Vigotsky, AD, Schoenfeld, BL, Beardsley, C, McMaster, DT, Reyneke, JHT, and Cronin, JB. Effects of a six-week hip thrust vs. front squat resistance training program on performance in adolescent males: A randomized controlled trial. *J Strength Cond Res* 31(4), 999-1008, 2017.

14. Cormie, P, McBride, JM, and McCaulley, GO. Power-time, force-time, and velocity-time curve analysis of the CMJ: Impact of training. *J Strength Cond Res* 23(1):177-186, 2009.

15. Costigan, SA, Eather, N, Plotnikoff, RC, Hillman, CH, and Lubans, DR. High-intensity interval training for cognitive and mental health in adolescents. *Medicine and Science in Sports and Exercise* 48(10):1985-1993, 2016.

16. de Freitas, MC, Gerosa-Neto, J, Zanchi, NE, Lira, FS, and Rossi FE. Role of metabolic stress for enhancing muscle adaptations: Practical applications. *World J Methodol* 7(2):46, 2107.

17. de Paula Simola, RÁ, Harms, N, Raeder, C, Kellmann, M, Meyer, T, Pfeiffer, M, and Ferrauti, A. Assessment of neuromuscular function after different strength training protocols using tensiomyography. *J Strength Cond Res* 29(5):1339-1348, 2015.

18. Douglas, J, Pearson, S, Ross, A, and McGuigan, M. Effects of accentuated eccentric loading on muscle properties, strength, power, and speed in resistance-trained rugby players. *J Strength Cond Res* 32(10):2750-2761, 2018.

19. Duplanty, AA, Levitt, DE, Hill, DW, McFarlin, BK, DiMarco, NM, and Vingren, JL. Resistance

training is associated with higher bone mineral density among young adult male distance runners independent of physiological factors. *J Strength Cond Res* 32(6):1594-1600, 2018.

20. Fahs, CA, Rossow, LM, and Zourdos, MC. Analysis of factors related to back squat concentric velocity. *J Strength Cond Res* 32(9):2435-2441, 2018.

21. Farrar, RE, Mayhew, JL, and Koch, AJ. Oxygen cost of kettlebell swings. *J Strength Cond Res* 24(4):1034-1036, 2010.

22. Figueroa A, Okamoto T, Jaime SJ, Fahs CA. Impact of high- and low-intensity resistance training on arterial stiffness and blood pressure in adults across the lifespan: A review. *Pflugers Arch* 471(3):467-478, 2019.

23. Frost, DM, Bronson, S, Cronin, JB, and Newton, RU. Changes in maximal strength, velocity, and power after 8 weeks of training with pneumatic or free weight resistance. *J Strength Cond Res* 30(4):934-944, 2016.

24. Gothe, NP, Keswani, RK, and McAuley, E. Yoga practice improves executive function by attenuating stress levels. *Biological Psychology* 121:109-116, 2016.

25. Gual, G, Fort-Vanmeerhaeghe, A, and Romero-Rodríguez, D. Volleyball and basketball players can be considered as a population at risk for patellar tendinopathy. *J Strength Cond Res* 30(7):1834-1842, 2016.

26. Gomes, APF, Correia, MA, Soares, AHG, Cucato, GG, Lima, AHRA, Cavalcante, BR, Sobral-Filho, DC, and Ritti-Dias, RM. Effects of resistance training on cardiovascular function in patients with peripheral artery disease: A randomized controlled trial. *J Strength Cond Res* 32(4):1072-1080, 2018.

27. Gonzalez-Badillo, J, Marques, M, and Sanchez-Medina, L. The importance of movement velocity as a measure to control resistance training intensity. *Journal of Human Kinetics* 29(special issue):15-19, 2011.

28. Groennebaek, T, and Vissing, K. Impact of resistance training on skeletal muscle mitochondrial biogenesis, content, and function. *Front Physiol* 8:713, 2017.

29. Haff, G, and Triplett, NT. *Essentials of Strength Training and Conditioning*. 4th ed. Champaign, IL: Human Kinetics, 2016.

30. Hartley, DR, and McMahon, JJ. The role of strength training for lower extremity tendinopathy. *Strength and Conditioning Journal* 40(4):85-95, 2018.

31. Haun, CT, Mumford, PW, Roberson, PA, Romero, MA, Mobley, CB, Kephart, WC, Anderson, RG, Colquhoun, RJ, Muddle, TW, Luera, MJ, and Mackey, CS. Molecular, neuromuscular, and recovery responses to light versus heavy resistance exercise in young men. *Physiological Reports* 5(18), 2017.

32. Hausswirth, C, and Mujika, I. *Recovery for Performance in Sport*. Champaign, IL: Human Kinetics, 2013.

33. Hernández-Preciado, JA, Baz, E, Balsalobre-Fernández, C, Marchante, D, and Santos-Concejero, J. Potentiation effects of the French contrast method on vertical jumping ability. *J Strength Cond Res* 32(7):1909-1914, 2018.

34. Hill, EC, Housh, TJ, Smith, CM, Keller, JL, Schmidt, RJ, and Johnson, GO. High-vs. low-intensity fatiguing eccentric exercise on muscle thickness, strength, and blood flow. *J Strength Cond Res* 13:15, 2018.

35. Jenkins, ND, Housh, TJ, Buckner, SL, Bergstrom, HC, Cochrane, KC, Hill, EC, Smith, CM, Schmidt, RJ, Johnson, GO, and Cramer, JT. Neuromuscular adaptations after 2 and 4 weeks of 80% versus 30% 1 repetition maximum resistance training to failure. *J Strength Cond Res* 30(8):2174-2185, 2016.

36. Jenkins, ND, Miramonti, AA, Hill, EC, Smith, CM, Cochrane-Snyman, KC, Housh, TJ, and Cramer, JT. Greater neural adaptations following high-vs. low-load resistance training. *Front Physiol* 8:331, 2017.

37. Kraemer, W, Ratamess, N, Nindl, B. Recovery responses of testosterone, growth hormone, and IGF-1 after resistance exercise. *J Appl Physiol* 122:549-558, 2017.

38. Lesinski, M, Prieske, O, and Granacher, U. Effects and dose-response relationships of resistance training on physical performance in youth athletes: A systematic review and meta-analysis. *British Journal of Sports Medicine* 50:781-795, 2016.

39. Luk, HY, Winter, C, O'Neill, E, and Thompson, BA. 2014. Comparison of muscle strength imbalance in powerlifters and jumpers. *J Strength Cond Res* 28(1):23-27.

40. Mann, B, Ivey, P, and Sayers, S. Velocity-based training in football. *Strength and Conditioning Journal* 37(6):52-57, 2015.

41. McBride, JM, Nimphius, S, and Erickson, TM. The acute effects of heavy-load squats and loaded countermovement jumps on sprint performance. *J Strength Cond Res* 19(4):893-897, 2005.

42. McGill, SM. *Ultimate Back Fitness and Performance*. 5th ed. Waterloo, Canada: Backfitpro, 2014.

43. Mikkelsen, K, Stojanovska, L, Polenakovic, M, Bosevski, M, and Apostolopoulos, V. Exercise and mental health. *Maturitas* 106:48-56, 2017.

44. Mitchell, CJ, Churchward-Venne, TA, West, DW, Burd, NA, Breen, L, Baker, SK, and Phillips, SM. Resistance exercise load does not determine training-mediated hypertrophic gains in young men. *Journal of Applied Physiology* 113(1):71-77, 2012.

45. Muddle, TW, Colquhoun, RJ, Magrini, MA, Luera, MJ, DeFreitas, JM, and Jenkins, ND. Effects of fatiguing, submaximal high-versus low-torque isometric exercise on motor unit recruitment and firing behavior. *Physiological Reports* 6(8):13675, 2018.

46. Neto, GR, Novaes, JS, Dias, I, Brown, A, Vianna, J, and Cirilo-Sousa, MS. Effects of resistance training with blood flow restriction on haemodynamics: A systematic review. *Clinical Physiology and Functional Imaging* 37(6):567-574, 2017.

47. Silva, JCG, Aniceto, RR, Oliota-Ribeiro, LS, Neto, GR, Leandro, LS, and Cirilo-Sousa, MS. Mood effects of blood flow restriction resistance exercise among basketball players. *Percept Mot Skills* 125(4):788-801, 2018.

48. Paulo, AC, Tricoli, V, Queiroz, ACC, Laurentino, G, and Forjaz, CLM. Blood pressure response during resistance training of different work to rest ratio. *J Strength Cond Res* 33(2):399-407, 2017.

49. Patil, SG, Mullur, LM, Khodnapur, JP, Dhanakshirur, GB, and Aithala, MR. Effect of yoga on short-term heart rate variability measure as a stress index in subjunior cyclists: A pilot study. *Indian J Physiol Pharmacol* 57(2):153-8, 2013.

50. Prestes, J, Tibana, RA, de Araujo Sousa, E, da Cunha Nascimento, D, de Oliveira Rocha, P, Camarço, NF, de Sousa, NMF, and Willardson, JM. Strength and muscular adaptations following 6 weeks of rest-pause versus traditional multiple-sets

51. Ratamess, NA, Rosenberg, JG, Klei, S, Dougherty, BM, Kang, J, Smith, CR, Ross, RE, and Faigenbaum, AD. Comparison of the acute metabolic responses to traditional resistance, body-weight, and battling rope exercises. *J Strength Cond Res* 29(1):47-57, 2015.

52. Romero-Arenas, S, Ruiz, R, Vera-Ibanez, A, Colomer-Poveda, D, Guadalupe-Grau, A, and Marquez, G. Neuromuscular and cardiovascular adaptations in response to high-intensity interval power training. *J Strength Cond Res* 32(1):130-138, 2018.

53. Salonikidis, K, and Zafeiridis, A. The effects of plyometric, tennis drills, and combined training on reaction, lateral and linear speed, power, and strength in novice tennis players. *J Strength Cond Res* 22(1):182-191, 2008.

54. Sanz-Lopez, F, Berzosa, C, Hita-Contreras, F, Cruz-Diaz, D, and Martınez-Amat, A. Ultrasound changes in Achilles tendon and gastrocnemius medialis muscle on squat eccentric overload and running performance. *J Strength Cond Res* 30(7):2010-2018, 2016.

55. Secomb, JL, Lundgren, LE, Farley, ORL, Tran, TT, Nimphius, S, and Sheppard, JM. Relationships between lower-body muscle structure and lower-body strength, power, and muscle-tendon complex stiffness. *J Strength Cond Res*, 29(8):2221-2228, 2015.

56. Schelling, X, Calleja-González, J, and Torres-Ronda, L. Using testosterone and cortisol as biomarker for training individualization in elite basketball: A 4-year follow-up study. *J Strength Cond Res* 29(2):368-378, 2015.

57. Schoenfeld, BJ, Grgic, J, Ogborn, D, and Krieger, JW. Strength and hypertrophy adaptations between low- vs. high-load resistance training: A systematic review and meta-analysis. *J Strength Cond Res* 31(12):3508-3523, 2017.

58. Sole, CJ, Moir, GL, Davis, SE, and Witmer, CA. Mechanical analysis of the acute effects of a heavy resistance exercise warm-up on agility performance in court-sport athletes. *Journal of Human Kinetics* 39:147-156, 2013.

59. Spiteri, T, Nimphius, S, Hart, NH, Specos, C, Sheppard, JM, and Newton, RU. Contribution of strength characteristics to change of direction and agility performance in female basketball athletes. *J Strength Cond Res* 28(9): 2415-2423, 2014.

60. Styles, WJ, Matthews, MJ, and Comfort, P. Effects of strength training on squat and sprint

resistance training in trained subjects. *J Strength Cond Res* (published ahead of print), 1-28, 2019.

performance in soccer players. *J Strength Cond* Res 30(6):1534-1539, 2016.

61. Townsend, J, Bender, D, Vantrease, W, Hudy, J, Huet, K, Williamson, C, Bechke, E, Serafini, P, and Mangine, G. Isometric mid-thigh pull performance is associated with athletic performance and sprinting kinetics in Division I men and women's basketball players. *J Strength Cond Res* (Epub ahead of print), 2017.

62. Wagle, JP, Cunanan, AJ, and Carroll, KM. Accentuated eccentric loading and cluster set configurations in the back squat: A kinetic and kinematic analysis. *J Strength Cond Res* (Epub ahead of print), 2018.

63. Wen, N, Dalbo, VJ, Burgos, B. Power testing in basketball: Current practice and future recommendations. *J Strength Cond Res* 32(9):2677-2691, 2018.

64. Wilson, JM, and Flanagan, EP. The role of elastic energy in activities with high force and power requirements: A brief review. *J Strength Cond Res* 22(5):1705-1715, 2008.

65. Zatsiorsky, VM, and Kraemer, WJ. *Science and Practice of Strength Training*. 2nd ed. Champaign, IL: Human Kinetics, 2006.

66. Zouita, S, Zouita, ABM, Kebsi, W, Dupont, G, Ben Abderrahman, A, Ben Salah, FZ, and Zouhal, H. Strength training reduces injury rate in elite young soccer players during one season. *J Strength Cond Res* 30(5):1295-1307, 2016.

Chapter 2

1. Abdelkrim, NB, Castagna, C, Fazaa, SE, Tabka, Z, and Ati, JE. Blood metabolites during basketball competitions. *J Strength Cond Res* 23(3):765-773, 2009.

2. Abe, T, Kitaoka, Y, Kikuchi, DM, Takeda, K, Numata, O, and Takemasa, T. High-intensity interval training-induced metabolic adaptation coupled with an increase in Hif-1α and glycolytic protein expression. *Journal of Applied Physiology* 119(11):1297-1302, 2015.

3. Bale, P. Anthropometric, body composition and performance variables of young elite female basketball players. *Journal of Sports Medicine and Physical Fitness* 31(2):173-177, 1991.

4. Bernstein, NA. *The Coordination and Regulation of Movement*. Oxford, UK: Pergamon Press, 1967.

5. Bosch, TA, Steinberger, J, Sinaiko, AR, Moran, A, Jacobs Jr, DR, Kelly, AS, and Dengel, DR. Identification of sex-specific thresholds for accumulation of visceral adipose tissue in adults. *Obesity* 23(2):375-382, 2015.

6. Bishop, DC, and Wright, C. A time-motion analysis of professional basketball to determine the relationship between three activity profiles: High, medium and low intensity and the length of the time spent on court. *International Journal of Performance Analysis in Sport* 6(1):130-139, 2006.

7. Buytendijk, FJJ. *Les Différences essentielles des Fonctions psychiques de L'homme et des Animaux*. Paris: Librairie philosophique J. Vrin., 1930.

8. Caprio, S. Relationship between abdominal visceral fat and metabolic risk factors in obese adolescents. *American Journal of Human Biology: The Official Journal of the Human Biology Association* 11(2):259-266, 1999.

9. Chow, JY, Davids, K, Button, C, and Renshaw, I. *Nonlinear Pedagogy in Skill Acquisition. An Introduction*. New York: Routledge, 2016.

10. Davids, K. The constraints-based approach to motor learning: Implications for a non-linear pedagogy in sport and physical education. In *Motor Learning in Practice*. New York: Routledge, 23-36, 2010.

11. Davids, K, Araújo, D, Correia, V, and Vilar, L. How small-sided and conditioned games enhance acquisition of movement and decision-making skills. *Exercise and Sport Sciences Reviews* 41(3):154-161, 2013.

12. Deneweth, JM, Pomeroy, SM, Russell, JR, McLean, SG, Zernicke, RF, Bedi, A, and Goulet, GC. Position-specific hip and knee kinematics in NCAA football athletes. *Orthopaedic Journal of Sports Medicine* 2:6, 2014.

13. Drakos, MC, Domb, B, Starkey, C, Callahan, L, and Allen, AA. Injury in the National Basketball Association: A 17-year overview. *Sports Health* 2(4):284-290, 2010.

13b. ESPN. NBA player stats. https://www.espn.com/nba/stats/player. Accessed September 10, 2019.

14. Flatt, AA, Esco, MR, Allen, JR, Robinson, JB, Earley, RL, Fedewa, MV, Bragg, A, Keith, CM, and Wingo, JE. Heart rate variability and training load among National Collegiate Athletic Association Division 1 college football players throughout spring camp. *J Strength Cond Res* 32(11):3127-3134, 2018.

15. Hartley, EM, Hoch MC, and Boling MC. Y-balance test performance and BMI are associated with ankle sprain injury in collegiate male athletes. *Journal of Science and Medicine in Sport* 21(7):676-680, 2018.

16. Hewett TE, Myer GD, Ford KR, Paterno MV, and Quatman CE. Mechanisms, prediction, and prevention of ACL injuries: Cut risk with three sharpened and validated tools. *J Orthopaedic Research* 34:1843-1855, 2016.

17. Kim, S, Cho, B, Lee, H, Choi, K, Hwang, SS, Kim, D, Kim, K, and Kwon, H. Distribution of abdominal visceral and subcutaneous adipose tissue and metabolic syndrome in a Korean population. *Diabetes Care* 34(2):504-506, 2011.

18. Moran, LR, Hegedus, EJ, Bleakley, CM, and Taylor, JB. Jump load: Capturing the next great injury analytic. *Br J Sports Med* 53(1):8-9, 2019.

19. Narazaki K, Berg K, Stergiou N, Chen B. Physiological demands of competitive basketball. *Scand J Med Sci Sports* 19(3):425-432, 2009.

19b. National Heart, Lung, and Blood Institute. Classification of overweight and obesity by BMI, waist circumference, and associated disease risks. https://www.nhlbi.nih.gov/health/educational/lose_wt/BMI/bmi_dis.htm. Accessed September 10, 2019.

19c. NBA Advanced Stats. Draft combine. https://stats.nba.com/draft/combine/. Accessed September 10, 2019.

20. Nye, NS, Carnahan, DH, Jackson, JC, Covey, CJ, Zarzabal, LA, Chao, SY, Bockhorst, AD, and Crawford, PF. Abdominal circumference is superior to body mass index in estimating musculoskeletal injury risk. *Medicine & Science in Sports & Exercise* 46(10):1951-1959, 2014.

21. Padua DA, DiStefano LJ, Beutler AI, De La Motte SJ, DiStefano MJ, and Marshall SW. The landing error scoring system as a screening tool for an anterior cruciate ligament injury-prevention program in elite-youth soccer athletes. *Journal of Athletic Training* 50(6):589-595, 2015.

22. Parolin, ML, Chesley, A, Matsos, MP, Spriet, LL, Jones, NL, and Heigenhauser, GJF. Regulation of skeletal muscle glycogen phosphorylase and PDH during maximal intermittent exercise. *American Journal of Physiology-Endocrinology and Metabolism* 277(5):E890-900, 1999.

23. Paterno, MV, Schmitt, LC, Ford, KR, Rauh, MJ, Myer, GD, Huang, B, and Hewett TE. Biomechanical measures during landing and postural stability predict second anterior cruciate ligament injury after anterior cruciate ligament reconstruction and return to sport. *American Journal of Sports Medicine* 38(10):1968-1978, 2010.

24. Richmond, SA., Kang, J, Doyle-Baker, PK, Nettel-Aguirre, A, and Emery, CA. A school-based injury prevention program to reduce sport injury risk and improve healthy outcomes in youth: A pilot cluster-randomized controlled trial. *Clinical Journal of Sport Medicine* 26(4):291-298, 2016.

25. Roos, KG, Kerr, ZY, Mauntel, TC, Djoko, A, Dompier, TP, and Wikstrom, EA. The epidemiology of lateral ligament complex ankle sprains in National Collegiate Athletic Association sports. *Am J Sports Med* 45(1):201-209, 2017.

26. Scanlan, A, Dascombe, B, and Reaburn, P. A comparison of the activity demands of elite and sub-elite Australian men's basketball competition. *Journal of Sports Sciences* 29(11):1153-1160, 2011.

27. Schinkel-Ivy, A, Burkhart, TA, and Andrews, DM. Differences in distal lower extremity tissue masses and mass ratios exist in athletes of sports involving repetitive impacts. *Journal of Sports Sciences* 32(6):533-541, 2014.

28. Skazalski C. A valid and reliable method to measure jump-specific training and competition load in elite volleyball players. *Scand J Med Sci Sports* 28(5):1578-1585, 2018.

29. Solfest, AL, Raymond-Pope, CJ, Carbuhn, A, Stanforth, PR, Oliver, JM, Ransone, JW, Bosch, TA, and Dengel, DR. Body composition of Division I collegiate basketball athletes, Consortium of College Athlete Research (C-CAR) Study: 1647 Board# 5 May 31. *Medicine & Science in Sports & Exercise* 50:382, 2018.

30. Stojanović, E, Stojiljković, N, Scanlan, AT, Dalbo, VJ, Berkelmans, DM, and Milanović, Z. The activity demands and physiological responses encountered during basketball match-play: A systematic review. *Sports Medicine* 48(1):111-135, 2018.

31. Weber, DR, Leonard, MB, Shults, J, and Zemel, BS. A comparison of fat and lean body mass index to BMI for the identification of metabolic syndrome in children and adolescents. *Journal of Clinical Endocrinology & Metabolism* 99(9):3208-3216, 2014.

32. Visnes, H. Training volume and body composition as risk factors for developing jumper's knee among young elite volleyball players. *Scand J Med Sci Sports* 23:607-613, 2013.

33. Zazulak BT, Hewett TE, Reeves NP, Goldberg B, and Cholewicki J. Deficits in neuromuscular control of the trunk predict knee injury risk. A prospective biomechanical-epidemiologic study. *American Journal of Sports Medicine* 35(7):1123-1130, 2009.

34. Ziv, G, and Lidor, R. Physical attributes, physiological characteristics, on-court performances and nutritional strategies of female and male basketball players. *Sports Med* 39(7):547-568, 2009.

35. Žumbakytėermukšnienė, R, Kajėnienė, A, Berškienė, K, Daunoravičienė, A, and Sederevičiūtė-Kandrataviciene, R. Assessment of the effect of anthropometric data on the alterations of cardiovascular parameters in Lithuanian elite male basketball players during physical load. *Medicina* 48(11):83, 2012.

Chapter 3

1. Alemdaroğlu, U. The relationship between muscle strength, anaerobic performance, agility, sprint ability and vertical jump performance in professional basketball players. *Journal of Human Kinetics* 31:149-158, 2012.

2. Almuzaini, KS, and Fleck, SJ. Modification of the standing long jump test enhances ability to predict anaerobic performance. *J Strength Cond Res* 22:1265-1272, 2008.

3. Andrews, AW, Thomas, MT, and Bohannon, RW. Normative values for isometric muscle force obtained with hand-held dynamometers. *Physical Therapy* 76(3):248-259, 1996.

4. Ashworth, B, Hogben, P, Singh, N, Tulloch, L, and Cohen, DD. The athletic shoulder (ASH) test: Reliability of a novel upper body isometric strength test in elite rugby players. *BJM Open Sport Exerc Med*, 2018.

5. Brady, CJ, Harrison, AJ, Flanagan, EP, Haff, GG, and Comyns, TM. A comparison of the isometric midthigh pull and isometric squat: Intraday reliability, usefulness, and the magnitude of difference between tests. *IJSPP* 13:844-852, 2018.

6. Brown, AE. *The reliability and validity of the lane agility test for collegiate basketball players.* Doctoral dissertation, University of Wisconsin-La Crosse, 2012.

7. Bruce, R, Kusumi, F, and Hosmer, D. Maximal oxygen intake and nomographic assessment of functional aerobic impairment in cardiovascular disease. *American Heart Journal* 85(4):546-562, 1973.

8. Chaouachi, A, Brughelli, M, Chamari, K, Levin, GT, Abdelkrim, NB, Laurencelle, L, and Castagna, C. Lower limb maximal dynamic strength and agility determinants in elite basketball players. *J Strength Cond Res* 23(5):1570-1577, 2009.

9. Comfort, P, Jones, PA, McMahon, JJ, and Newton, R. Effect of knee and trunk angle on kinetic variables during the isometric midthigh pull: Test-retest reliability. *IJSPP* 10:58-63, 2014.

10. Cormack, SJ, Newton, RU, and McGuigan, MR. Neuromuscular and endocrine responses of elite players to an Australian rules football match. *Int J Sports Physiol Perform* 3:359-374, 2008.

11. Dawes, JJ, Marshall, M, and Spiteri, T. Relationship between pre-season testing performance and playing time among NCAA DII basketball players. *Sports Exer Med* 2(2):47-54, 2016.

12. Delextrat, A, and Cohen, D. Physiological testing of basketball players: Toward a standard evaluation of anaerobic fitness. *J Strength Cond Res* 22:1066-1072, 2008.

13. Delextrat, A, and Cohen, D. Strength, power, speed, and agility of women basketball players according to playing position. *J Strength Cond Res* 23(7):1974-1981, 2009.

14. Dos'Santos, T, Thomas, C, Jones, PA, McMahon, JJ, and Comfort, P. The effect of hip joint angle on isometric midthigh pull kinetics. *J Strength Cond Res* 31(10):2748-2757, 2017.

15. Ebben, WP, and Petushek, EJ. Using the reactive strength index modified to evaluate plyometric performance. *J Strength Cond Res* 24:1983-1987, 2010.

16. Flanagan, EP, and Comyns, TM. The use of contact time and the reactive strength index to optimize fast stretch-shortening cycle training. *Strength & Conditioning Journal* 30(5):32-38, 2008.

17. Frank, B, Bell, DR, Norcross, MF, Blackburn, JT, Goerger, BM, and Pauda, DA. Trunk and hip biomechanics influence anterior cruciate loading mechanism in physical active participants. *Am J Sports Med* 41(11):2676-83, 2013.

18. Gabbett, TJ, Kelly, JN, and Sheppard, JM. Speed, change of direction speed, and reactive agility of rugby league players. *J Strength Cond Res* 22:174-181, 2008.

19. Giffin, VC, Everett, T, and Horsley, IG. A comparison of hip adduction and abduction strength ratios, in the dominant and non-dominant limb, of elite football academy players. *Journal of Biomedical Engineering and Informatics* 2:(1), 2016.

20. Harper, D, Hobbs, S, and Moore, J. The ten to five repeated jump test: A new test for evaluating reactive strength. *British Association of Sports and Exercises Sciences Student Conference*, Chester, 2011.

21. Hoffman, J. *Norms for Fitness, Performance, and Health.* Champaign, IL: Human Kinetics, 2006.

22. Hunter, JP, Marshall, RN, and McNair, PJ. Relationship between ground reaction force impulse and kinematics of sprint-running acceleration. *J Appl Biomech* 21:31-43, 2005.

23. Jackson, TJ, Starkey, C, McElhiney, D, and Domb, BG. Epidemiology of hip injuries in the National Basketball Association: A 24-year overview. *Orthop J Sports Med*, 2013.

24. Jakovljevic, ST, Karalejic, MS, Pajic, ZB, Macura, MM, and Erculj, FF. Speed and agility of 12-and 14-year-old elite male basketball players. *J Strength Cond Res* 26(9):2453-2459, 2012.

25. Kaminsky, LA, Arena, R, and Myers, J. Reference standards for cardiorespiratory fitness measured with cardiopulmonary exercise testing: Data

from the fitness registry and the importance of exercise national database. *Mayo Clinic Proceedings* 90(11):1515-1523, 2015.

26. Latin, RW, Berg, K, and Baechle, T. Physical and performance characteristics of NCAA division I male basketball players. *J Strength Cond Res* 8(4):214-218, 1994.

27. Leger, LA, Mercier, D, Gadoury, C, and Lambert, J. The multistage 20-meter shuttle run test for aerobic fitness. *J Sport Sci* 6:93-101, 1988.

28. Manske, R, and Reiman, M. Functional performance testing for power and return to sports. *Athletic Training*, 2013.

29. National Basketball Conditioning Coaches Association. *Complete Conditioning for Basketball.* Champaign, IL: Human Kinetics, 2007.

30. Noyes, FR, Barber-Westin, SD, Smith, ST, Campbell, T. and Garrison, TT. A training program to improve neuromuscular performance indices in female high school basketball players. *J Strength Cond Res* 26:709-719, 2012.

31. Paine, R and Voight, ML. The role of the scapula. *Int J Sports Phys Ther* 8(5):617-629, 2013.

32. Pehar, M, Sekulic, D, Sisic, N, Spasic, M, Uljevic, O Krolo, A, Milanovic, Z, and Sattler, T. Evaluation of different jumping tests in defining position-specific and performance-level differences in high level basketball players. *Biol Sport* 34(3):263-27, 2017.

33. Roe, G, Shaw, W, Darrall-Jones, J, Phibbs, PJ, Read, D, Weakley, JJ, Till, K, and Jones, B. Reliability and validity of a medicine ball-contained accelerometer for measuring upper-body neuromuscular performance. *J Strength Cond Res* 32(7):1915-1918, 2018.

34. Scanlan, A, Madueno, M, Guy, J, Giamarelos, K, Spiteri, T, and Dalbo, V. Measuring decrement in change-of-direction speed across repeated sprints in basketball: Novel vs. traditional approaches. *J Strength Cond Res.* Published ahead of print, 2018.

35. Scanlan, AT, Dascombe, BJ, Reaburn, P, and Dalbo, VJ. The physiological and activity demands experienced by Australian female basketball players during competition. *J Sci Med Sport* 14:341-347, 2012.

36. Scanlan, AT, Wen, N, Pyne, DB, Stojanović, E, Milanović, Z, Conte, D, Vaquera, A, and Dalbo, VJ. Power-related determinants of modified agility T-test performance in male adolescent basketball players. *J Strength Cond Res* (Published ahead of print), March 2019.

37. Schweigert, D. Normative values for common preseason testing protocols: NCAA Division II women's basketball. *Strength & Conditioning Journal* 18(6):7-10, 1996.

38. Sekulic, D, Pehar M, Krolo A, Spasic M, Uljevic O, Calleja-González J, and Sattler, T. Evaluation of basketball-specific agility: Applicability of preplanned and nonplanned agility performances for differentiating playing positions and playing levels. *J Strength Cond Res* 31(8):2278-2288, 2017.

39. Spiteri, T, Binetti, M, Scanlan, A, Dalbo, V, Dolci, F, and Specos, C. Physical determinants of Division 1 collegiate basketball, Women's National Basketball League, and Women's National Basketball Association athletes: With reference to lower body sidedness. *J Strength Cond Res* (Published ahead of print), 2017.

40. Spiteri, T, McIntyre, F, Specos, C, and Myszka, S. Cognitive training for agility: The integration between perception and action. *Strength & Conditioning Journal* 40(1):39-46, 2018.

41. Spiteri, T, Newton, RU, Binetti, M, Hart, NH, Sheppard, JM, and Nimphius, S. Mechanical determinants of faster change of direction and agility performance in female basketball athletes. *J Strength Cond Res* 29:2205-2214, 2015.

42. Spiteri, T, Nimphius, S, Hart, NH, Specos, C, Sheppard, JM, and Newton, RU. Contribution of strength characteristics to change of direction and agility performance in female basketball athletes. *J Strength Cond Res* 28(9):2415-2423, 2014.

43. Sugimoto, D, Mattacola, CG, Millineaux, DR, and Palmer, TG, and Hewett, TE. Comparison of isokinetic hip adduction and adduction peak torques and ratios between sexes. *Clin J Sports Med* 24(5):422-428, 2014.

44. Thorborg, K, Serner, A, Petersen, J, Madsen, TM, Magnusson, P, and Hölmich, P. Hip adduction and abduction strength profiles in elite soccer players: Implications for clinical evaluation of hip adductor muscle recovery after injury. *Am J Sports Med* 39(1):121-6, 2011.

45. Toohey, LA, De Noronha, M, Tayler, C, and Thomas J. Is a sphygmomanometer a valid and reliable tool to measure the isometric strength of hip muscles? A systematic review. *Physiother Theory Pract* 31:2114-119, 2015.

46. Townsend, RJ, Bender, D, Vantrease, W, Hudy, J, Heut, K, Williamson, C, Bechke, E, Serafini, P, and Mangine, GT. Isometric mid-thigh pull performance is associated with athletic performance and sprinting kinetics in Division I men and women's basketball players. *J Strength Cond Res*, July 2017.

47. Walker, O. Reactive strength index. www.science-forsport.com/reactive-strength-index. Accessed August 27, 2019.

48. Wang, R, Hoffman, JR, Sadres, E, Bartolomei, S, Muddle, TWD, Fukuda, DH, and Stout, JR. Evaluating upper-body strength and power from a single test: The ballistic push-up. *J Strength Cond Res* 31(5):1338-1345, 2017.

49. Wen, N, Dalbo, VJ, Burgos, B, Pyne, DB, and Scanlan, AT. Power testing in basketball: Current practice and future recommendations. *J Strength Cond Res* 32(9):2677-2691, 2018.

Chapter 4

1. Balyi, I, Way, R, and Higgs, C. *Long-Term Athlete Development*. Champaign, IL: Human Kinetics, 2013.

2. Bird, S, and Markwick, WJ. Musculoskeletal screening and functional testing: Considerations for basketball athletes. *Int J Sports Phys Ther* 11(5):784–802, 2016.

3. Bompa, T, and Buzzichelli, C. *Periodization: Theory and Methodology of Training*. 6th ed. Champaign, IL: Human Kinetics, 2018.

4. Bondarchuk, AP. *Transfer of Training*. Michigan: Ultimate Athlete Concepts, 2007.

5. Boone J, and Bourgois, J. Morphological and physiological profile of elite basketball players in Belgian. *Int J Sports Physiol Perform* 8(6):630-8.

6. Brenner, JS. Sports specialization and intensive training in young athletes. *American Academy of Pediatrics* 138(3), 2016.

7. Burd, N. Muscle time under tension during resistance exercise stimulates differential muscle protein sub-fractional synthetic responses in men. *J Physiol* 590(Pt 2):351–362, 2012.

8. Clemente, FM, González-Víllora, S, Delextrat, A, Martins, FML, and Vicedo, JCP. Effects of the sports level, format of the game and task condition on heart rate responses, technical and tactical performance of youth basketball players. *Journal of Human Kinetics* 58(1):141-155, 2017.

9. Dietz, C, and Peterson, B. *Triphasic Training: A Systematic Approach to Elite Speed and Explosive Strength Performance*. Vol 1. Hudson, WI: Bye Dietz Sports Enterprise, 2012.

10. Edwards, T, Spiteri, T, Piggott, B, Bonhotal, J, Haff, G, and Joyce, C. Monitoring and managing fatigue in basketball. *Sports* 6(1):19, 2018.

11. Epstein, D. *The Sports Gene*. New York: Penguin Books, 2013.

12. Haff, GG, and Triplett, NT, eds. *Essentials of Strength and Conditioning*. 4th ed. Champaign, IL: Human Kinetics, 2016.

13. Fox, JL, Stanton, R, and Scalan, AST. A comparison of training and competition demands in semi-professional male basketball players. *Res Q Exerc Sport* 89:103-111, 2018.

14. Fyfe, JJ, Bishop, DJ, and Stepto, NK. Interference between concurrent resistance and endurance exercise: Molecular bases and the role of individual training variables. *Sports Medicine* 44(6):743-762, 2014.

15. Gabbe, BJ, Finch, CF, Bennell, KL, and Wajswelner, H. How valid is a self-reported 12-month sports injury history? *British Journal of Sports Medicine* 37(6):545-547, 2003.

16. Gambetta, V. *Athletic Development: The Art and Science and Functional Sports Conditioning*. Champaign, IL: Human Kinetics, 2007.

17. Grabara, M. Comparison of posture among adolescent male volleyball players and non-athletes. *Biol Sport* 32(1):79–85, 2015.

18. Harries, SK, Lubans, DR, and Callister, R. Systematic review and meta-analysis of linear and undulating periodized resistance training programs on muscular strength. *J Strength Cond Res* 29(4):1113-1125, 2015.

19. Hawley, JA. Specificity of training adaptation: time for a rethink? *Journal of Physiology* 586(1):1-2, 2008.

20. Jones, TW, Smith, A, Macnaughton, LS, and French, DN. Strength and conditioning and concurrent training practices in elite rugby union. *J Strength Cond Res* 30(12):3354-3366, 2016.

21. Kawamori, N, and Haff, GG. The optimal training load for the development of muscular power. *J Strength Cond Res* 18(3):675-684, 2004.

22. Koklu, Y, Alemdaroglu, U, Kocak, FU, Erol, AE, and Findikoglu, G. Comparison of chosen physical fitness characteristics of Turkish professional basketball players by division and playing position. *J Hum Kinet* 30:99-106, 2011.

23. Komi, P. Stretch shortening cycle: A powerful model to study normal and fatigued muscle. *J Biomech* 33(10):1197-206, 2000.

24. Kraemer, WJ, Ratamess, NA, and French, DN. Resistance training for health and performance. *Current Sports Medicine Reports* 1(3):165-171, 2002

25. Kravitz, L, and Bubbico, A. *Essentials of Eccentric Training*. Champaign, IL: Human Kinetics, 2015.

26. Kucera, KL, Marshall, SW, Kirkendall, DT, Marchak, PM, and Garrett, WE. Injury history as a

risk factor for incident injury in youth soccer. *British Journal of Sports Medicine* 39(7):462-462, 2005.

27. Lindh, M. Increase of muscle strength from isometric quadriceps exercises at different knee angles. *Scandinavian Journal of Rehabilitation Medicine* 11(1):33-36, 1979.

28. McGuine, TA, Post, EG, Hetzel, SJ, Brooks, MA, Trigsted, S, and Bell, DR. A prospective study on the effect of sport specialization on lower extremity injury rates in high school athletes. *American Journal of Sports Medicine* 45(12):2706-2712, 2017.

29. Mendell, L. The size principle: A rule describing the recruitment of motoneurons. *J Neurophysiol* 93:3024–3026, 2005

30. Narazaki, K, Berg, K, Stergiou, N, and Chen, B. Physiological demands of competitive basketball. *Scandinavian Journal of Medicine & Science in Sports* 19(3):425-432, 2009.

31. National Strength and Conditioning Association. *NSCA's Guide to Tests and Assessments*. Champaign, IL: Human Kinetics, 2012.

32. Nikolaos, K. Anthropometric and fitness profiles of young basketball players according to their playing position and time. *Journal of Physical Education and Sport* 15(1):82, 2015.

33. Plisk, SS, and Stone, MH. Periodization strategies. *Strength & Conditioning Journal* 25(6):19-37, 2003.

34. Sabag, A, Najafi, A, Michael, S, Esgin, T, Halaki, M, and Hackett, D. The compatibility of concurrent high intensity interval training and resistance training for muscular strength and hypertrophy: A systematic review and meta-analysis. *J Sports Sci* 36(21):2472-2483, 2018.

35. Sapolsky, RM. *Why Zebras Don't Get Ulcers*. New York: Owl Book/Henry Holt, 2004.

36. Schelling, X, and Torres-Ronda, L. Accelerometer load profiles for basketball specific drills in elite players. *J Sports Sci Med* 15:585-591, 2016.

37. Siff, M, and Verkhoshansky, Y. *Supertraining*. 6th ed, Verkhoshansky.com, 2009.

38. Taylor, K. Fatigue monitoring in high performance sport: A survey of current trends. *J Aust Strength Cond* 20(1):12-23, 2012.

39. USA Basketball. *Defining the Positions*. www.usab.com/youth/news/2012/08/defining-the-positions.aspx.

40. Weiss, KJ, Allen, SV, McGuigan, MR, and Whatman, CS. The relationship between training load and injury in men's professional basketball. *International Journal of Sports Physiology and Performance* 12(9):1238-1242. 2017.

41. Williams, TD, Tolusso, DV, Fedewa, MV, and Esco, MR. Comparison of periodized and non-periodized resistance training on maximal strength: A meta-analysis. *Sports Medicine* 47(10):2083-2100, 2017.

42. Zatsiorsky, V, and Kraemer, W. *Science and Practice of Strength Training*. 2nd ed. Champaign, IL: Human Kinetics. 2006.

Chapter 5

1. Hori, N, Newton, RU, Nosaka, K, and Stone, MH. Weightlifting exercises enhance athletic performance that requires high-load speed strength. *Strength and Conditioning Journal* 24(4):50-55, 2005.

2. National Basketball Conditioning Coaches Association. *Complete Conditioning for Basketball*. Champaign, IL: Human Kinetics, 63, 127, 171, 2007.

3. Sigmon, C. *52-Week Basketball Training*. Champaign, IL: Human Kinetics, 127, 187, 2003.

4. Ziv, G, and Lidor, R. Physical attributes, physiological characteristics, on-court performances and nutritional strategies of female and male basketball players. *Sports Medicine* 39(7):547-568, 2009.

Chapter 6

1. Caulfield, S, and Berninger, D. Exercise technique for free weight and machine training. In *Essentials of Strength Training and Conditioning*. 4th ed. Haff, G, and Triplett, T, eds. Champaign, IL: Human Kinetics, 352-357, 2016.

2. McBride, J. Nature of power. In *Developing Power*. McGuigan, M, ed. Champaign, IL: Human Kinetics, 11-12, 2017.

3. Sato, K, and Shimokochi, Y. Basketball. In *Functional Training Handbook*. Liebenson, C, ed. Tokyo, Japan: Wolters Kluwer Health, 135-136, 2014.

Chapter 7

1. Chen, WH, Wu, HJ, Lo, SL, Chen, H, Yang, WW, Huang, CF, and Liu, C. Eight-week battle rope training improves multiple physical fitness dimensions and shooting accuracy in collegiate basketball players. *J Strength Cond Res* 32(10):2715-2724, 2018.

2. Erculj, F, and Supej, M. Impact of fatigue on the position of the release arm and shoulder girdle over a longer shooting distance for an elite basketball player. *J Strength Cond Res* 23(3):1029-1036, 2009.

3. Ikeda, ER, Borg, A, Brown, D, Malouf, J, Showers, KM, and Li, S. The Valsalva maneuver revisited: The influence of voluntary breathing on isometric muscle strength. *J Strength Cond Res* 23(1):127, 2009.

4. Pryor, RR, Sforzo, GA, and King, DL. Optimizing power output by varying repetition tempo. *J Strength Cond Res* 25(11):3029-3034, 2011.

Chapter 8

1. Boyle, M. *New Functional Training for Sports.* 2nd ed. Champaign, IL: Human Kinetics, 115-120, 2016.

2. Cole, B, and Panariello, R. *Basketball Anatomy.* Champaign, IL: Human Kinetics, 31-32, 2016.

3. Komi, P. *Strength and Power in Sport.* 2nd ed. Malden, MA: Blackwell Science, 5, 2003.

4. McGill, S. Core training: Evidence translating to better performance and injury prevention. *Strength and Conditioning Journal* 32:33-46, 2010.

Chapter 9

1. Alcaraz, PE, Perez-Gomez, J, Chavarrias, M, and Blazevich, AJ. Similarity in adaptations to high-resistance circuit vs. traditional strength training in resistance-trained men. *J Strength Cond Res* 25(9):2519-2527, 2011.

2. Bogdanis, G, Nevill, M, Boobis, L, and Lakomy, H. Contribution of phosphocreatine and aerobic metabolism to energy supply during repeated sprint exercise. *J Appl Physiol* 80:876-884, 1996.

3. Buchheit, M, Morgan, W, Wallace, J, Bode, M, and Poulos, N. Physiological, psychometric, and performance effects of the Christmas break in Australian football. *Int J Sports Physiol Perform* 10(1):120-3, 2015.

4. DePhillipo, NN, Kennedy, MI, Aman, ZS, Bernhardson, AS, O'Brien, L, and LaPrade, RF. Blood flow restriction therapy after knee surgery: Indications, safety considerations, and postoperative protocol. *Arthrosc Tech* 7(10):e1037-e1043, 2018.

5. Franchi, MV, Reeves, ND, and Narici, MV Skeletal muscle remodeling in response to eccentric vs. concentric loading: Morphological, molecular, and metabolic adaptations. *Front Physiol* 8:447, 2017.

6. Gastin, P. Energy system interaction and relative contribution during maximal exercise. *Sports Med* 31:725-741, 2001.

7. Gettman, L, Ward, P, and Hagan, RD. Conditioning report: Strength and endurance changes through circuit weight training. *NSCA J* 3:12-14, 1981.

8. Iodice, P, Ripari, P, and Pezzulo, G. Local high-frequency vibration therapy following eccentric exercises reduces muscle soreness perception and posture alterations in elite athletes. *Eur J Appl Physiol* 119(2):539-549, 2019.

9. Joo, CH. The effects of short-term detraining and retraining on physical fitness in elite soccer players. *PLoS One* 13(5), 2018

10. Lixandrão, ME, Ugrinowitsch, C, Berton, R, Vechin, FC, Conceição, MS, Damas, F, Libardi, CA, and Roschel, H. Magnitude of muscle strength and mass adaptations between high-load resistance training versus low-load resistance training associated with blood-flow restriction: A systematic review and meta-analysis. *Sports Med* 48(2):361-378, 2018.

11. Lloyd, RS, Faigenbaum, AD, Stone, MH, Oliver, JL, Jeffreys, I, Moody, JA, Brewer, C, Pierce, KC, McCambridge, TM, Howard, R, Herrington, L, Hainline, B, Micheli, LJ, Jaques, R, Kraemer, WJ, McBride, MG, Best, TM, Chu, DA, Alvar, BA, and Myer, GD. Position statement on youth resistance training: The 2014 International Consensus. *Br J Sports Med* 48(7):498-505, 2014.

12. Magallón, S, Narbona, J, and Crespo-Eguílaz, N. Acquisition of motor and cognitive skills through repetition in typically developing children. *PLoS One* 11(7), 2016.

13. Magoffin, RD, Parcell, AC, Hyldahl, RD, Fellingham, GW, Hopkins, JT, and Feland, JB. Whole-body vibration as a warmup before exercise-induced muscle damage on symptoms of delayed-onset muscle soreness in trained subjects. *J Strength Cond Res* (Epub ahead of print), 2018.

14. Mattocks, KT, Buckner, SL, Jessee, MB, Dankel, SJ, Mouser, JG, and Loenneke, JP. Practicing the test produces strength equivalent to higher volume training. *Med Sci Sports Exerc* 49(9):1945-1954, 2017.

15. Maughan, R, and Gleeson, M. *The Biochemical Basis of Sports Performance.* New York, NY: Oxford University Press, 2004.

16. Miller, T, Mull, S, Aragon, AA, Krieger, J, and Schoenfeld, BJ. Resistance training combined with diet decreases body fat while preserving lean mass independent of resting metabolic rate: A randomized trial. *Int J Sport Nutr Exerc Metab* 28(1):46-54, 2018.

17. Peitz, M, Behringer, M, and Granacher, U. A systematic review on the effects of resistance and plyometric training on physical fitness in youth: What do comparative studies tell us? *PLoS ONE* 13(10), 2018.

18. Pope, ZK, Willardson, JM, and Schoenfeld, BJ. Exercise and blood flow restriction. *J Strength Cond Res* 27(10): 2914-2926, 2013.

19. Ratel, S, Kluka, V, Vicencio, SG, Jegu, AG, Cardenoux, C, Morio, C, Coudeyre, E, and Martin, V Insights into the mechanisms of neuromuscular fatigue in boys and men. *Med Sci Sports Exerc* 47(11):2319-28, 2015.

20. Rodríguez-Fernández, A, Sánchez-Sánchez, J, Ramirez-Campillo, R, Rodríguez-Marroyo, JA, Villa Vicente, JG, and Nakamura, FY. Effects of short-term in-season break detraining on repeated-sprint ability and intermittent endurance according to initial performance of soccer player. *PLoS One* 13(8), 2018.

21. Sabag, A, Najafi, A, Michael, S, Esgin, T, Halaki, M, and Hackett, D. The compatibility of concurrent high intensity interval training and resistance training for muscular strength and hypertrophy: A systematic review and meta-analysis, *Journal of Sports Sciences* 36(21):2472-2483, 2018.

22. Sakai, K, Sheahan, J, and Takamatsu, K. The relationship between high power output during intermittent exercise and three energy delivery systems. *Japanese Journal of Physical Fitness and Sports Medicine* 48:453-466, 1999.

23. Slimani, M, Paravlic, A, and Granacher, U. A meta-analysis to determine strength training related dose-response relationships for lower-limb muscle power development in young athletes. *Frontiers of Physiol* 9:1155, 2018.

24. Steele, J, Fisher, JP, Assunção, AR, Bottaro, M, and Gentil, P. The role of volume-load in strength and absolute endurance adaptations in adolescent's performing high- or low-load resistance training. *Appl Physiol Nutr Metab* 42(2):193-201, 2017.

25. Sternad, D. It's not (only) the mean that matters: Variability, noise and exploration in skill learning. *Current Opinion in Behavioral Science* 20:183-195, 2018.

26. Stone, WJ, and Steingard, P. Year-round conditioning for basketball. *Clinics in Sports Medicine* 12:173-191, 1993.

27. Taipale, RS, Mikkola, J, Salo, T, Hokka, L, Vesterinen, V, Kraemer, WJ, Nummela, A, and Hakkinen, K. Mixed maximal and explosive strength training in recreational endurance runners. *J Strength Cond Res* 28(3): 689–699, 2014.

28. Veqar, Z, and Imtiyaz S. Vibration therapy in management of delayed onset muscle soreness (DOMS). *J Clin Diagn Res* 8(6), 2014.

29. Walker, S, Hulmi, JJ, Wernbom, M, Nyman, K, Kraemer, WJ, Ahtiainen, JP, and Häkkinen, K. Variable resistance training promotes greater fatigue resistance but not hypertrophy versus constant resistance training. *European Journal of Applied Physiology* 113(9):2233-44, 2013.

30. Wiesinger, HP, Kosters, A, Muller, E, and OR Seyennes. Effects of increased loading on in vivo tendon properties: A systematic review. *Med Sci Sports Exerc* 47(9):1885-1895, 2015.

31. Yessis, M. *Biomechanics and Kinesiology of Exercise.* Muskegon, MI: Ultimate Athlete Concepts, 2013.

Chapter 10

1. Aagard, P, Simonsen, E, Andersen, J, Magnusson P, and Dyhre-Poulsen, P. Increased rate of force development and neural drive of human skeletal muscle following resistance training. *J Appl Physiol* 93:1318-1326, 2002.

2. American College of Sports Medicine. American College of Sports Medicine position stand: Progression models in resistance training for healthy adults. *Med Sci Sports Exerc* 41(3):687-708, 2009.

3. Andersen, LL, and Aagard, P. Influence of maximal muscle strength and intrinsic muscle contractile properties on contractile rate of force development. *Eur J Appl Physiol* 96(1):46-52, 2006.

4. Asadi, A, Arazi, H, Young, WB, and Sáez de Villarreal, E. The effects of plyometric training on change-of-direction ability: A meta-analysis. *Int J Sports Physiol Perform*11(5):563-73, 2016.

5. Asadi, A, Ramirez-Campillo, R, Meylan, C, Nakamura, FY, Cañas-Jamett, R, and Izquierdo, M. Effects of volume-based overload plyometric training on maximal-intensity exercise adaptations in young basketball players. *J Sports Med Phys Fitness* 57(12):1557-1563, 2017.

6. Bailey, CA, Suchomel, TJ, and Beckham GK. A comparison of reactive strength index-modified between six U.S. collegiate athletic teams. *J Strength Cond Res* 29(5):1310-1316, 2015.

7. Baker, D, and Newton, RU. Methods to increase the effectiveness of maximal power training for the upper body. *Strength Cond J* 27:24-32, 2005.

8. Bartolomei S, Fukuda DH, Hoffman JR, Stout JR, and Merni F. The influence of isometric preload on power expressed during bench press in strength-trained men. *Eur J Sport Sci* 17(2):195-199, 2017.

9. Beckham, G, Sato, K, Santana, HA, Mizuguchi, S, Haff, GG, and Stone, MH. Effect of body position

on force production during the isometric midthigh pull. *J Strength Cond Res* 32(1):48-56, 2018.

10. Behm, DG, Young, JD, Whitten, JHD, Reid, JC, Quigley, PJ, Low, J, Li, Y, Lima, CD, Hodgson, DD, Chaouachi, A, Prieske, O, and Granacher, U. Effectiveness of traditional strength vs. power training on muscle strength, power and speed with youth: A systematic review and meta-analysis. *Front Physiol* 30(8):423, 2017.

11. Boffey, D, Sokmen, B, Sollanek, K, Boda, W, and Winter, S. Effects of load on peak power output fatigue during the bench throw. *J Strength Cond Res* 33(2):355-359, 2019.

12. Bompa, T. *Periodization: Theory and Methodology of Training.* 4th ed. Champaign, IL: Human Kinetics, 1999.

13. Byrne, PJ, Moody, JA, Cooper, SM, Callanan, D, and Kinsella, S. Potentiating response to drop jump protocols on sprint acceleration: Drop-jump volume and intrarepetition recovery duration. *J Strength Cond Res* (Epub ahead of print), July, 2018.

13b. Colquhoun, RJ, Gai, CM, Aguilar, D, Bove, D, Dolan, J, Vargas, A, Couvillion, K, Jenkins, ND, and Campbell, BI. Training volume, not frequency, indicative of maximal strength adaptations to resistance training. *J Strength Cond Res* 32(5):1207-1213, 2018.

14. Del Balso, C, and Cafarelli, E. Adaptations in the activation of human skeletal muscle induced by short-term isometric resistance training. *J Appl Physiol* 103:402-411, 2007.

15. Dos' Santos, T, Thomas, C, Jones, PA, McMahon, JJ, and Comfort, P. The effect of hip joint angle on isometric midthigh pull kinetics. *J Strength Cond Res* 31(10):2748-2757, 2017.

16. Douglas J, Pearson S, Ross A, and McGuigan M. Chronic adaptations to eccentric training: A systematic review. *Sports Med* 47(5):917-941, 2017.

17. Fleck, SJ, and Falkel, JE. Value of resistance training for the reduction of sports injuries. *Sports Med* 3(1):61-68, 1986.

18. Ford, P, De Ste Croix, M, Lloyd, R, Meyers, R, Moosavi, M, Oliver, J, Till, K, and Williams, C. The long-term athlete development model: Physiological evidence and application. *J Sports Sci* 29(4):389-402, 2011.

19. Garhammer, J, and Gregor, R. Propulsion forces as a function of intensity for weightlifting and vertical jumping. *J Strength Cond Res* 6(10):1519, 1992.

20. Häkkinen, K, Pakarinen A, Alen, M, Kauhanen, H, and Komi, P. Neuromuscular and hormonal adaptations in athletes to strength training in two years. *J Appl Physiol* 65:2406-2412, 1988.

21. Häkkinen, K, Komi, P, Alen, M, and Kauhanen, H. EMG, muscle fibre and force production characteristics during a 1-year training period in elite weightlifters. *Eur J Appl Phys* 56:419-427, 1987.

22. Harden, M, Wolf, A, Russell, M, Hicks, K, French, D, and Howatson, G. An evaluation of supramaximally loaded eccentric leg press exercise. *J Strength Cond Res* 32(10):2708-2714, 2018.

23. Jeffreys, MA, Croix, MBDS, Lloyd, RS, Oliver, JL, and Hughes, JD. The effect of varying plyometric volume on stretch-shortening cycle capability in collegiate male rugby players. *J Strength Cond Res* 33(1):139-145, 2019.

23b. Jenkins, N, Miramonti, AA, Hill, EC, Smith, CM, Cochrane-Snyman, KC, Housh, TJ, and Cramer, JT. Greater neural adaptations following high- vs. low-load resistance training. *Front Physiol* 8:331, 2017.

24. Jensen, RL, and Ebben, WP. Impulses and ground reaction forces at progressive intensities of weightlifting variations. In *ISBS-Conference Proceedings Archive* (Vol. 1, No. 1), 2002.

25. Johnson, BA, Salzberg, CL, and Stevenson, DA. A systematic review: Plyometric training programs for young children. *J Strength Cond Res* 25(9):2623-2633, 2011.

26. Kawamori, N, and Haff, G. The optimal training load for the development of muscular power. *J Strength Cond Res* 18:675-684, 2004.

27. Lee, BCY, and McGill, SM. Effect of long-term isometric training on core/torso stiffness. *J Strength Cond Res* 29(6):1515-1526, 2015.

28. Lepley, LK, Lepley, AS, Onate, JA, and Grooms, DR. Eccentric exercise to enhance neuromuscular control. *Sports Health* 9(4):333-340, 2017.

29. Maffiuletti, NA, Aagaard, P, Blazevich, AJ, Folland, J, Tillin, N, and Duchateau, J. Rate of force development: Physiological and methodological considerations. *Eur J Appl Physiol* 116(6):1091-116, 2016.

30. McMaster, DT, Gill, N, Cronin, J, and McGuigan, M. The development, retention and decay rates of strength and power in elite rugby union, rugby league and American football. *Sports Medicine* 43(5):367-384, 2013.

31. Mike, JN, Cole, N, Herrera, C, Van Dusseldorp, T, Kravitz, L, and Kerksick, CM. The effects of eccentric contraction duration on muscle strength, power production, vertical jump, and soreness. *J Strength Cond Res* 31(3):773-786, 2017.

32. Munger, CN, Archer, DC, Leyva, WD, Wong, MA, Coburn, JW, Costa, PB, and Brown, LE. Acute effects of eccentric overload on concentric front squat performance. *J Strength Cond Res* 31(5):1192-1197, 2017.

33. Newton, R, and Dugan, E. Application of strength diagnosis. *Strength Cond J* 24:50-59, 2002.

34. Nosaka, K., and Newton, M. Concentric or eccentric training effect on eccentric exercise-induced muscle damage. *Med Sci Sports Exerc* 34:63-69, 2002.

35. Pearson, S, Stadler, S, Menz, H, Morrissey, D, Scott, I, Munteanu, S, and Malliaras, P. Immediate and short-term effects of short- and long-duration isometric contractions in patellar tendinopathy. *Clin J Sport Med* Aug, 2018.

36. Sabag A, Najafi A, Michael S, Esgin T, Halaki M, and Hackett D. The compatibility of concurrent high intensity interval training and resistance training for muscular strength and hypertrophy: A systematic review and meta-analysis. *Journal of Sports Sciences* 36(21):2472-2483, 2018.

36b. Schoenfeld, BJ, Grgic, J, and Krieger, J. How many times per week should a muscle be trained to maximize muscle hypertrophy? A systematic review and meta-analysis of studies examining the effects of resistance training frequency. *Journal of Sports Sciences* 37(11):1286-1295, 2019.

37. Schoenfeld, BJ, Ogborn, D, and Krieger, JW. Effect of repetition duration during resistance training on muscle hypertrophy: A systematic review and meta-analysis. *Sports Med* 45(4):577-85, 2015.

38. Schoenfeld, BJ, Ogborn, D, and Krieger, JW. Effects of resistance training frequency on measures of muscle hypertrophy: A systematic review and meta-analysis. *Sports Med* 46(11):1689-1697, 2016.

39. Stone, MH, Stone, M, and Sands, W. *Principles and Practice of Resistance Training*. Champaign, IL: Human Kinetics, 2007.

40. Thibaudeau, C, and Schwartz, T. *Theory and Application of Modern Strength and Power Methods*. Lepine, 2007.

41. Tillin, NA, and Folland, JP. Maximal and explosive strength training elicit distinct neuromuscular adaptations, specific to the training stimulus. *Eur J Appl Physiol* 114(2):365-74, 2014.

42. Tsoukos, A, Bogdanis, GC, Terzis, G, and Veligekas, P. Acute improvement of vertical jump performance after isometric squats depends on knee angle and vertical jumping ability. *J Strength Cond Res* 30(8):2250-2257, 2016.

43. Wagle, JP, Taber, CB, Cunanan, AJ, Bingham, GE, Carroll, KM, DeWeese, BH, Sato, K, and Stone, MH. Accentuated eccentric loading for training and performance: A review. *Sports Med* 47(12):2473-2495, 2017.

43b. Walker, S, Blazevich, AJ, Haff, GG, Tufano, JJ, Newton, RU, and Häkkinen, K. Greater strength gains after training with accentuated eccentric than traditional isoinertial loads in already strength-trained men. *Front Physiol* 7:149, 2016.

44. Williams, TD, Tolusso, DV, Fedewa, MV, and Esco, MR. Comparison of periodized and non-periodized resistance training on maximal strength: A meta-analysis. *Sports Med* 47:2083-2100, 2017.

45. Xenofondos, A, Bassa, E, Vrabas, IS, Kotzamanidis, C, and Patikas, D. Muscle twitch torque during two different in volume isometric exercise protocols: Fatigue effects on postactivation potentiation. *J Strength Cond Res* 32(2):578-586, 2018.

46. Zając A, Chalimoniuk M, Maszczyk A, Gołaś A, and Lngfort, J. Central and peripheral fatigue during resistance exercise: A critical review. *Journal of Human Kinetics* 49:159-69, 2015.

47. Zatsiorsky, V, and Kraemer, W. *Science and Practice of Strength Training*. 2nd ed. Champaign, IL: Human Kinetics, 2006.

Chapter 11

1. Balabinis, CP, Psarakis, CH, Moukas, M, Assiliou, MP, and Behrakis, PK. Early phase changes by concurrent endurance and strength training. *J Strength Cond Res* 17(2):393-401, 2003.

2. Bridgeman, LA, McGuigan, MR, Gill, ND, and Dulson, DK. The effects of accentuated eccentric loading on the drop jump exercise and the subsequent postactivation potentiation response. *J Strength Cond Res* 31(6):1620-1626, 2017.

3. Douglas, J, Pearson, S, Ross, A, and McGuigan, M. Effects of accentuated eccentric loading on muscle properties, strength, power, and speed in resistance-trained rugby players. *J Strength Cond Res* 32(10):2750-2761, 2018.

3b. French, DN. Advanced power techniques. In *Developing Power*. McGuigan, M. ed. Champaign, IL: Human Kinetics, 195-196, 2017.

4. Gołaś, A, Maszczyk, A, Zajac, A, Mikołajec, K, and Stastny, P. Optimizing post activation potentiation for explosive activities in competitive sports. *J Hum Kinet* 52:95-106, 2016.

5. Haff, GG, Burgess, S, and Stone, MH. Cluster training: Theoretical and practical applications for the strength and conditioning professionals. *Prof Strength and Conditioning* 12:12-17, 2008.

6. Haff, GG, Hobbs, RT, Haff, EE, Sands, WA, Pierce, KB, and Stone, MH. Cluster training: A novel method for introducing training program variation. *Strength and Conditioning Journal* 30:60-76, 2008.

7. Haff, GG, Whitley, A, McCoy, LB, O'Bryant, HS, Kilgore, JL, Haff, EE, Pierce, K, and Stone, MH. Effects of different set configurations on barbell velocity and displacement during a clean pull. *J Strength Cond Res* 17:95-103, 2003.

8. Haff, GG. Periodization and power integration. In *Developing Power*. McGuigan, M, ed. Champaign, IL: Human Kinetics, 33-61, 2017.

9. Hernandez-Preciado, JA, Baz, E, Balsalobre-Fernandez, C, Marchante, D, and Santos-Concejero, J. Potentiation effects of the French contrast method on the vertical jumping ability. *J Strength Cond Res* 32(7):1909-1914, 2018.

10. Hough, P, Ross, E, and Howatson, G. Effects of dynamic and static stretching on vertical jump performance and electromyographic activity. *J Strength Cond Res* 23(2):507-512, 2009.

11. Lim, JJ, and Barley, CI. Complex training for power development. *Strength and Conditioning Journal* 38(6):33-43, 2016.

12. Lorenz, D. Post-activation potentiation: An introduction. *International Journal of Sports Physical Therapy* 6(3):234-40, 2011.

13. Mann, JB. Olympic lifts: The importance of peak velocity and recommended guidelines. https://simplifaster.com/articles/olympic-lifts-importance-peak-velocity-recommended-guidelines. Accessed July 17, 2019.

14. Mann, JB. Power and bar velocity measuring devices and their use for autoregulation. *NSCA's Hot Topic Series*, 2011.

15. Ratamess, N, Alvar, B, Evetoch, T, Housh, T, Kibler, W, and Kraemer, W. Progression models in resistance training for healthy adults. *Med Sci Sports Exerc* 41(3):687-708, 2009.

16. Rivière, M, Louit, L, Strokosch, A, and Seitz, LB. Variable resistance training promotes greater strength and power adaptations than traditional resistance training in elite youth rugby league players. *J Strength Cond Res* 31(4):947-955, 2017.

17. Seitz, L, and Haff, G. Factors modulating post-activation potentiation of jump, sprint, throw, and upper-body ballistic performances: A systematic review with meta-analysis. *Sports Medicine* 46(2), 2016.

18. Soria-Gila, MA, Chirosa, IJ, Bautista, IJ, Baena, S, and Chirosa, LJ. Effects of variable resistance training on maximal strength: A meta-analysis. *J Strength Cond Res* 29(11):3260-3270, 2015.

19. Turki, O, Chaouachi, A, Drinkwater, E, Chtara, M, Chamari, K, Amri, M, and Behm, D. Ten minutes of dynamic stretching is sufficient to potentiate vertical jump performance characteristics. *J Strength Cond Res* 25(9):2453-63, 2011.

Chapter 12

1. Boucher, D. *Citadel Football S&C*. Presented at the NSCA Coaches Conference, Indianapolis, IN, January 2014.

2. Bridgeman, LA, McGuigan, MR, Gill, ND, and Dulson, DK. The effects of accentuated eccentric loading on the drop jump exercise and the subsequent postactivation potentiation response. *J Strength Cond Res* 31(6): 620-1626, 2017.

3. Cushion, EJ, Goodwin, JE, and Cleather, DJ. Relative intensity influences the degree of correspondence of jump squats and push jerks to countermovement jumps. *J Strength Cond Res* 30(5):1255-1264, 2016.

4. Day, ML, McGuigan, MR, Brice, G, and Foster, C. Monitoring exercise intensity during resistance training using the session RPE scale. *J Strength Cond Res* 18(2):353-358, 2004.

5. French, DN. Advanced power techniques. In *Developing Power*. McGuigan, M, ed. Champaign, IL: Human Kinetics, 191, 2017.

6. Helms, ER, Cronin J, Storey, A, and Zourdos, MC. Application of the repetitions in reserve-based rating of perceived exertion scale for resistance training. *Strength and Conditioning Journal* 38(4):42-49, 2016.

7. Laputin, NP, and Oleshko, VG. *Managing the Training of Weightlifters*. Kiev, Ukraine: Zdorov'ya, 1982.

8. Mann, B. *Developing Explosive Athletes: Use of Velocity Based Training in Training Athletes*. CreateSpace Independent Publishing Platform, 2016.

9. Mann, J, Ivey, P, and Sayers, S. Velocity-based training in football. *Strength and Conditioning Journal* 37(6):52-57, 2015.

10. McMaster, DT, Gill, N, Cronin, J, and McGuigan, M. The development, retention, and decay rates of strength and power in elite rugby union, rugby league and American football. *Sports Medicine* 43(5):367-384, 2013.

11. Seitz, L, and Haff, G. Factors modulating post-activation potentiation of jump, sprint, throw, and upper-body ballistic performances: A systematic review with meta-analysis. *Sports Medicine* 46(2), 2016.

12. Sole, CJ, Moir, GL, Davis, SE, and Witmer, CA. Mechanical analysis of the acute effects of a heavy resistance exercise warm-up on agility performance in court-sport athletes. *Journal of Human Kinetics* 39:147-156, 2013.

13. Soria-Gila, MA, Chirosa, IJ, Bautista, IJ, Baena, S, and Chirosa, LJ. Effects of variable resistance training on maximal strength: A meta-analysis. *J Strength Cond Res* 29(11):3260-3270, 2015.

14. Sweet, TW, Foster, C, McGuigan, MR, and Brice, G. Quantitation of resistance training using the session rating of perceived exertion method. *J Strength Cond Res* 18(4):796-802, 2004.

15. Turki, O, Chaouachi, A, Drinkwater, E, Chtara, M, Chamari, K, Amri, M, and Behm, D. Ten minutes of dynamic stretching is sufficient to potentiate vertical jump performance characteristics. *J Strength Cond Res* 25(9):2453-63, 2011.

16. Zourdos, MC, Klemp, A, Dolan, C, Quiles, JM, Schau, KA, Jo, E, Helms, E, Esgro, B, Duncan, S, Merino, SG, and Blanco, R. Novel resistance training–specific rating of perceived exertion scale measuring repetitions in reserve. *J Strength Cond Res* 30:267-275, 2016.

Note: The italicized *f* and *t* following page numbers refer to figures and tables, respectively.

The National Strength and Conditioning Association (NSCA) is the world's leading organization in the field of sport conditioning. Drawing on the resources and expertise of the most recognized professionals in strength training and conditioning, sport science, performance research, education, and sports medicine, the NSCA is the world's trusted source of knowledge and training guidelines for coaches and athletes. The NSCA provides the crucial link between the lab and the field.

ABOUT THE EDITORS

Javair Gillett, MS, CSCS, RSCC*E, is the director of athletic performance for the Houston Rockets and has 20 years of experience working as a strength and conditioning coach at the collegiate and professional levels. Prior to joining the Rockets, Gillett spent 14 years with the Detroit Tigers, and he has worked with the Orlando Magic, Indiana University, and Penn State University.

Gillett is certified as a registered strength and conditioning coach (RSCC*E) by the National Strength and Conditioning Association (NSCA). He has a master's of science degree in human movement from A.T. Still University and completed his bachelor's degree at DePauw University, majoring in health and human performance with an emphasis in exercise science. He lettered four seasons with DePauw University's baseball team and was given All-Conference honors two of those four years as well as All-American Honorable Mention his final season.

Gillett dedicates himself to sharing his knowledge in sports and exercise science with youth athletes, parents, and coaches. In 2017, he was named the National Basketball Strength & Conditioning Association's Strength & Conditioning Coach of the Year. Gillett has co-authored several NSCA books, been a speaker at numerous educational events, and has published research articles and other educational content for a variety of resources.

Courtesy of Houston Rockets.

Bill Burgos, MS, CSCS, RSCC*D, is the head strength and conditioning coach for the Minnesota Timberwolves. Burgos is also an adjunct professor for Austin Peay State University, where he created an online course discussing the current trends of sport science and strength and conditioning. He has over 15 years of experience in collegiate and professional sports, including as head of strength and conditioning for the Orlando Magic and the New York Knicks.

Burgos has obtained two master of science degrees. The first of these, in exercise science, was obtained from Austin Peay State University, where he also obtained his undergraduate degree in exercise science. His second MS, in human movement, was obtained from A.T. Still University. He is currently pursuing a doctorate in health sciences, with an emphasis on leadership and organizational behavior and electronic medical record (EMR) modernization, from A.T. Still University. In addition, Burgos is certified by the National Strength and Conditioning Association (NSCA) as a certified strength and conditioning specialist (CSCS) and a registered strength and conditioning coach (RSCC). Burgos also has the functional movement screen (FMS) certification, is an EXOS performance specialist, is MWOD certified, and is certified in myokinematics by the Postural Restoration Institute (PRI).

Burgos is the immediate past president of the National Basketball Strength and Conditioning Association (NBSCA) and served on several committees in the NBA such as the NBA Sports Science Committee and the Junior NBA Leadership Council. Additionally, Burgos serves on the NBA Gatorade Advisory Board. Burgos resides in Minneapolis with his wife Noemi, two boys Jesus and Joel, and son-in-law and daughter Quandre and Cynthia King. His oldest daughter Atia lives in Los Angeles, California.

Andrew Barr, DPT, CSCS, is an established leader in the field of high performance and injury risk reduction with over 20 years of experience working in professional sports. He has held director of medicine and performance roles with Bolton Wanderers F.C., Southampton F.C., and Manchester City F.C. in the EPL; New York Knicks in the NBA; and New York City F.C. in the MLS. Barr is the founder of Quantum Performance, a Los Angeles-based elite level physical therapy and high-performance consultancy company (www.Quantumperformance.co; @andybarrPT). He holds a BSc in physiotherapy, an MSc in sports science, and a doctorate in physical therapy.

©Andrew Barr

Joshua Bonhotal, MS, CSCS, is the vice president of operations with Future, an emerging fitness technology startup which has raised nearly $12M in funding to date. Previously, he was the director of sports performance for Purdue men's basketball, where he was in charge of training and development for a program that perennially ranked in the Top 25, won the 2017 Big Ten Championship, earned two Sweet Sixteen appearances, and had multiple All-American selections during his tenure. Prior to Purdue, Bonhotal served as the assistant strength and conditioning coach for the Chicago Bulls. During that time, he worked with Derrick Rose—while Rose won Rookie of the Year (2009) and MVP (2011)—and he contributed to the team's 62-win season in 2010-2011. Bonhotal has been featured in *The Wall Street Journal*, *ESPN*, and *Sports Illustrated*.

Courtesy of Future Research. Photographer Kaare Iverson.

Tyler Bosch, PhD, earned his master's and doctoral degree from the school of kinesiology at the University of Minnesota. Following his doctorate, he completed a two-year post-doctoral fellowship at the University of Minnesota medical school studying the effect of exercise on glucose and lipid metabolism using isotopic tracer techniques. In between his master's and PhD work, Bosch served as the director of sports performance for Fitness Revolution in Chicago, IL. During his PhD, he served as the director of coaching and curriculum at Leftfoot Coaching Academy, a dedicated soccer training facility in Minneapolis, MN. Bosch serves as a research scientist in the college of education and human development and cofounder of Dexalytics, a software application for body composition data that provides sport and position specific analyses for athletes. In addition to Dexalytics, he works with collegiate and professional sports teams to improve how they collect, analyze, and interpret the data on their athletes.

Courtesy of University of Minnesota.

Bryce Daub, MS, CSCS, serves as the director of basketball strength and performance at the University of Oklahoma. Before joining the Sooners, Daub spent the previous four seasons as the strength and conditioning coach for the University of Oregon men's basketball program. Also, Daub spent the 2010-11 season as an athletic performance coach with the Oklahoma City Thunder basketball franchise. Prior to his time in OKC, he served as a strength and conditioning intern with the Seattle Supersonics. Daub earned both his BS and MS degrees in exercise science from Central Washington University.

Courtesy of University of Oklahoma.

Bryan D. Doo, MS, CSCS, RSCC, is the former head strength and conditioning coach for the Boston Celtics for 14 seasons. Doo continues to operate the company he founded in 1997, Optimal Fitness: Professionals in Health and Human Performance. Doo consults for the National Basketball Players Association (NBPA), Bose, and New Balance on various projects dealing with innovation, biomechanics, and HR monitoring. He has consulted and trained various NHL, EPL, Olympic athletes. Doo is a frequent and eloquent speaker regarding sports and athletic development, injury prevention, and team training at local and national conferences.

©Bryan Doo

Bill Foran, MS, CSCS, RSCC*E, has been with the Miami Heat for all its 32 seasons. For the first 29 seasons, he was the head strength and conditioning coach. Prior to the Heat, Foran was the head strength and conditioning coach at the University of Miami where he was part of two football national championships. Before the Hurricanes, Foran was the head strength and conditioning coach at Washington State University. He has a bachelor's degree from Central Michigan University and a master's degree in exercise physiology from Michigan State University. In 2009, Foran was voted the NBA Strength Coach of the Year. In 2014, he was inducted into the USA Strength and Conditioning Coaches Hall of Fame. In 2017, Foran was named the NSCA Professional Strength and Conditioning Coach of the Year.

Courtesy of Miami Heat.

Eric Foran, MS, CSCS, RSCC, is in his eight season with the Miami Heat, and his third season as the head strength and conditioning coach. Prior to his current role, Foran served as a strength and conditioning intern and an assistant strength and conditioning coach for the team. He earned a master's degree in applied physiology and kinesiology from the University of Florida, where he competed as a pole vaulter on the NCAA champion track and field team.

Courtesy of Miami Heat.

Katie Fowler, MEd, CSCS, is a sports performance coach who spent seven years working with NCAA Division I women's basketball teams and is currently privately training athletes of all ages in Charlotte, North Carolina. She has worked with women's basketball teams at the University of South Carolina, University of Maryland, and the University of Virginia. Fowler has had the opportunity to be a part of one NCAA National Championship team, three Final Fours teams, and four regular season and conference tournament championship teams. Fowler obtained her undergraduate degree in exercise science from Truman State University and graduate degree from the University of Washington.

Courtesy of Just Workout.

Nic Higgins, CSCS, joined the University of Washington Olympic strength and conditioning staff in June 2017 and is responsible for men's rowing, softball, and throwers for track and field, and he assists with men's basketball. Higgins came to Washington from DePaul University where he served as the assistant director of sports performance and oversaw women's soccer, men's golf, and track and field while assisting men's basketball. Previous to DePaul, he spent two and a half years assisting at the University of Texas in both the football and athletic performance departments. Higgins holds a MS degree in exercise and science and health promotion with a concentration in performance enhancement and injury prevention from California University of Pennsylvania in 2013. He earned his bachelor's degree in exercises science from the University of Wisconsin-La Crosse in 2012.

Courtesy of University of Washington.

Amanda Kimball, MEd, CSCS, LMT, is the director of sports performance for women's basketball at the University of Connecticut. Kimball has coached athletes from women's basketball to 6 national championships, 12 consecutive Final Four appearances, 12 consecutive NCAA tournament appearances, and 15 regular season and conference tournament championships. Previously, Kimball worked with women's lacrosse, women's rowing, women's volleyball, softball, and the 2-time national championship field hockey team. In her time with field hockey, she coached athletes to 2 national championships, 5 Final Four appearances, 9 NCAA tournament appearances, and 13 regular season and conference championships. Since 2004, Kimball has coached 50 All-Americans.

Courtesy of University of Connecticut.

Mubarak Malik, MS, CSCS,*D, is in his fifth year as director of performance for the New York Knicks. In this role, he oversees all aspects of the strength and conditioning program, supervises the implementation of the sports science program, and works closely with the player development coaches to help build a robust NBA player. Malik has over 10 years of experience working with professional athletes in both the MLB and the NBA. His master's degree is from A.T. Still University and he is a certified strength and conditioning specialist (with distinction) by the National Strength and Conditioning Association. Malik served as the treasurer for the National Basketball Strength and Conditioning Association for four years and he has written articles on strength training for *Men's Health and Men's Fitness*. He has been featured in *Sports Illustrated* and in 2018, Malik was nominated as the Strength Coach of the Year by the National Strength and Conditioning Association.

© Mubarak Malik

Alexander (Alex) Reeser, MS, CSCS, TSAC-F, is the director of biomechanics at Sports Rehab LA in Los Angeles, CA. Reeser previously was the head performance coach for Quantum Performance and an assistant strength and conditioning coach for the USA women's national soccer team. He holds a MS in biokinesiology from the University of Southern California and is pursuing a PhD in exercise science from Texas A&M University.

© Alexander Reeser

John Shackleton, MS, CSCS, completed his seventh season as Villanova's strength and conditioning coach in 2018-19. In his tenure, he has been part of a staff that has led the Wildcats to 211 victories, seven NCAA Tournament appearances, five BIG EAST Tournament regular season titles, four BIG EAST Tournament championships, and two NCAA national championships (2016 and 2018). Along the way, Shackleton has been praised for his innovative approach to player development and nutrition. He was featured in a segment on NBC's "Today" show in March 2019. Shackleton works closely with the Villanova coaching staff on nutrition, strength training, and recovery. He earned BS (magna cum laude) in kinesiology in 2008 from Temple University and an MS in exercise science in 2010 from George Washington University.

Courtesy of Villanova University.

Robby Sikka, MD, is the CEO of Sports Medicine Analytics Research Team (SMART), an organization that has assisted NBA, NFL, MLB, and NHL clubs with injury data, return to play planning, and player evaluation and development. He also serves as a consultant to the National Basketball Player's Association and has served as a consultant to the NFL. Sikka is the associate director for data analytics for Mayo Clinic Sports Medicine, and is also the lead clinical research scientist, and serves on the fellowship faculty at TRIA Orthopaedic Center. He attended the University of Pennsylvania for his undergraduate studies and USC Keck School of Medicine for medical school. Sikka was named a Rising Star in *Minneapolis/St. Paul Magazine* in 2016, 2017, and 2018 in anesthesiology, and was named to the 40 under 40 list by *Minneapolis/St. Paul Business Journal* in 2017.

©Robby Sikka

Steve Smith, PT, DPT, SCS, CSCS, Pn1, is the senior director of health wellness and performance for the Washington Wizards. Prior to his current role, Smith worked for the Los Angeles Dodgers first as the medical/rehabilitation coordinator and then as the team's major league physical therapist. Before making the jump into the professional team environment, Smith was the lead physical therapist for Athletes' Performance (now EXOS) in Florida. There he worked mainly with high level tactical athletes from a variety of special operations units, professional and collegiate athletes in American football and baseball, and professional rugby as well as several other international team and individual sports. Smith earned his master's and doctorate degree in physical therapy from the University of Maryland Baltimore and he is a board-certified specialist in sports physical therapy through the American Board of Physical Therapy Specialties and a certified strength and conditioning specialist through the National Strength and Conditioning Association.

Courtesy of Washington Wizards.

Tania Spiteri, PhD, is the head of sport science at the World Basketball Academy. She received a PhD in biomechanics from Edith Cowan University and is a level two certified strength and conditioning coach with the Australian Strength and Conditioning Association. Spiteri is also an adjunct lecturer in exercise and sport science at Edith Cowan University.

©Tania Spiteri

Scott Thom, MA, CSCS, USAW, started his coaching journey in 2003 as the head coach for boys' basketball and PE teacher at Vintage High in Napa, California. He coached and taught at Vintage until 2010 in which he was hired at University of California Berkeley as the head strength coach/player development for the men's basketball team. He coached at Cal until 2014 in which he was hired at Washington State University as the head strength coach/player development. In 2016, Thom was selected as one of the coaches to accompany a group of Pac-12 All-Stars to Australia to prepare the Australian National Team for the 2016 Olympics. In 2016, he wrote his first book, *Season of Strength*, before leaving WSU to become the head men's basketball coach and director of strength and conditioning at College of Marin.

Courtesy of College of Marin.

TAKE THE
NEXT
STEP

A continuing education course
is available for this text.
Find out more.